BUSINESS ON TRIAL

BUSINESS ON TRIAL

THE CIVIL JURY
AND
CORPORATE RESPONSIBILITY

VALERIE P. HANS

Yale University Press / New Haven and London

Designed by Mary Valencia. Set in Bodoni type by Keystone Typesetting, Inc., Orwigsburg, Pennsylvania. Printed in the United States of America by Edwards Brothers, Inc., Ann Arbor, Michigan.

Library of Congress Cataloging-in-Publication Data

Hans, Valerie P.
    Business on trial : the civil jury and corporate responsibility / Valerie P. Hans.
        p.   cm.
    Includes bibliographical references and index.
    ISBN 0-300-08206-1 (cloth : alk. paper)
    1. Jury—United States—Decision making.   2. Tort liability of corporations—United States.   3. Social responsibility of business.   I. Title.
    KF8972 .H267 2000
    347.73′752—dc21   99-087513

A catalogue record for this book is available from the British Library.

The paper in this book meets the guidelines for permanence and durability of the Committee on Production Guidelines for Book Longevity of the Council on Library Resources.

10   9   8   7   6   5   4   3   2   1

To
Michael and Zachary

CONTENTS

ACKNOWLEDGMENTS

I have many people and some corporate entities to thank as I conclude this challenging research project on how the civil jury treats business corporations. A memorable sabbatical at Stanford Law School gave me some of the legal background I needed to frame the questions for the research project, and for that I thank Barbara Babcock, Robert Ellickson, Phoebe Ellsworth, Lawrence Friedman, Bob Rabin, and David Rosenhan. With the support of Felice Levine, the National Science Foundation funded the data collection through grant SES-8822598; a subsequent year to analyze and write at the Wharton School of Business was funded through NSF Visiting Professorship for Women grant GER-9350498. I am grateful for a fellowship in the Center for Advanced Study at the University of Delaware, which allowed me the time to make significant headway on this manuscript. So much for Virginia Woolf's *A Room of One's Own; this* is the kind of support that a mother with a young child needs to finish a book!

Conducting the research incurred debts as well. The judges and staff of the court whose jurors I interviewed, who shall remain nameless at their own request, provided the kind of assistance and access that enabled me to do a scientifically sound study of civil jurors. The jurors my students and I interviewed spoke with candor and eloquence about their experiences with, and views of, the work of the civil jury. Many of my students at the University of Delaware participated enthusiastically in the project. It would be impossible to name them all, but the roles of Bill Lofquist, Andrea Appel, Michelle Hallerdin, Valerie Stevenson, and Kerrie Finneran deserve special mention.

Finally, my family, friends, and colleagues have been generous with their advice and encouragement as I have worked to make sense of 269 juror interviews, several experiments, and survey data. The manuscript benefited from the insightful critiques of Shari Diamond, Dave Ermann, Betsy Hans, Stephan Landsman, Dick Paul, Eric Rise, and Neil Vidmar. I also appreciate the assistance and persistence of John Covell throughout the editorial review process at Yale University Press, and Jenya Weinreb's excellent editorial work.

BUSINESS ON TRIAL

1

THE DEBATE OVER THE JURY'S
ROLE IN BUSINESS CASES

In 1987 Georgia farmer William Lawson was pleased to learn from the salesman at his local supply store that an improved version of the fungicide Benlate, called Benlate DF, had become available. For twenty years Lawson had been using the original version of Benlate successfully at his Bush Ranch, where he grew juniper bushes. He quickly ordered the new product. Lawson had a good deal of confidence in the fungicide's manufacturer, E. I. DuPont de Nemours and Company. So when some of his juniper bushes began to sicken and die, he did not at first think to blame the new fungus killer. But the problems with his juniper bushes spread. The output of his farm dropped, and he was forced to lay off half of his twenty-six employees. Examining the possible causes for the destruction of his plants, Lawson became convinced that Benlate DF was responsible. Six years later, Lawson was the lead plaintiff in a $450-million lawsuit against the company in which he had once expressed such confidence. Lawson joined with the owners of three other nurseries to sue the giant corporation.[1]

As the first in a series of lawsuits against DuPont for damages allegedly resulting from Benlate DF, the farmers' case attracted considerable attention. The jury trial took place in Columbus, Georgia. Lawson and the other farmers testified that after using the new version of Benlate, their crops had deteriorated and died. In their view, the most likely culprit was the fungicide. They presented scientists who reported tests showing that some samples of Benlate were tainted with deadly herbicides called sulfonylureas.

In turn, DuPont called its chief executive officer, other DuPont employees, and independent experts who testified that Benlate was not to blame for the farmers' crop failures. In his testimony, the vice president and general manager of DuPont's agricultural chemicals division recounted how, after some reports of crop failures, DuPont had pulled Benlate DF from the market and begun paying out more than half a billion dollars to farmers who reported crop damage after using Benlate. The company then spent sixteen months and nearly $12 million testing Benlate on plants, trying to identify the problem with the fungicide. The company could find nothing wrong with its product.[2]

The outlook appeared bleak for the chemical company in the early stages of the trial. The judge in the case expressed anger at DuPont's lawyers for what he labeled "stonewalling."[3] He made a number of unfavorable rulings against the company, levying a substantial fine for withholding evidence and barring a key DuPont scientist from testifying about her tests of Benlate.[4] To make matters worse, the plaintiffs introduced evidence of secret company memos, orders to delete computer files after printing out their contents, and other documents that suggested to some observers that there had been a cover-up in the Benlate case. During the closing arguments, the plaintiffs' attorney exhorted the jurors to send DuPont "to the woodshed" to teach the giant corporation a lesson. Likening the jury's task to that of parents of a disobedient child, the plaintiffs' attorney argued: "DuPont, like any large child, can become a bully, can become a monster unless it is disciplined. Your job is going to be to discipline DuPont."[5]

But with all the emphasis on demonstrating a cover-up, as the trial progressed the main weakness of the plaintiffs' case started to emerge: they were having difficulty demonstrating that the Benlate used on *their* crops had actually been contaminated. Both sides observed that the evidence seemed to be going DuPont's way, but both were unsure what the citizens of the jury would decide. Stereotypes of the civil jury as a modern-day Robin Hood, biased against wealthy businesses and eager to redistribute funds from large corporations to injured plaintiffs, gave the attorneys on both sides pause.[6] Would sympathy for the growers lead the Georgia jurors to ignore the problems in the evidence and decide the case in favor of the plaintiffs? Would jurors tap the deep pockets of the wealthy DuPont corporation to compensate the farmers for their losses?

Notwithstanding the stereotypes suggesting that the jury would decide in the plaintiffs' favor, the plaintiffs' lead attorney reported that he was uneasy. During jury deliberations, he approached DuPont with an offer to settle the case. The lawyers for the two sides came up with an acceptable figure—$4.25 million, a substantial sum, but only a fraction of the amount the farmers had asked for initially.[7] It was reportedly less than the plaintiffs' lawyers had spent preparing the case.[8] The company's chairman and CEO described the settlement as a "victory for DuPont, our employees, and our science."[9]

Two jurors, who spoke with reporters after the settlement had been reached, said that they were about to decide the case in favor of DuPont.[10] One of the jurors stated that the settlement came in the nick of time for the farmers: "We were pretty close to bringing down a verdict." The other juror observed that the plaintiffs had failed to substantiate their case: "The plaintiffs did not present any evidence that proved that Benlate was the cause of the damage."[11] Both jurors believed that the plaintiffs were counting on sympathy for the growers.[12] In contrast, DuPont had "very credible witnesses," including company chairman Edgar Woolard.[13]

There were disagreements on the jury. Two or three pro-plaintiff jurors reportedly felt that *something* must have caused the crop damage. Several jurors also gave weight to the memos purporting to show that DuPont was engaged in a cover-up. But the two jurors who were interviewed by reporters said that a full reading of the documents did not support the cover-up claims. Some of the memos were unrelated to the issues at trial, and most were not as significant as they had first appeared to be when only parts of them were read during the trial.[14] As for the witnesses whom the judge would not allow to testify, the jurors did not know exactly what testimony was prohibited but suspected that it was something favorable to the defense.[15]

Since the opening salvo fired in the Georgia courtroom, DuPont has continued to defend its product and the company's integrity before American juries, experiencing both wins and losses. Although the lawsuits have differed in location and specifics, the major charge in most lawsuits has been that Benlate caused crop failures. In May 1994, in a scenario strikingly reminiscent of the Georgia trial, a Florida jury was in the midst of deliberations in a Benlate case when DuPont lawyers reached settlements with four of the five plaintiffs. The timing of the settlements was propitious for the plaintiffs; shortly thereafter, the jury came back with a verdict in favor of DuPont.[16] Yet in a contrasting pair of cases, one in 1994 in South Carolina and the other in 1995 in Hawaii, juries found DuPont liable for crop damages.[17]

As these cases developed, questions arose about whether DuPont had complied sufficiently with judicial orders to turn over its Benlate test results to the plaintiffs. Responding to claims that DuPont had withheld documents during the pretrial discovery process, a DuPont representative replied: "We have handed over 3 million pages of documents. It's simply not the DuPont way to stonewall anybody. That sort of statement impugns the reputation of the company."[18] The judge in the Hawaii case, however, hit DuPont with a $1.5 million penalty for withholding toxicity tests of Benlate.[19] The Georgia plaintiffs who had settled the Bush Ranch case then came back to court to argue that they had been tricked into accepting a low settlement because DuPont had failed to inform them fully about the results of their tests.[20] Now facing criminal investigation as well as civil litigation over discovery errors, DuPont signed an $11 million consent decree in Georgia in which it agreed to fund law school professorships and lectures on legal ethics.[21] But as of 1999 it continues to face other disgruntled plaintiffs on similar charges.[22]

In 1996 a new and far more ominous claim about Benlate surfaced at trial. In a case involving a six-year-old boy born with no eyes, a Florida jury heard expert testimony linking ingredients in Benlate with the possibility of birth defects. The family claimed, specifically, that prenatal exposure to Benlate DF fungicide had caused the unusual birth defect. Although the plaintiff's expert testimony was derided as "junk science," the jury found DuPont liable and awarded the boy's family $4 million in damages.[23] A Florida appeals court that cited flaws in the scientific evidence overturned the verdict and award in 1999.[24] Yet the courts are still considering claims about the effects of Benlate on health.[25]

Benlate DF was withdrawn from the market in 1991. DuPont, however, faces continuing litigation for crop damages and personal injury as well as legal challenges over its conduct in the lawsuits. As of 1999, the total cost to the company for the Benlate litigation had been estimated at more than a billion dollars.[26]

In addition to the court costs, lawyers' fees, and payments to successful plaintiffs, the company also faces the worrisome possibility that the Benlate litigation may damage the public's view of DuPont. Whether the lawsuits are successful or not, the litigation claims alleging that a DuPont product caused substantial harm to farmers' crops and was linked to birth defects taint the company's standing as a trustworthy, safety-conscious institution. That image is critical to product credibility and sales. And the charges that the company withheld relevant information make negative impressions more likely. DuPont's concerns about the effect of litigation on the company's image are echoed by such other business executives as a public relations chief from Mitsubishi: "Too many litigators think too much like the good lawyers they are and how they can win in court. My concern is that they will win the battle but lose the war. What good does it do to save the company several hundred thousand dollars in attorneys' fees, maybe a few million dollars in awards, but ruin its public image [so that] the company is no longer able to sell its product, and tens of millions of dollars are lost?"[27]

A History of Business Corporations in the Courtroom

The Benlate litigation, costly and troublesome to the parties and the courts, illustrates the central role of the civil justice system, and of juries, in resolving contemporary business disputes. A number of analyses have found that lawsuits involving business are more frequent now than in the past. Although product liability cases like the Benlate ones constitute a very small proportion of civil lawsuits, they, too, have been increasing in recent decades. Product liability cases may be small in number, but they can have enormous impact. Indeed, concerns about product liability and other mass torts have played a disproportionately large role in debates about the soundness and future of the civil jury.

This book examines the contemporary jury's treatment of businesses and corporations. Its particular focus is on cases in which individual plaintiffs sue business defendants, the most common pattern of lawsuits involving business corporations. Before I present a picture of the business litigants and cases that jurors see in court today, it will be useful to look at how the legal world of businesses has changed over time.[28] From the early nineteenth century to the present, there has been a broad shift in the extent to which business corporations are held legally accountable for injury. In nineteenth-century America, a variety of legal rules and societal and judicial attitudes supported an ethic of individual responsibility. This ethic worked against liability for corporate entities. The eminent legal historian Willard Hurst documented widespread sentiment among community leaders that rapid business expansion was in the best interest of society, and that the law should do everything possible to facilitate its development. Legislatures and courts, highly reluctant to place legal restrictions on business, erected bars against compensation for injuries that occurred in corporate settings. Inspection and licensing laws were weak and erratically enforced. If individual citizens did not complain about the transgressions of businesses, the state did little or nothing about them.[29] The developing law of torts, primarily designed to deal with injuries stemming from the industrial revolution, had a pro-business, pro-enterprise slant. Excessive lawsuits, it was feared then, might strangle the growing economy.

Legal historian Lawrence Friedman has observed that in the nineteenth century,

5

Americans were used to living with adversity. They rather fatalistically considered injuries a normal, if undesirable, part of life. They took responsibility themselves if things went wrong—or at least, they did not tend to look elsewhere for guilty parties. For example, nineteenth-century workers were presumed to have assumed any risks or dangers of their jobs, particularly if they were aware of those risks.[30] There was a purported economic rationale for this. Highly dangerous jobs—say, working with dynamite—generally paid higher salaries than less dangerous but otherwise comparable jobs. Thus, some economists argued that salaries in high-risk occupations included financial compensation for the greater likelihood of injury on the job. Judicial opinions of the time reflected this perspective.

In addition, the legal doctrine of contributory negligence made it difficult for citizens to recover for business-related injuries. Contributory negligence is behavior on the part of the plaintiff that is at least a partial cause of his or her own injury. In the nineteenth and early twentieth centuries, any fault on the part of the plaintiff generally absolved the defendant completely.[31] Another legal rule that businesses relied on during this time was the fellow-servant rule, which precluded an employee from suing his or her employer for injuries that were caused by another employee.[32] Juries who heard cases involving a plaintiff's contributory negligence occasionally interpreted the law and the facts to allow some compensation. More often, though, judicial rulings based on contributory negligence and fellow-servant doctrines barred the jury from hearing such cases at all.

Parallel legal developments reduced the jury's once-unquestioned prominence in the civil justice system; some of the jury's power shifted to an increasingly professionalized, legally trained judiciary.[33] The Seventh Amendment to the U.S. Constitution established the right to a jury trial in civil cases, so the civil jury could not readily be eliminated outright. Instead, rules and practices chipped away at the jury's authority. The law began to differentiate more sharply between the factual issues appropriate for jury consideration and the legal issues that were the province of the judge. Judges in some civil cases limited the jury to answering specific factual questions rather than reaching a general verdict. Although it was still a rare occurrence, judges became more willing to overturn civil jury verdicts they viewed as inconsistent with the evidence. All these practices operated to constrict the role of the jury, which was presumed to be strongly pro-plaintiff in business cases.

Nevertheless, a variety of factors produced legal changes placing more responsibility on business corporations. Historian Peter Karsten notes a tension in nineteenth-century cases between what he labels a "jurisprudence of the head" and a "jurisprudence of the heart." Whereas it was true that many judges interpreted and enforced laws that precluded corporate liability for injuries, a number of judges, especially in the midwestern and western United States, practiced a jurisprudence of the heart, interpreting laws and precedents so that corporations would be liable for plaintiffs' injuries.[34]

A significant factor that led judges and the public toward greater business accountability was the skyrocketing number of industrial accidents. The industrial revolution produced record numbers of injuries. And no invention of the industrial age was more damaging than the railroad. As Lawrence Friedman put it: "Almost every leading case in tort law was connected, mediately or immediately, with this new and dreadful presence. [In the early period] the railroad was the prince of machines, both as symbol and as fact. It was the key to economic development. It cleared an iron path through the wilderness. It bound cities together, and tied the farms to the cities and the seaports. Yet, trains were also wild beasts; they roared through the countryside, killing livestock, setting fires to houses and crops, smashing wagons at grade crossings, mangling passengers and freight. Boilers exploded; trains hurtled off tracks; bridges collapsed; locomotives collided in a grinding scream of steel."[35]

At the beginning of the twentieth century, industrial accidents were causing about 2 million injuries and 35,000 deaths a year.[36] Because legal doctrines and practice favored businesses, most of those injured were never compensated. But the extent of the injuries increasingly challenged the wisdom of the day, which ascribed causal responsibility to the victims and deflected responsibility away from businesses.

Historian Arthur McEvoy argues that high-visibility cases of industrial injury were an important stimulus for legal change. McEvoy's compelling essay about an infamous industrial accident, the Triangle Shirtwaist Factory fire of 1911, describes a fire that broke out in a New York City garment factory, killing 146 workers, most of them young immigrant women. Although the company had committed numerous safety violations, including locked exit doors and fire escapes so inadequate that they collapsed as the women tried to flee, a jury acquitted the company's owners of all criminal charges. Just one survivor of the fire went to a civil trial, where the jury was unable to agree on a verdict and the court dismissed the case. Twenty-three wrongful death actions were settled for seventy-five dollars each.[37]

These legal outcomes, though harsh by today's standards, reflected prevailing assumptions about causality and responsibility in the workplace. As one of the Triangle

Shirtwaist trial jurors observed: "I can't see that any one was responsible . . . it must have been an act of God. I think the factory was well managed, and was as good or better than many others. I think that the girls, who undoubtedly have not as much intelligence as others might have in other walks of life, were inclined to fly into a panic."[38]

Analyzing the jurors' reaction, McEvoy maintains that their explanation for the trial and the deaths of so many workers was embedded in a view of the world that placed overwhelming importance on individual responsibility. People were supposed to look after themselves, and if they made choices that had negative consequences, they were presumed to have accepted those consequences. The fact that the Triangle Shirtwaist factory workers were primarily immigrant women did not mean that their employer had greater responsibility for these vulnerable workers. Rather, it suggested that the limitations of the workers themselves had contributed to their deaths.[39] By the laws and the mores of the day, the Triangle victims were seen as having assumed the risks of their jobs; their panic in response to the fire was assigned a contributory role in their deaths. Nevertheless, McEvoy argues that the very public nature of the fire and subsequent investigations of the garment industry helped to shape new understandings of the causes of industrial accidents, ultimately changing who the public found responsible for these accidents.

During the course of the nineteenth and early twentieth centuries, then, the sheer number of business-related injuries tended to undermine the clarity of such doctrines as assumption of risk, contributory negligence, and the fellow-servant rule. Ultimately their importance and power diminished. Changes on the political front, including increasing calls to regulate the business community, also altered the legal landscape. Workers organized to protest unfair and dangerous conditions, and pressured legislatures to curb the worst excesses of industry. The Progressive Movement and the New Deal swept in new attitudes about the collective responsibilities of businesses and government for dealing with the problems of the citizenry. The advent of workers' compensation in the early decades of the twentieth century was especially significant. Both the workers and the business community obtained substantial benefits in the deal that created workers' compensation. By covering the medical expenses and lost wages of injured workers and following a preset schedule of payments for injuries, employers purchased freedom from most lawsuits. Workers' compensation also signaled the business community's acknowledgment of its own responsibility for workers injured on the job.

Although a general trend toward greater liability for business can be observed over the nineteenth and twentieth centuries, a dramatic acceleration began in the 1960s. A tort "revolution" generated novel theories of liability, which allowed business corporations to be held liable under a wider range of circumstances.[40] Product liability laws underwent substantial change. Companies were held to a standard of strict liability for defective products.[41] The idea of market-share liability, in which companies would pay a proportion of the claims for injuries stemming from a defective product according to their market share of the product rather than their demonstrated negligence toward specific plaintiffs, was proposed.[42] Criminal charges against corporations for wrongdoing in the course of business also increased.[43]

All these modifications enhanced the role of law in regulating business transactions and increased business presence in the courts. Large business corporations constitute a notable presence in the federal courts today.[44] Overall, studies of federal court filings show that business litigation has increased since the 1960s. Most of the public attention has been focused on cases in which individual plaintiffs sue business defendants, and that is the major focus of this book. However, there have also been some marked changes in the extent to which businesses use the courts to resolve disputes among themselves.[45] The Benlate cases, for example, often pitted small-business users of the product against the much larger manufacturer. Even though some types of business litigation have leveled off or even decreased somewhat since the mid-1980s, certain kinds of high-visibility cases involving businesses, such as product liability and class actions, continue to expand. And one study of federal litigation in the 1990s found that business disputes ranked first among the most intractable cases confronting the judiciary, comprising about a third of the cases that were three or more years old.[46]

Analysts have attempted to explain the increased presence of business corporations in the courtroom. Some commentators focus on why people now appear to be more willing to sue businesses over defective products, workplace and consumer injuries, and discrimination than they were in the past. Some trace this increased propensity to sue to a changed legal culture with the basic tenet that innocent victims of injury should receive compensation.[47] Others assert that standards of personal responsibility have eroded and that Americans are an overly litigious people who hobble businesses with lawsuits. Still other scholars focus on why businesses themselves are more apt to bring their disputes against other businesses into the courtroom. This greater willingness to sue other businesses has been attributed to changes

9

in business practices that encourage reliance on the law.[48] It has also been linked with the degree to which businesses face competition, instability, and uncertainty.[49]

The Contemporary Jury in Business Cases

Whatever the reasons for increased business presence in the courts, the result of the historical trends that I have just described is that ordinary citizens sitting on juries today decide a substantial number of cases involving a corporate party. The Benlate litigation demonstrates the often demanding role that the United States asks citizens to play in the resolution of complex disputes involving one or more business corporations.

In one of the earliest studies of the use of civil juries in business cases, Mark Peterson analyzed state and federal jury trials in Cook County, Illinois, and San Francisco, California, from 1960 to 1984.[50] Jury trials in business-contract cases increased over the two decades in both jurisdictions,[51] tracking the increase in business litigation.

Other studies show significant numbers of jury trials with business litigants in state trial courts.[52] In an analysis of the civil jury trials during 1992 in forty-five state courts participating in the Civil Trial Court Network Project organized by the National Center for State Courts, just over half of the civil jury trials listed a corporation as a defendant. Another 9% listed a hospital or medical company as a defendant.[53] Thus, business corporations account for more than half of the defendants in civil jury trials in state courts nationwide. They also appear as plaintiffs, but much less frequently— in 11% of the civil jury trials.[54] Yet little is known about how the jury responds to and copes with these kinds of trials, or how jurors are affected by the presence of business corporations in litigation.

One important point must be mentioned. Most business lawsuits, like other kinds of civil and criminal litigation, settle rather than go to trial.[55] In contrast to the jury's dominant role in the legal systems of earlier times, today jury verdicts constitute only a small fraction of case resolutions. The Civil Trial Court Network Project showed that jury verdicts accounted for just 2.7% of the outcomes of tort cases (both business and nonbusiness) in the state courts,[56] while a study of large corporate litigation in federal courts found that jury verdicts constituted about 5% of all case outcomes.[57]

Some observers might assert that the relatively small percentage of business cases resolved by a jury (or a judge, for that matter) indicates the overall unimportance of the jury in business litigation. It's a reasonable point. Yet what happens in those relatively few jury trials helps to determine what will occur in the far more numerous settlements.[58] The civil jury provides signals that litigants, potential litigants, lawyers, and others read to assess their chances at trial, informing their decisions about pursuing claims, accepting cases, and reaching settlements.[59] Of course, the signals can be fuzzy: in the Benlate cases in Georgia and Florida that settled during jury deliberations, uncertainty over the jury verdict and the award were much on the minds of the parties as they engaged in settlement negotiations while the jury was deliberating. The jury's presence in the civil justice system also influences the nature of the litigation. Whether juries actually decided the Benlate cases or not, a significant amount of the legal activity in such cases was and continues to be structured around the possibility that a jury might evaluate the case. Litigation procedures, rules of evidence, and decisions about whether certain experts might testify are all predicated on the potential fact-finding jury. Then, too, the jury is the visible tip of the iceberg; public attention to jury verdicts in business cases heightens their impact.

Some people argue that there are good reasons for the jury's continuing involvement in these civil cases. One of the prime justifications for the jury is its political role. Usually when people discuss the political role of the jury, they focus on criminal cases. The criminal jury is seen as a vehicle for protecting individuals against biased or oppressive government, and as a way of infusing community notions of fairness and equity into court outcomes. The civil jury also serves important political purposes.[60] Jury judgments of corporate negligence reflect public expectations about responsibility in the marketplace and send messages about desirable standards of business conduct. The balance of responsibility between workers and consumers, on the one hand, and business enterprises, on the other hand, has changed over time. The civil jury decides negligence cases in line with these shifting ideas about the power of citizens over businesses. By jury verdicts or by the threat of them, the citizens on the jury control (albeit imperfectly) corporate and business conduct. Through their awards, juries also have the ability to respond to changes in the value of life and work.

Wall Street Journal reporter Stephen Adler has observed that when cases pit an individual against a business corporation, the jury operates as a kind of equalizer: "Though the company is typically richer and more powerful than the individual, its wealth provides it no particular advantage before a jury that is randomly picked from the community. The company can't buy the jury's protection, as it conceivably might buy the loyalty of an elected state judge who's dependent on campaign contributions. And it can't benefit from social connections at the top tier of society that's shared by corporate and judicial officials but not by the average juror. The playing field is level."[61]

Consumer activist Ralph Nader and his colleagues may be identified as one end of the continuum of views about the importance of the civil jury's exertion of control over the business community. Believing that business corporations are privileged in the legal system, they critique the tort reform movement for its attempt to seek "a radical dismembering of the justice system's ability to hold corporations accountable to people they have wronged."[62] Nader and his colleagues champion the ability of the jury to speak out against corporations engaging in activities that have the potential to harm consumers: "Following a single decade, 1965–75, when consumer, environmental, and other laws protecting individuals were enacted and judicial decisions rendered to hold corporations more accountable, corporate power domestically and internationally has been in ascendance for the past twenty years. . . . The imbalances between real people and artificial persons called corporations are growing fast. . . . The momentum in Congress and state legislatures has been . . . to weaken the very laws that restrained the abuses of companies and channeled their energy toward less destructive paths or, at best, into more singularly productive outcomes such as adopting safety technologies."[63]

For precisely this reason, as well as others, there are many criticisms of the jury's role in business and corporate lawsuits. Some critics argue that experts or business people should resolve these disputes rather than the lay public, many of whom are unfamiliar with technical material or business operations. The Benlate trials are a good example of the challenging types of evidence juries must consider, including scientific and technical evidence and conflicting expert testimony. The Benlate juries learned about such company undertakings as memos, orders to erase computer files, and communications between the legal branch and the agricultural products branch of DuPont. They had to judge whether the documents and actions represented benign business dealings or attempts to cover up negligent behavior. To understand this evidence requires a fair amount of sophistication about standard operating procedures within companies. For instance, in the Benlate case there was dispute about the meaning of a DuPont directive to delete computer files. DuPont's attorneys presented it as normal business activity, but the plaintiffs' attorneys saw it as evidence of an attempted cover-up. Can jurors grasp the significance of evidence of company activity, especially when it is presented within an adversarial context?

And what about the purported "junk science" linking Benlate to birth defects?

How does a jury largely unschooled in medical and scientific research reach a sound decision about highly technical and hotly disputed expert evidence? The appellate order overturning the Florida jury's decision in the birth-defect case observed that allowing the plaintiffs to refer to an alleged but undocumented link between Benlate and birth-defect clusters had great potential to affect the jury adversely.[64]

Other critics question the civil jury's fairness rather than its competence. Many business people believe that the public is prejudiced against corporations and that this slant is reflected in jury decisions. Some business leaders, perhaps the majority, would disagree strongly with Adler's metaphor of a level playing field in the jury trial, instead believing that businesses face significant disadvantages before a jury because of jurors' inherent tendency to empathize with individual plaintiffs who have been injured.[65] As Marcia Angell, the executive editor of the prestigious *New England Journal of Medicine*, observed in a book about breast implant litigation: "The presence of juries increases the lottery aspects of the tort system. Skillful plaintiffs' attorneys may select only the most appealing clients, and focus their efforts primarily on mobilizing the sympathy of the jury. . . . The resultant verdict may have little to do with the merits of the case, and everything to do with theater."[66]

Related to this is a prevailing notion that the jury acts as Robin Hood, redistributing wealth from the rich to the injured poor. A ubiquitous belief is that jurors are so sympathetic to injured plaintiffs who sue big companies that they reach into the deep pockets of wealthy corporations and grant huge awards, even though the companies may not be negligent. A recent national survey asked senior corporate executives for their views about the reasons that litigation and civil justice costs were high. The number-one reason listed was "the knowledge that major corporate defendants and their insurance companies have deep pockets."[67] "Juries that hand out excessively high awards" was ranked third as an explanation for high costs. Was the Florida jury's decision against DuPont in the birth-defect case based more on their heartstrings and the company's deep pockets than on the scientific evidence linking the boy's lack of eyes to prenatal Benlate exposure? Just how true is it that juries penalize businesses in court for having substantial resources?

Even those who believe that juries are competent and fair point to the unpredictability of jury verdicts as a serious problem. Not atypically, the Benlate litigation shows that juries in different trials sometimes reach opposite verdicts, even when the bulk of the evidence is similar.[68] The post-trial interviews with Benlate jurors revealed that even in the same trial, jurors responded differently. Of course, the most likely alternative to the jury is the judge. Judicial decision making may also vary from case to case. Studies of judges on sentencing councils and appellate courts reveal substantial disagreement among judges on factual, normative, and legal matters.[69] Whether judges would be more predictable than juries in their resolution of business cases, then, is debatable. The variability across judges, jurors, trials, and jurisdictions makes it challenging to gauge the likely outcomes of litigation.

The unpredictability of citizen control in the form of civil jury verdicts is blamed for interfering with American business competitiveness and innovation. Eight out of ten senior corporate executives in the survey previously described said that the fear of lawsuits has more impact on company decision making now than it did ten years ago, and six out of ten agreed that the U.S. civil justice system significantly hampers the ability of U.S. companies to compete effectively with Japanese and European companies.[70] Whether civil litigation has in fact interfered with international competitiveness has been questioned. Although the evidence so far is limited, some scholars conclude that it's unlikely that the costs associated with liability have materially affected trade balances.[71]

Perhaps more significant is the charge that the threat of litigation discourages companies from making risky but useful products.[72] Facing the prospect of multiple lawsuits, many companies decide to abandon otherwise sound products. Consider the anti-nausea drug Bendectin. This prescription medication was given to pregnant women to counteract morning sickness. A set of initial animal studies appeared to implicate Bendectin as a cause of birth defects, and massive numbers of lawsuits were launched against the manufacturer. Even though later epidemiological studies showed no statistical link between taking Bendectin during pregnancy and having a baby with birth defects, the company removed the drug from the market.[73] The extensive testing of Benlate, too, produced results that DuPont proclaimed as a clean bill of health but which plaintiffs' experts disputed. The final chapter on the effects of Benlate DF is not yet written; in fact, as a scientific matter we may never know its exact effects. Whether or not it could have been a valuable fungicide, it is no longer available.

Efforts to Limit the Civil Jury

The debate about citizen control over the corporation via the jury has intensified in recent times. During the Reagan, Bush, and Clinton administrations, there were concerted efforts to pass tort-reform legislation that would make it more difficult for plaintiffs to recover from civil defendants in the tort system.[74] Various business concerns, especially the insurance industry, undertook advertising campaigns decrying a litigation explosion, a tort crisis, and the jury at the root of it all.[75] In arguments reminiscent of nineteenth-century views, excessive litigation was charged with interfering with American competitiveness. Although the civil jury was not the only culprit, it was a frequent target of tort reform efforts. For example, in the *Contract with America*, Republicans pointed to the civil jury as a serious problem: "It is news to no one that juries have been out of control over the past decade in awarding punitive damages far in excess of what is recovered to make a plaintiff whole."[76]

Although federal tort-reform efforts have been largely unsuccessful, many statehouses across the nation have changed their tort systems, imposing new restrictions on the civil jury, including modification of liability rules and limits on monetary awards.[77] Business interests have been well represented among the groups urging both state and federal lawmakers to pass tort reforms.[78]

Efforts to limit the civil jury in business cases are not confined to the political arena. Combined with the legislative actions just described, judicial decision making in product liability cases has resulted in what two scholars labeled a "quiet revolution."[79] In contrast to the loudly announced expansion of product liability law starting in the 1960s, during the 1970s and 1980s judicial decisions quietly but effectively eroded the reach of product liability law.

More recently, the U.S. Supreme Court has placed new constraints on the scope of the civil jury's decision making, and I believe it is no accident that each of the cases in which it did so was a business dispute.[80] In 1996 a unanimous Court decided *Markman v. Westview Instruments*,[81] which restricted the jury's role in patent cases. The key issue in the case was whether the judge or the jury should determine claim terms in patent lawsuits. Even though there was no empirical evidence about jurors' abilities in patent cases, the Supreme Court concluded that "the construction of written instruments is one of those things that judges often do and are likely to do better than jurors."[82] The Supreme Court stated that the significant goal of uniformity would be better served by giving the task of claim interpretation to judges as opposed to jurors.

In another important case, the Supreme Court imposed controls on jury discretion, this time over jury decisions about punitive damages. The Supreme Court found a jury's punitive damage award in a case against the car manufacturer BMW to be grossly excessive and struck it down.[83] Justice Stephen Breyer observed that unregulated jury decision making about damages encouraged results that "jar one's constitutional sensibilities."[84]

The Supreme Court has also given judges greater control over determining who should testify as expert witnesses. At least part of the justification is the perception that judges need to act as gatekeepers so that juries will not be unduly influenced by junk-science experts. In the *Daubert* case involving claims about the drug Bendectin, the Court held that federal judges should subject a potential scientific expert's proposed testimony to critical review in the process of determining whether the expert should be allowed to testify in a case;[85] the *Kumho* case expanded that approach to other expert witnesses who rely on their experience, such as tire specialists.[86] The end result is that experts whose credibility was assessed in the past by juries are now likely to be heard (and perhaps excluded) only by the judge. Thus the credibility of expert testimony becomes more a judicial matter than a jury matter, in a power shift reminiscent of the nineteenth-century constriction of jury powers and concomitant expansion of judicial authority. It is worth emphasizing that both the *Daubert* and *Kumho* decisions granting greater judicial control over expert witnesses were cases with corporate defendants.

Whatever the outcome of political and legal conflicts over the shape of the civil justice system, there are sure to be continuing efforts to limit the role of the jury in cases involving businesses and corporations. The stakes in this debate are high. If one takes the advocates of each position seriously, on one side is the strength and soundness of the U.S. business community. On the other is the ability of citizens to send messages about the acceptability of business conduct and to control and punish irresponsible and harmful actions in the corporate world.

Notwithstanding the high stakes, much of the debate over the citizen's role as jurors in business litigation has consisted of the presentation of flashy anecdotes rather than careful study and analysis. Many commentators on the problems of the civil justice system have noted the lack of extensive factual knowledge about how the system operates.[87] Two scholars of corporate litigation, Terence Dunworth and Joel Rogers, observe: "We lack a clear understanding of the scope and character of business litigation. . . . The information vacuum makes it extremely difficult to create a satisfactory empirical context for even the most basic questions raised by those on either side of the issues. Despite this, policies are formed and legislation is passed, often seemingly rationalized by little more than carefully selected anecdotes. . . . The empirically degraded character of the discussion virtually ensures excess combativeness and policy mistakes."[88]

This book is intended as a corrective. It provides, for the first time, systematic information about how jurors and the public respond to civil lawsuits with business and corporate parties.

An Overview of the Business Jury Project

A number of scholars, energized by the policy debate, have begun to study how the civil jury operates in practice. I draw on their important work in this book. The book's major focus, though, is the presentation of results from a set of interrelated studies that I conducted specifically to determine the reactions of juries and the public to business corporations in court.[89] The research concentrates (though not exclusively) on the most controversial type of case, tort cases in which individual plaintiffs sue corporate defendants for personal injuries.

As part of the research project, I interviewed civil jurors who decided cases in state courts with business and corporate litigants. This unique set of interviews is analyzed to determine how jurors react to business defendants and to the plaintiffs who sue them. In this book I describe how jurors treat corporations in civil cases, how they decide on business liability and damages, and how a corporation's financial and other resources influence them.

I also undertook a statewide survey in which respondents gave their opinions about business regulation and litigation. This poll of public opinion provides information about how the public thinks and feels about business at a relatively abstract level. By presenting these data together with the reactions of the lay public when they serve as jurors in specific trials, I am able to draw comparisons and links between these two different sources of information about the public's responses to business litigation.

Finally, I conducted a series of experiments designed to determine *why* people might respond differently when a corporation is the defendant in a lawsuit. Experiments are not as realistic as the courtroom, but they are ideal for teasing apart some of the factors that influence public judgments of business and corporate responsibility. The research approach of triangulation, in which several different methods are employed to answer the same questions, is often the best way to uncover complex reasons for human behavior. This research strategy helps to overcome the inevitable weaknesses in any one research method.

To obtain a sense of the strengths and limitations of the research project, it is important to provide more detailed description of the studies. This is particularly true of the juror study, because the types of cases heard by these jurors limit the relevance of their observations. During a one-year period at a state trial court of general juris-diction, I identified every civil jury trial that had a business or corporate party in which the jury deliberated to a verdict or declared itself hung.[90] With the court's cooperation, my research team contacted each juror from these trials and requested a personal interview. The overall participation rate was 64%, with approximately 7 out of every 12 jurors from each case interviewed for the study. A total of 269 jurors from 36 different cases involving businesses and corporations were interviewed. The trials and interviews spanned the time period from 1989 to 1991. Because the judges in the court requested that I preserve the confidentiality of the cases and jurors as much as possible, the book does not identify the court, the specific case names, or the exact start and end dates of the study.

The cases, which included twenty-eight tort cases and eight contract cases, repre-sented a broad spectrum of business issues. This book often focuses on the tort jurors because tort cases against businesses have occasioned the greatest criticism. Tort trials included one product liability case, two cases of premises liability, three as-bestos trials, four cases of worker injuries, eight cases involving automobile accidents with business vehicles, and ten medical malpractice cases.

In all the tort cases, an individual plaintiff or a group of plaintiffs sued business or corporate defendants, which is consistent with the pattern found in national studies.[91] All but three cases involved multiple plaintiffs; most typically, an injured party's spouse or other family member joined the injured person as a party in the lawsuit. The asbestos cases included from six to nine plaintiffs apiece.

The contract cases included three trials involving alleged breaches of contract for construction or other home improvements, one employment contract case, a lemon law case, and three other trials of business disputes, including disagreements over service fees, a supplier's contract, and a shipment delivery. Four of the eight contract cases pitted individual plaintiffs against defendant corporations, another involved a corporate plaintiff suing individual defendants (who prevailed on counterclaims), and the remaining three contract cases were disputes between business corporations.

Because the study included every relevant case over the time period, it reflects the sort of civil jury cases typically heard in the state court. The types of cases are fairly typical of the trials that civil juries decide in other states as well.[92] About three-quarters of my sample and the usual civil jury caseload consists of tort cases, with automobile torts one of the most frequent types of cases. My sample included relatively more medical malpractice cases and fewer premises liability cases than is typical of state court juries hearing cases with business and corporate parties.

Most of the cases involved business corporations of moderate size and financial resources. Eight of the cases, including the three asbestos trials, had parties that were Fortune 500 companies or other major national corporations. Eighteen cases included regional or local companies; several had only a single place of business. Nevertheless, virtually all the businesses were incorporated. In the medical and dental malpractice cases, the doctors and dentists frequently were sued both individually and as part of their medical corporations; such additional defendants as hospitals were included in a few cases.

Overall, the plaintiffs prevailed in twenty-six of the thirty-six trials, including one directed verdict for the plaintiff, for a win rate of 72%. There were nine defense verdicts, and in one medical malpractice case the jury could not reach a unanimous verdict. Although the small number of cases does not permit us to make meaningful statistical comparisons with other studies of tort litigation, the win rate in my study of 72% is higher than that found in other projects. In the National Center for State Courts study, for example, the win rate in civil jury tort trials with business defendants was 52%. American Bar Foundation researchers Stephen Daniels and Joanne Martin found striking variability in civil jury win rates in their study of eighty-two jurisdictions, ranging from a low of 31% to a high of 76%. Most sites had win rates between 50% and 65%, but a not insignificant number (fourteen out of eighty-two) exceeded 65%, as my study sample did. The win rate does not necessarily suggest that jurors in this jurisdiction favor plaintiffs; it could just as easily reflect state law, local settlement practices, the mix of cases going to jury trial, or other factors. The case mix seems a particularly likely candidate, given that in this study I purposefully selected only cases with business or corporate parties.

As in other studies of civil jury awards, the awards in most of the cases in this project were moderate, although there were several very substantial awards. The median award for all cases was $115,000. The mean award was substantially higher, at $697,556, reflecting the five awards of one million dollars or more. The National Center for State Courts study found that cases involving corporations resulted in higher mean and median awards compared to the mean and median awards in all tort cases, and that was true in this study as well.[93]

Using a semi-structured interview format, we interviewed each of the jurors individually and asked about their reactions to the parties and evidence in the case. A number of questions revolved around how juries evaluated the liability of businesses and corporations. We asked jurors about their general impressions of the parties, about the impact of the presence of a corporation, and about their general views of corporate responsibility. After the interviews, jurors completed questionnaires that probed their attitudes toward civil litigation and business. This gave us general information about the views of civil jurors and also permitted us to examine whether these attitudes affected their decision making as jurors.

Interviews constitute an excellent way to obtain detailed accounts of jurors, but they have some limitations. The accuracy of self-reports is debatable because of potential for memory problems or systematic biases. Participants who want to present themselves as "good jurors," for example, might consciously or unconsciously slant their responses in a socially desirable direction. Jurors might adjust their memory for events so that it is more consistent with the outcome of the case or so that it reflects more positively on them.[94] In designing the project, I attempted to minimize these problems. I asked a series of open-ended questions about the jury experience, with witness lists and specific trial benchmarks to aid jurors' memory. Key issues were explored with several different questions, which were posed in ways to lessen automatic, socially desirable responses. Interviews were completely confidential, so that jurors would feel freer to express their true views. Multiple jurors were interviewed from each case, providing an opportunity to confirm or disconfirm jurors' recollections. The candor reflected in many of the quotations from jurors in this book attest to at least the partial success of these features of the interviews. Perhaps most significant, however, is that for key issues the interview data were supplemented by the findings of two other research approaches.

The first of these approaches, a mock jury study of premises liability, tested whether people would respond differently to a tort case that included a business defendant rather than an individual defendant. It used a "slip-and-fall" case, where a woman plaintiff was injured in a fall occurring either in a furniture store or at a tag sale in a private home. Thus, in one experimental condition, the defendant was an individual; in the other condition, all the facts were the same except that the defendant was a corporation. The study was conducted in the real-life setting of a public courthouse, and community residents read the case materials, made individual judgments, and deliberated in mock juries to reach a group decision on the verdict and award. A total of 216 people participated in the study. Videotaped discussions of the deliberations provided insights about how people evaluate cases that include a corporate defendant. Participants in the study also completed questionnaires probing their attitudes toward civil litigation and business, and thus we were able to examine whether these attitudes affected subjects' decisions in the mock jury trial. Because the decisions of mock juries have no real impact on either a plaintiff or a defendant, these experiments may not completely reflect how actual juries respond to a real trial of premises liability, but they allow the researcher control over the key features of a trial, in this case, whether the defendant was a business corporation.

In a final study, we examined several theoretical ideas about why people might treat corporations differently from individuals. Respondents were 450 residents of a northeastern state, contacted by telephone in a study of attitudes toward civil litigation and business.[95] As in the other two studies, a questionnaire was used to obtain information about attitudes toward business and civil litigation. In addition, a scenario experiment testing several key hypotheses was included. Respondents were first asked to indicate their agreement or disagreement with a number of items pertaining to civil litigation, business, and other social attitudes. Then, each respondent listened to a single scenario and answered questions about their evaluations of the incident described by the scenario. Various scenarios were constructed to test the study's hypotheses. To examine the impact of corporate identity, the defendant to a personal injury claim was described in different scenarios as an individual, a nonprofit corporation or association, or a for-profit business corporation. Financial resources were varied to test the "deep pockets" hypothesis. Finally, two different types of tort claims were employed to explore the generality of the phenomenon. Statistical analyses of attitudes toward business and civil litigation were conducted to determine whether and how these attitudes influenced judgments of corporate responsibility. Combining the findings of the public opinion survey with the results from the juror interviews and the mock jury study was a powerful research approach that provided a wealth of information about how jurors and the public react to business corporations in the courtroom. When the findings from this original research are placed in the context of the work of other scholars and analysts of the civil justice system, they present a fuller portrait of juries in business cases than has ever been available before.

2

BLAMING THE VICTIM IN CIVIL
LAWSUITS AGAINST BUSINESS

There is a widespread presumption that juries are naturally sympathetic to injured plaintiffs, particularly those hurt by the actions of a business corporation. The assumption goes back a long way. In the mid-nineteenth century, Judge Barculo observed in *Haring v. New York and Erie Railroad* (1852): "We can not shut our eyes to the fact than in certain controversies between the weak and the strong—between a humble individual and a gigantic corporation, the sympathies of the human mind naturally, honestly, and generously, run to the assistance and support of the feeble, and apparently oppressed; and that compassion will sometimes exercise over the deliberations of a jury, an influence which, however honorable to them as philanthropists, is wholly inconsistent with the principles of law and the ends of justice."[1]

Similarly, the eminent American jurist Jerome Frank wrote in the 1930s that the facts that the "defendant is a wealthy corporation and the plaintiff is a poor boy . . . often determine who will win or lose."[2] In a scathing indictment of the civil justice system written in 1988, popular writer Peter Huber argued that juries are often overwhelmed with sympathy when they decide a business case involving a seriously injured victim: "Juries face accidents up close, viewing them in the lurid setting of an individual tragedy already completed. . . . The only human reaction to the individual tragedy viewed close up, is unbounded generosity, which any large corporation or insurer can surely afford to underwrite."[3]

This common belief that people naturally sympathize with injured victims is presumed to make juries more prone than judges to find for the plaintiff, especially when the plaintiff sues a corporation. More than half the respondents in a national poll said that plaintiffs had a better chance of winning a case if the fact finder was a jury rather than a judge.[4] Legal experts seem to agree. In one poll, law professors, dispute experts, and law students were asked whether juries or judges were likely to be more favorable to the plaintiffs in product liability cases, medical malpractice cases, and contract cases. Although these legally sophisticated respondents perceived that juries would not favor plaintiffs in contract trials, the participants predicted that plaintiffs would have much greater success before juries than before judges in product liability cases and medical malpractice cases. For instance, in product liability trials, the law professors predicted that the plaintiff would prevail 63% of the time before a jury but only 44% before a judge.[5]

Relatively recent court decisions also appear to be based in part on assumptions about the jury's overwhelming sympathy for the injured victim, which is thought to interfere with its effort to decide cases on the objective facts. In a case involving the anti-nausea agent Bendectin, alleged to have caused birth defects in children whose mothers had ingested the drug during pregnancy, the trial judge barred from the courtroom plaintiffs under ten years of age and those with visible birth defects.[6] He argued that the jury's sympathy for children with birth defects would be too prejudicial and would interfere with its fact finding.

Beliefs about the problem of jury sympathy toward plaintiffs in corporate cases is so widespread that the Federation of Insurance and Corporate Counsel put together an informative videotape for its members entitled *Handling Sympathy in Jury Trials*. The hour-long tape instructs corporate counsel on methods for counteracting the natural compassion that jurors feel for severely injured plaintiffs. Among the tips are suggestions that corporate attorneys desensitize jurors to the plaintiff's injuries, avoid grilling the victim (which would make him or her an even more sympathetic figure), and show that even people who suffer debilitating injuries can lead productive lives.[7]

Assumptions that jury decisions in civil cases are based largely on sympathy to injured plaintiffs, rather than on rational assessments of the defendant's negligence, have fueled a move in the United States to restrict the jury's role in civil cases (see Chapter 1). Considering all of these perspectives, there seems to be a consensus that juries are highly sympathetic to the injured people who sue businesses.

In this chapter, I argue that this apparent consensus is wrong. The belief that jurors are universally compassionate to injured plaintiffs is simplistic. It does not capture the complexity of the approach that jurors take in assessing the claims of the injured party in a lawsuit against a corporation. Jurors often show doubts about, and sometimes even hostility toward, injured plaintiffs. This is not to say that jurors are *never* sympathetic. Rather, they have a highly differentiated reaction to the civil plaintiff that flies in the face of the conventional wisdom that jurors are nothing more than bleeding hearts.

The Boy in the Paint Store

The case of the boy in the paint store reveals the varied ways jurors examine the victim's responsibility in a lawsuit. A five-year-old boy accompanied his mother to a paint store. While she was looking at wallpaper samples, he was getting into trouble. Even before the accident that became the subject of the lawsuit, the clerk had apparently complained to the mother that the boy was messing up his displays. Before long, the boy got hold of a spring-loaded knife on the store counter. It was bright orange and looked a lot like a toy. Trying to open the knife, he cut one of his fingers through the tendon. The mother took the boy to his pediatrician, who simply sewed the skin without repairing the tendon. As a result the boy lost the full use of his finger. The family sued the store for negligence on the grounds that it had dangerous items that were accessible to children. The task for the jury was to determine whether the store was negligent. In making that decision, they also had to consider whether the boy's mother was negligent.

The doctor who mismanaged the boy's initial care was a phantom in the case. Jurors reported having discussed why a prime culprit was not a defendant in the litigation before them: "Hey, this lady's suing the wrong person, she's suing the store, and she should be suing the doctor" (C20-J7).[8] Jurors, though frustrated by the doctor's absence, resigned themselves to addressing the issue before them: the relative culpability of the mother and the store.

The jury contained a range of individuals—young and old, men and women, some with little education or modest jobs, and others with extensive resumes. From the start, there were striking contrasts in the ways various jurors allocated the responsibility for the injury between the store and the mother. A few of the jurors, who were older men, thought that although a parent is always responsible for his or her child, the situation is different in a store with hazardous materials. One man stated:

> The defense [tried] to create the impression to the jury that this was a busybody kid. And he'd gotten into trouble in other ways. He'd fallen off this at the school and he'd gotten into that kind of a jam. . . . He was a busy guy. . . . The clerk doesn't know how busy this kid is, but he ought to know that five-year-olds generally are pretty busy. I think the clerk and the store share a greater responsibility in this regard for watching the child because the mother doesn't know that in a paint store and wallpaper store there are any hazardous materials, things are in cans and there are brushes and there are rolls and she can see that in the displays. I'm sure that it would never dawn on her that the kid could really get into any more trouble than to just handle a paint or a roll or a brush or what have you. (C20-J2)

This juror saw the mother as having little knowledge of the potential dangers the store posed to her child, whereas the clerk was in a position to be aware of the trouble spots. The juror criticized the defense attorney, who "wanted to make it look as if the child was negligent. . . . He wanted to put the blame on [the mother and the boy]." The defense attorney tried to "blame the victim" by emphasizing the active role of the child and by pointing out that he had to reach across the counter to get the knife and had to work hard to get the knife open. In addition, defense suggestions that the mother was too preoccupied with her wallpaper to attend to the child bordered on charges of maternal neglect. This older male juror took issue with the defense's blaming the child and the mother: "I'm assuming that it's perfectly all right and not negligent to release the child from your hand. She did not have him by the hand. But then kids get lost in stores for God's sake, it happens all the time. People's kids are wandering around getting themselves into hopefully not very serious trouble. So it's an accepted part of the custom for the kids to be let alone. In this case I didn't think that she was negligent. It was pretty much a nonhazardous type of situation, and she said she had him out of the corner of her eye while she was looking at the book, she was looking up periodically" (C20-J2). In the words of another juror, who was a grandfather of two: "You know a mother is going to go in there to look at a book of wallpaper, her mind is on what she wants to get and the kid runs off this and that. Kids do that, I've seen that all over the place, then the company should definitely not have anything out where a kid might get hurt on it." Likening the store's role to that of a grandparent, he observed: "I have two granddaughters, and when my daughter used to come my wife would check right away to make sure she doesn't have anything out for the kids to hurt themselves on, any pills or anything like that" (C20-J1).

Even so, the grandfather continued to acknowledge the responsibility of the parent: "The mother is definitely responsible for your kid . . . especially when she walked in the store. . . . If you take a kid in a hardware store, you definitely got to keep an eye on him because they got all kinds of stuff in a hardware store that you can get hurt on. You know that" (C20-J1). Another man in his fifties was initially drawn to the plaintiffs. Left on his own, he admitted that he would have given them some money.

In contrast to these older men, other jurors argued that the store was not negligent at all. They maintained that the responsibility was entirely the mother's, not the store's. The strongest advocates for the mother's responsibility were women jurors. Holding her baby during the interview, one young woman asserted that the mother should have known of the danger: "Knowing the accessories that come with

25

wallpaper, she should have been a little more careful than to let her son run around. I mean that would have been the same thing if he had got a hold of a can of spray paint and sprayed it in his eye, I mean she just wasn't watching him, he was over there tearing up all the other stuff before he ran over there to the counter. . . . She was at fault for just letting him run around. . . . Some people let their kids do what they wanna do because they're spoiled. . . . I learned a lot from the case not to just let her [the juror's own baby daughter] wander off. I think it's a shame that his hand is like that, but if he could play softball and bowl, what else does he do?" (C20-J3).

This juror complained that the plaintiff's attorney was oriented toward eliciting sympathy from the jury, selecting a lot of old people for the jury "because they would feel sorry because he was a little five-year-old when it happened." Every time the plaintiff's attorney spoke, "it was about how much pain [the child] was in. How much pain his parents have gone through and they sound like they've been having a ball to me. Going to see ball games and swim meets. . . . " She was surprised that many of the other jurors initially saw the store as having some responsibility: "I really convinced them that they had to sort out more facts and that they couldn't just go by the way that they stood. I mean you can make tears come out of your eyes if you sit there and just dwell on the sympathy part" (C20-J3).

The new mother was not alone. Another woman juror, a mother of nine children, complained that the plaintiff's attorney was "trying to put a guilt trip on us all . . . for the poor kid, the poor kid . . . 'I want you to take a good look at this kid,' and all this, he was really putting the pity on. And I thought no, no, no, no, you don't do that." She said that she was pretty strict with her own children: "I would not take one of my kids out to a store with me, because I felt if I can't make it mind, it's not going with me. And they didn't go with me either." The mother "should have had him, five years old, right by her side" and by the hand, because fifteen feet away was too far for a young child, and "I know what kids can get into" (C20-J4). In addition to her strong belief that the mother alone was responsible for her children, this juror questioned the plaintiff's claims about the severity of the injury to the boy's hand, because he was very active in sports.

A third woman who strongly supported the defense was an older, unmarried nurse, who said of the mother: "She should have been watching her child. You don't let a kid run around in a store, a five year old, without keeping an eye on him. [The store clerks] aren't baby-sitters. . . . The knives were up by the cash register. How do they know some kid was gonna come around, picking up knives? It would have been different if it were laying on the floor with the blade exposed" (C20-J8).

This juror's assumptions about what the clerk was likely to have known in advance contrast strongly with the assumptions of the first juror quoted above, who believed that the clerk was quite likely to know the store's danger spots. She complained that a number of the gentlemen on the jury "fell for the sympathy ploy." "They made a big issue out of the boy's finger, about it being sensitive, but it was nothing but a sympathy ploy, and he plays baseball, he pitches" (C20-J8).

The other jurors fell somewhere in the middle, seeing the dual responsibilities of store and mother. Nevertheless, several commented unfavorably on the mother: "My impression of the mother was that she was a person who saw an opportunity to recover a lot of money, a significant amount of money, and was taking every opportunity she had to do that. . . . The mother should have known that she had an active five-year-old and either left him in the car, the mother had a tough choice to make, or if she had him in the store she had him tied to her belt or took him to his grandmother's house and then went back to the store. But the mother was the one responsible for the safety of that child in the store, and she did not exercise the right or reasonable care. That story which was not presented by either side but was generated in the jury room, was seen to be credible by all of the jurors" (C20-J5).

Another man found the mother's testimony "not believable because she clearly had a vested interest in the outcome of the case. My impression of her was not that she was intentionally lying, but that she was distorting, but unintentionally, what actually happened" (C20-J9). He was initially on the fence, but the mother's own evidence convinced him that she was distorting what had happened.

An older woman juror gave her reactions to the mother's testimony: "She was emotional and she would break down. I think she just made a big thing out of it, and I almost agreed with the defense lawyer that she was the cause of it, because I didn't think it was that big a thing." She observed: "There was an older man [in the jury deliberation] who said, 'I'd like to see them get something.' And sure, we'd all like to have happy endings, but we've got to face facts, that mother was wrong" (C20-J6). Jurors thus policed one another to stick to what they regarded as "the facts" rather than give in to their desires to help out the plaintiff's family.

Jurors relied on their own experiences—and their areas of special knowledge and expertise—in trying to reach a conclusion about the appropriate level of responsibility of the mother. The three strongest opponents of the mother were women, two of whom were immersed in child rearing (one with nine children, the other with a new baby). Others, more at a distance, seemed to take a more generous view of the mother's behavior, seeing it as normal. Jurors with managerial experience drew on their knowledge of business safety practices to infer that the defendant company bore some responsibility.

Another issue that divided jurors was their contrasting beliefs about what each of the parties knew or should have known about the hazards of the store. Those who favored the mother suggested that she may not have known about the danger, while those who opposed her maintained that she should have known because she had gone to other similar stores.

All the jurors acknowledged that "kids will be kids," but what implications stemmed from the perceived uncontrollability of children differed. The mothers who were the strongest advocates for the store claimed that they would not take a child into a potentially hazardous place without having the child firmly in hand. In contrast, advocates for the plaintiffs acknowledged that because kids sometimes can't be controlled, others—such as store owners—must try to anticipate potential accidents and arrange their stores to minimize them.

In the end, as the divergent perspectives suggest, the jury concluded that both the store and the mother bore some responsibility for the boy's injury. The negligence of the mother was held to be an intervening cause of the injury, offsetting the negligence of the store, and the ultimate result was a defense verdict.

Similar Trends in Other Cases

The paint-store case is a bit unusual in that the person who was injured, the boy, was not the one the jurors focused on the most in allocating responsibility. That prize went to the boy's mother. But similar tendencies to blame the victim—to locate responsibility in injured persons and their families rather than corporate actors—were apparent in most cases in the research project. In fact, in virtually every tort case there was at least some critical scrutiny of the plaintiff. Of course, the serious assessment of the claims of both sides is a legitimate part of the jury's role. But at times, the light cast on the plaintiffs was a particularly harsh one.

Jurors' suspicions about plaintiffs' claims led them in most cases to dissect the personal behavior of plaintiffs, with seemingly no limits. Jurors criticized plaintiffs who did not act or appear as injured as they claimed, those who did not appear deserving, and those with preexisting or complicated medical conditions. The state of their marriages, their treatment of their children and coworkers, and their financial status were all subject to close examination. Jurors held plaintiffs to high standards of comportment.

At the time of the jury interview study, the courts were processing a substantial number of claims from men who had been exposed to asbestos in the workplace. Asbestos had become a mass tort, with attorneys and medical experts specializing on both sides of the asbestos litigation. Jurors sometimes took a dim view of the merits of the claims generated in this litigation: "Some lawyers were running around getting clients to sue companies who sold asbestos and installed asbestos and were trying to make somewhat of a killing out of it. We didn't have very much sympathy for the plaintiffs because we figured this bordered on being an unethical procedure. These lawyers went and found these people, [who] filed a grievance to get something out of it, because the lawyer is going to get about 40% or more of anything they get" (C4-J3). Jurors discredited the motives of the plaintiffs' attorneys, which in turn threw the issue of the legitimacy of the plaintiffs' claims about their injuries into doubt.

A similar theme, voiced by jurors in the paint-store case as well as those in other cases, was the money-hungry plaintiff. One asbestos juror, noting that there were a large number of defendant companies listed in the case, observed: "I think [the plaintiffs] were out to get money, all they could get, because they sued a lot of companies" (C22-J2). Another asbestos juror stated: "I just thought as though they felt they were going to come into a big sum of money and just live the rest of their life on easy street. . . . They figured they were going to take the companies for a large amount, and they really played a good part. And, of course, if they had to pay out any large sums, it's gonna affect you and me, because they'll raise their prices in prod-ucts" (C4-J1). A juror in a trial involving a motor-vehicle accident speculated about the motives of the plaintiff: "She worked for an insurance company and she did medical claims. So, I think probably, looking at these medical claims, she said, 'Well, maybe I can cash in on this knee injury' " (C2-J2).

A juror in a case in which a worker had been injured on the job and was suing the owner of the facility in which the injury had occurred, remarked that her first impression of the plaintiff was negative: "Well, my first impression was that he was suing the wrong party. To me, he should have been suing his employer, but they stated that from the beginning that he couldn't sue his employer. And then I just got the impression that he was, just that it was known that he drank a lot and that he hadn't accumulated much throughout his life, and he just hit rock bottom. And this was his chance to make some money and that's what he was going for. That's the impression that I got" (C14-J8).

One of the most surprising cases in which we found critical views was a case in which a teenager had been severely injured in an athletic contest sponsored by his high school. As a result of his injury, he was a paraplegic. He and his family sued the equipment manufacturer, and ultimately the jury found for the plaintiff and gave a substantial award. This is just the kind of case in which one might predict that sympathy and pity would overwhelm jurors. And indeed, several jurors in the case reported feeling pity for a young man struck down in his prime: "It was pity. I really pitied him. . . . I really felt sorry for him" (C1-J3); "I just was sympathetic toward him because of the condition he was in" (C1-J4);[9] "I felt sorry for the boy" (C1-J5).

Jurors also observed, however, that sympathy had to be kept in check, as shown by some of their initial impressions of this badly injured plaintiff: "Pitiful. But you can't let sympathy . . . , you must find a point of negligence if there is one" (C1-J1); "I felt empathy, or sympathy for the guy, for what happened and stuff . . . and that's natural. Because, the lawyers said, you can't help feeling sympathy, but don't let that affect your decision" (C1-J2).

The jurors examined the plaintiff's behavior in great detail. They discussed the possibility that the plaintiff's own actions had violated sports rules, contributing directly to his injuries. They debated the argument that he assumed the risk of injury by playing: "If you decide that you're going to play any sport, I feel as though any consequence coming from playing that sport and getting hurt, that's the way it is" (C1-J1);[10] "That's a risk you always take. . . . I can remember before I played football that I took the risk. If you step out on the field, you have to sign a paper saying you took the risk" (C1-J6).

In addition to pointing out the assumption of risk, this juror also complained that the plaintiff had done little to help himself become more highly functioning after his injury, and that he had taken too long to start physical therapy: "After this long with him being in that position he could have been farther along in his growth, as far as income-wise, occupation-wise. I think he could have been a lot farther along, but who's to say how long it takes a person to get over something that traumatic, like he'd gone through? . . . I feel that he could have been somewhere along the lines of doing more than he'd done. He hadn't done a whole lot" (C1-J6).

Although this case generated sympathy among jurors and resulted in a substantial award in line with the severe injury, it would be a mistake to attribute the award solely to compassion. Jurors' own accounts suggest that they engaged in a complex assessment of responsibility, balancing the plaintiff's role and responsibility against those of the manufacturer.

As in the paint-store case, jurors in a wide variety of trials frequently relied on their own personal experiences to judge the plaintiff's behavior, the injury, and the legitimacy of the claim. In an asbestos case that resulted in a very low award, pro-defense jurors in the majority argued that workplace dangers are commonplace and that the workers themselves have a responsibility to change jobs or the environment. As one asbestos juror pointed out: "I worked in a dental laboratory, and I've been exposed to acrylics. But I don't feel as though I should sue the company, because if I didn't like the smell or thought it was doing any harm to me I could have quit" (C4-J1).

Plaintiff responsibility was a strong theme in another case involving a workplace accident. Jurors criticized the injured worker because he did not use all the safety equipment. Several jurors in this case had construction experience themselves. They admitted that in the construction industry, it was routine for workers not to use all the available safety equipment because to do so was often too time consuming and troublesome. Nevertheless, one of the men who had done construction in the past (and who frankly admitted that he periodically failed to use available safety equipment) was one of the loudest voices blaming the worker for his own injury.

Jurors calibrated the claims about plaintiff injury using their own experience and knowledge of the world. One juror deciding a car accident case in which the plaintiff claimed a knee injury revealed that she herself had a similar injury. Rather than leading her to sympathize, however, the injury led her to downgrade the plaintiff's situation: "I have a knee injury, and it seemed to me that what she was complaining about was the same thing I have. I mean, the weather bothers you, but basically it's just something that you live with" (C2-J2). Thus jurors sometimes compared their own situations with those of the plaintiff. These comparisons at times highlighted the apparent inequities in granting a money award to the plaintiffs while jurors themselves had not been compensated. In fact, research on accidental injuries suggests that a substantial number of jurors are likely to have been negligently injured at some point in their lives without bringing a claim (see Chapter 3). Thus, it's not at all uncommon for jurors to be considering their own decisions to refrain from litigation while assessing the worth of someone else's personal injury lawsuit.

Loss of Consortium Claims

Skepticism about plaintiffs' claims was especially apparent in jurors' discussions about loss of consortium claims, which were an element in some lawsuits.[11] A loss of consortium claim in a personal injury lawsuit is a request for compensatory money damages by the spouse or other family member of a physically injured party. Most frequently, it is a spouse who asserts that he or she has suffered the loss of companionship and services of the physically injured person. In general, jurors were not strongly supportive of loss of consortium claims. In the fifteen cases in my sample in which a family member claimed loss of consortium, there was some award in two-thirds of the cases, but the awards tended to be quite small (in seven of the fifteen cases it was five thousand dollars). Only three cases resulted in substantial consortium awards.

Many jurors we interviewed expressed a measure of hostility toward the plaintiffs requesting loss of consortium. Some jurors considered it to be an illegitimate request, which did not constitute "real" injury. Some jurors criticized attorneys who brought spouses to the stand to testify about their loss of companionship, seeing this tactic primarily as a sympathy gambit. Jurors who felt that lawyers and plaintiffs were trying to exploit their emotions expressed resistance to giving awards. One of the zero consortium-award cases elicited such quotations as: "And they, the women come up here figuring they would cry and we'd feel sorry for 'em and give them something" (C4-J1). In one of the asbestos cases, jurors expressed hostility for the wives of the plaintiffs. For example: "She was the yucky little bleached blonde, she was the one that wanted to tell you about her sex life and you really didn't want to care, care to hear about it 'cause you felt like she was trying to make you feel sympathy for her" (C4-J8). One juror in a workplace injury case characterized the wife's loss of consortium claim as "baloney," noting: "I didn't get the impression that they were lovey-dovey. To me they were just out for what they could get" (C14-J8).

Other jurors were not overtly hostile toward the plaintiff claiming loss of consortium but nevertheless felt that it was a marital duty to take care of an injured spouse. In many cases, especially lower-level injury cases, the duty of "for better or worse" was seen as negating the legal right to a loss of consortium award. Interestingly, women jurors expressed the duty ethic more frequently. Several women jurors who invoked the duty ethic compared the situation of the claimant to their own circumstances in having taken care of their spouses. As women jurors who had considered loss of consortium awards put it, they would never be up on the stand requesting money if their husbands fell. A woman shouldn't need money to take care of her husband.

Some men, especially married men who had previously been cared for by a spouse, expressed greater support for financial compensation for loss of consortium. A woman juror explained a male juror's support for a higher loss of consortium award by reporting that the male juror had had a heart attack and his wife had taken good care of him, so he held out for a higher consortium award for the plaintiff.

Typically, it was the wife who claimed loss of consortium. But in one case, the husband of a woman injured in a car accident claimed consortium. The jury assumed that the couple was having marital difficulties because they did not sit together in the courtroom. Virtually every juror we interviewed from this case speculated about why the husband was not sitting with his wife, concluding that there must have been problems in their marriage. These assumptions about the rocky state of their marriage translated into critical scrutiny of the husband's loss of consortium claim.

In two of the three cases involving substantial loss of consortium claims, the spouses were perceived as having a strong relationship. These were also cases in which the injured party experienced severe injury, so it is possible that the relatively high loss of consortium award reflected the jury's view of the necessity of a spouse's nursing services rather than the jury's sympathy for a loving couple. In most cases, however, jurors questioned the legitimacy of loss of consortium claims. Just as claims for other damages were sometimes seen as an avoidance of personal responsibility, loss of consortium claims were viewed as violations of marital responsibilities.

Are Jurors Completely Heartless?

Jurors frequently reported engaging in critical scrutiny of the plaintiffs and their claims, as the preceding scenarios suggest. Yet in many of these cases, even those in which plaintiffs were judged rather harshly, the jury ultimately decided in favor of the plaintiff and a money award. Some of the anti-plaintiff comments were made by jurors to support a defense verdict, while others used them to argue for lower awards. It was clear from the interviews that arguments centering on plaintiff responsibility and credibility resonated strongly with other jurors.

It would be misleading to suggest that jurors were entirely heartless when it came to the plaintiffs in their cases. More often, jurors reported that the issue of plaintiff blame led to spirited discussion and disagreement. As in the case of the paraplegic high school student, most jurors reported feeling sympathy and pity, although several cautioned about the need to hold sympathy in check and others pointed to areas of plaintiff responsibility. And recall the paint-store case, in which jurors expressed varying opinions about the mother's responsibility for her child's injury. In the work-place injury case in which the worker did not use the safety equipment, the jurors who favored liability for the company pointed out that he was new on the job and that his supervisor bore some of the responsibility for making sure that a new worker followed safety procedures when he undertook risky activities.

In a contract case in which a married couple sued a landscaping company for improper installation of grass sod, the plaintiffs were widely considered by jurors in a positive light: "They seemed like very reliable people and they seemed very honest. The impression that they made on me as a juror was one of the things that made me think they were not people who were trying to get something that wasn't theirs. But they were people who had been wronged, and I guess everyone's had that experience of being wronged by a business at some time or another, and maybe it was the feeling that this is what happened to them" (C8-J6).

Notice that the juror explicitly measures this couple against the expectation that many plaintiffs are out to get something that isn't rightfully theirs. Another juror from the same case also voiced a positive view of the plaintiff: "She was a very good witness, she knew what she was talking about, you could tell that she was still upset by all of this, that she was pretty indignant that this could have happened and that [the owner of the company] had the audacity to do some of the things that he did, but she was never rude or anything like that, so, after a while you definitely felt for the woman because the things that this guy did was just incredible" (C8-J1).

On the whole, however, the comments by jurors about their scrutiny of the plain-tiff's credibility stand in marked—and surprising—contrast to the rhetoric about the bleeding-heart tendencies of today's juries.

Lawyers and Jury Sympathy

Lawyers can affect the tendency of jurors to engage in victim blaming in civil trials. By downplaying or emphasizing a plaintiff's degree of control and extent of knowl-edge, plaintiff and defense attorneys may influence jurors' perceptions of the plain-tiff's role in the injury. In the adversary arena of the courtroom, it was routine for plaintiffs' lawyers to highlight, and in jurors' eyes exaggerate, the extent of the injuries of their clients. Corporate defendants, in turn, usually attempted to counter-act these strategies by minimizing the injury, pointing to inconsistencies in the testimony about the injury's impact and emphasizing areas in which the plaintiff was functioning well despite the injury. In the sports-injury trial, lawyers cautioned jurors about relying on sympathy. In the paint-store case, the defense tried (with some success) to show that the boy led an active life, casting doubt on the severity of the injury to his finger. Jurors, however, seemed mindful of the motives of the attorneys from both sides in their arguments over the extent of a plaintiff's injuries. A plaintiff attorney's excessive emotion over a relatively minor injury was derogated, as were defense attorneys' attempts to badger the witnesses or to minimize the suffering of severely injured plaintiffs.[12]

In the paint-store case, one juror suspected that the plaintiff's lawyer had instructed the injured boy's mother "how to act and react. . . . She was very emotional and upset about it. I mean, she acted like it was yesterday when his hand got cut" (C20-J3). In another case in which a woman had been injured as a result of a car accident, her attorney made a number of arguments that jurors believed were meant to appeal to their emotions, and the jurors resisted: "He was overly dramatic. You know what I'm talking about? Since it was about the case, he kept saying how perfect her body was before the accident. . . . he made her almost seem like a cripple, but we could all look at her and see that there was no neck brace, no wheelchair, nothing, you know? And we're all just like . . . she looks fine to me" (C6-J7).

In contrast, defense attorneys who went after the plaintiffs sometimes undercut their own efforts. When attorneys badgered witnesses, jurors felt uncomfortable, and the attacks occasionally led them to sympathize with the plaintiff more than they otherwise might have. In a case in which a woman suffered a knee injury, the defense attorney questioned her forcefully, attempting to show that the injury was not severe and did not interfere with her activities. This strategy backfired with some jurors: "The defense lawyer would cut down her credibility, which I didn't like. . . . I didn't like somebody trying to make somebody else look really bad, unless they really are. But I mean she didn't seem like she should be really cut down like that, you know, make her look like she's a liar" (C2-J4). Similarly: "Another thing the attorney did at that point was to ask her if she had walked to the courtroom. She said, 'Yes, I parked two blocks away.' He said, 'Do you have high heels on?' and she said, 'No.' And he, he frankly took her shoe off, and I would have been mortified if this were me, and showed it to the jury. And there was a small heel on there, but most working women do not wear flats. Even if you're in mortal pain, you're at least going to get a little bit of a heel out of it. And he really tried to rake, rake her over the coals over that. . . . So I really felt sorry for her there" (C2-J5). In this instance, the lawyer's attempt to undermine the plaintiff seems to have boomeranged.

Taken as a whole, however, the jurors' reactions to plaintiffs suggest that even when the actual degree of control that a plaintiff has over a situation is relatively modest, jurors are strongly motivated to examine how a plaintiff could bear responsibility for an injury. Attorneys' accounts stressing the plaintiff's personal responsibility are likely to find a sympathetic audience.

Attitudes toward Plaintiffs and Their Responsibility

The conclusion from the interviews is that jurors frequently focus on the plaintiffs and their responsibilities and actions. The broad message is that jurors often doubt plaintiffs' claims and report the need to balance their sympathies with a detailed assessment of the plaintiff's role in the injury.

Given the potential limits of juror interviews, it is important to compare these results with findings from other research approaches to assess whether a plaintiff-blaming orientation is common. Findings from all three studies that I conducted, as well as the research of other investigators, confirm that jurors and, to a lesser extent, lay observers often blame the victim. In my studies, I asked respondents whether they agreed that "most people who sue others in court have legitimate grievances." Figure 2-1 provides a graphic depiction of the responses that jurors, mock jurors, and participants in the state telephone poll gave to this statement. A substantial number within each group of respondents entertained serious questions about the legitimacy of plaintiff lawsuits. Notably, the jurors were much less sanguine about the legitimacy of lawsuits than the other two groups. Only about a third of the jurors agreed that most plaintiffs have legitimate grievances, compared to roughly half the mock jurors and the public opinion poll respondents. Although it may be that these differences reflect the diverging views of three distinct groups from the same community, I am inclined to think that there is something about the role of the juror—who is given the task of considering fully the legitimacy of the plaintiff's side and who is exposed to defense arguments attempting to undermine that credibility—that encourages jurors to adopt a more skeptical stance toward the plaintiff.

One other question, asked only of participants in the mock jury study and the public opinion poll, related to plaintiffs. The item took up the perception, which some jurors had expressed in the interviews, that "most people who sue companies are just trying to blame someone else for their problems." Here, there was a big difference between the mock jurors and the state poll respondents. Slightly more than half the

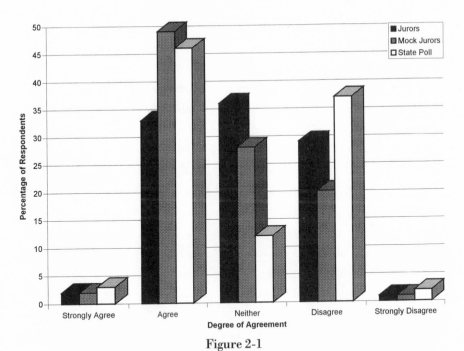

Figure 2-1

Responses to the statement "Most people who sue others in court have
legitimate grievances."

state poll participants (51%) agreed with the statement, whereas just 16% of the
mock jurors agreed with it. Mock jurors, we should remember, had just been asked to
decide the simulated case of a plaintiff allegedly injured through a defendant's negligence. Their overall assessment of plaintiff blame was consistent with the conclusion
of most mock juries that the defendant was negligent. Even so, as they decided the
mock trial case, they often brought up their general concerns about the legitimacy of
plaintiffs' claims.

As might have been expected from some of the quotations from jurors, general
predispositions about the legitimacy (or lack of legitimacy) of plaintiffs' claims were
related to the ways jurors and lay participants in my studies perceived the plaintiffs in
the cases they evaluated. In the mock jury study, in which participants evaluated a
case of personal injury, their responses to the questionnaire item about the general
legitimacy of plaintiffs' grievances were significantly related to their perceptions of
the plaintiff in the case before them.[13] The state opinion poll also gave participants a

chance to evaluate a case of personal injury. As with the mock jurors, the state poll respondents' answers to the general question about the legitimacy of plaintiff claims were related to their judgments in the scenario.[14]

Thus, a significant number of citizens, asked about their general views of plaintiff credibility, express some doubts. Broad concerns about the credibility of civil plaintiffs are not unique to the jurisdiction in the study. National studies tapping people's views of the civil litigation system frequently find that respondents doubt the credibility of plaintiffs as a general rule.[15] One national survey found that many respondents reported believing that more people bring lawsuits than should.[16] The most important reason people gave for the rise in lawsuit costs was "people who figure they can make a lot of money from such suits." In another survey, 62% said that the reason the number of lawsuits has gotten out of hand is that people always look for a culprit when something bad happens.[17] Fully 84% of the respondents in a national poll agreed that "when people are injured, they often try to blame others for their carelessness."[18]

In a study conducted in the 1970s, law professor David Engel interviewed members of a rural Illinois community, finding that plaintiffs in civil litigation were seen as troublemakers who were attempting to escape responsibility for their own actions.[19] His interviews revealed that community members often evaluated others' behavior using lay versions of assumption of risk and contributory negligence: "To the traditional individualists of Sander County, transforming a personal injury into a claim against someone else was an attempt to escape responsibility for one's own actions. The psychology of contributory negligence and assumption of risk had deep roots in the local culture. The critical fact of personal injuries in most cases was that the victims probably could have prevented them if they had been more careful, even if others were to some degree at fault."[20]

Finally, the widespread belief that juries are more favorable to plaintiffs than judges are finds no clear support in the verdict data on jury trials versus judge trials. A comparison of judge and jury verdicts in federal cases found that plaintiffs actually did better with judges than with juries.[21] The cases that are heard by juries and judges may not be strictly comparable, however, so it would be unwise to assume that this would be the result if judges and juries heard exactly the same cases.[22]

In the few studies that have asked judges to comment on the jury verdicts in cases over which they have presided, there is no strong pattern of pro-plaintiff jury behavior in cases with business litigants. A classic judge-jury agreement study by Harry

Kalven, Jr., and Hans Zeisel, dating from the 1950s, asked judges for their hypothetical verdicts in civil jury trials. Judges' hypothetical verdicts and juries' actual verdicts were similarly divided between the plaintiff and the defendant.[23] That study did not differentiate between business cases and other types of civil trials. A 1998 study of jury reform in Arizona contrasted judge-jury agreement in cases with business defendants versus cases with other defendants, and found that juries were no more likely to favor the plaintiff in cases with business defendants.[24]

A final study relevant to the question of plaintiff blame is an experiment conducted in the mid-1990s by Neil Feigenson and other scholars from Quinnipiac College School of Law and Yale University's Department of Psychology.[25] In a scenario experiment that varied the blameworthiness of the plaintiff and the severity of the plaintiff's injury, they found that their study participants (law students and college students) reflected an anti-plaintiff bias in their responses. In some of their experimental conditions, the plaintiff was legally blameless. In one instance, a worker was described as obeying all the rules. The students, however, allocated him 22% of the blame for his accident. In another scenario, a homeowner was given 14% of the blame for injuries from a faulty valve on a propane gas tank (located in his home) that belonged to the gas company.[26] Although neither of these plaintiffs would be considered legally negligent, the participants thought they deserved at least a small amount of blame.

The participants also reflected an anti-plaintiff bias by reducing the compensatory damage assessments when plaintiffs were blameworthy. Under a comparative negligence statute, this results in "double discounting," because the degree of plaintiff fault found by the jury is taken into account by the court when it arrives at a final damage award. For example, under a comparative negligence rule, if the jury finds the plaintiff 30% at fault and reaches an overall compensatory damage award of $90,000, the court would reduce the $90,000 by 30% to take into account the comparative fault of the plaintiff. What Feigenson and his colleagues suggest is that plaintiffs are doubly charged for their own negligence, once by jurors who decrease their estimate of what the injury is worth, and again by the judge who takes the comparative fault into account in reducing the award.

Drawing on both my research and that conducted in other jurisdictions, one can see that people across the nation come to the jury box prepared to consider plaintiff claims with some skepticism. We can have a fair amount of confidence in the phenomenon of plaintiff blame because it arises in multiple settings and research projects.

Why Do Jurors Blame the Victim?

The findings from the interviews, the questionnaire data, and other research, which suggest that jurors frequently blame the victim, may be surprising to those who have been following the tort reform debate, with its emphasis on the dangers of overly sympathetic jurors. But the findings are consistent with a body of literature from social psychology that shows a widespread tendency to hold an injured victim personally responsible. Psychologist Melvin Lerner has studied the phenomenon intensively.[27] He argues that psychological dynamics on the part of observers may predispose them to engage in victim blame. In Lerner's view, people need to believe in a just, stable, predictable, and controllable world. When an innocent person suffers, it challenges the belief that the world is just. Therefore, observers of suffering engage in a variety of strategies—including derogating the victim, reinterpreting the injury as victim-precipitated, and minimizing the injury—to reconcile the contradiction.[28]

A good deal of psychological research confirms that people do indeed at times blame the victim for unfortunate outcomes.[29] Being similar to a victim can be threatening to an observer. After all, if an accident injured the victim, why should the same thing not happen to the observer? Observing similarities may lead people to distinguish themselves from victims, searching for ways that victims themselves caused their injuries. Psychologists have labeled this phenomenon defensive attribution, and have speculated that the pressure to engage in defensive attribution will be heightened when a victim is severely injured. In the research described earlier, for example, Feigenson and his colleagues found the strongest tendencies to blame the victim in scenarios with the most severe injuries. Under certain circumstances, jurors who are similar to a plaintiff may actually take a harsher approach than less similar jurors. We saw that phenomenon in the paint-store case, where the three staunchest opponents of the boy's mother were women jurors.

One finding from the psychological studies is that if an observer has a chance to help or to compensate an innocent victim who has suffered, the observer tends to engage in less derogation of the victim. But in my research study of actual jurors, jurors had the opportunity to (and often did) compensate the injured plaintiffs. Still, I observed a fair amount of derogation and victim blame. In fact, in contrast to the psychological research, jurors who had the chance to compensate were *less* likely than the participants in my mock jury study and the public opinion poll to say that most claims brought by plaintiffs were legitimate. Certainly jurors' general views about plaintiff claims may have been affected by the evidence and personalities in the specific cases they decided. In addition, the fact that jurors have assumed a specific role, and consider part of that role to be scrutinizing the credibility of the parties, may lead them to take a more critical view of plaintiff claims than they otherwise would.

The phenomenon of victim blame can also be attributed to the pivotal American ethic of individualism, which emphasizes the individual's own role in events, whether they are positive or negative. The ideal of individual freedom and autonomy has contributed much of value to our society, but it may limit our recognition of the complex influence of business and the state. In *Habits of the Heart,* Robert Bellah and other social scientists observe: "This ideal of freedom has historically given Americans a respect for individuals; it has, no doubt, stimulated their initiative and creativity; it has sometimes even made them tolerant of differences in a diverse society and resistant to overt forms of political oppression. But it is an ideal of freedom that leaves Americans with a stubborn fear of acknowledging structures of power and interdependence in a technologically complex society dominated by giant corporations and an increasingly powerful state."[30]

What Personal Characteristics Relate to an
Individual's Attitudes toward Plaintiffs?

What was most striking to me as I interviewed jurors was that jurors who sat through the same trial often had different judgments of the responsibility and credibility of injured plaintiffs. One juror may disbelieve much of what the plaintiff says, while another may find it persuasive. How do people form their general impressions about plaintiff responsibility? Are there broad life experiences or sets of more general beliefs and predispositions that lead people to take a relatively generous, or relatively restrictive, view of a plaintiff who claims injury by a corporation? The case of the boy in the paint store certainly was a strong counterexample of the widespread view that women are more sympathetic than men, but what happens in general? Do women indeed have a soft spot in their hearts for an injured victim? What about jurors who are fortunate themselves, that is, the highly educated or wealthy? Psychologists have theorized about the factors—such as belief in a just world—that predispose people to blame victims for their own predicaments. Do these factors help to explain the juror's view of a plaintiff in a civil lawsuit?

I undertook to explore whether people's attitudes and personal factors were related to their general views about plaintiffs, using the item about the legitimacy of plaintiff claims that was asked in all three studies. In all three studies, whether people grant legitimacy to those who bring lawsuits is most strongly related to broad perceptions of a litigation crisis. I conducted regression analyses using a wide range of demographic and attitudinal factors as possible predictors of the legitimacy of plaintiff claims. Participants' views that we are in the midst of a litigation explosion constituted the only significant predictor that was common to all three studies.[31] In Chapter 3 I examine in greater detail this set of views about the litigation explosion, and say more about the determinants of these general perceptions that appear to be so significant in shaping predispositions about the legitimacy of plaintiff claims.

Just two demographic characteristics were significantly related to general views of plaintiff legitimacy, and each was a significant factor in only one study. First, participants' racial identification was related to judgments of plaintiff legitimacy in the state telephone poll.[32] Second, whether jurors reported that they were Protestants, as opposed to another religious identification, was related to judgments of plaintiff legitimacy.[33] Whites in the state poll, and Protestant jurors, were more likely to doubt plaintiff claims as a general matter. Gender, as it happens, was never a consistent predictor of reactions to plaintiffs in the statistical analyses. Trials like the paint-store case, in which the women's perspective seemed to lead to a harsher view of the mother's role, may be offset by other cases where the reverse occurs or no difference is found. Aside from attitudes toward litigation, however, none of the other attitudinal or demographic factors was a particularly strong predictor of attitudes toward plaintiffs. That is, attempts to pick a favorable jury on the basis of race, religion, or some other political, social, or psychological characteristic alone would likely be unsuccessful.[34]

Plaintiffs Injured in a Place of Business

Along with the decided tendency to blame the plaintiff that was apparent in the juror interviews and in the other research studies, the data I gathered also show a second important phenomenon: jurors take the organizational context into account when they decide how much the plaintiff is at fault. In some instances, the individual plaintiff is held to be *less* responsible for his or her own injury when the injury occurs in a place of business, or when a corporate actor is involved in the situation giving rise to the injury.

Teasing apart the factors that affect judgments of responsibility within a business or corporate environment is a complicated task. Consumer injuries from defective products, worker injuries on the job, hazards in places of business, and failures to follow contractual obligations might all result in lawsuits against business and corporate defendants. To begin to look at the larger question of the impact of a corporation in a lawsuit (an issue common to these different types of civil wrongs), I started research with a narrower focus, looking systematically at how injuries that occur in a place of business might be treated differently than injuries that occur in a private home.

To determine how people's decisions are affected by the corporate business setting, I used a mock jury experiment. In one of the mock jury studies that I conducted, a woman plaintiff was injured in a fall. Half the subjects in the study were told that the fall had occurred in a furniture store, whereas the remainder were told that the fall occurred at a tag sale in a private home. All the other details of the injury remained the same: Ms. Brown was reading the price list while walking around, when she suddenly tripped on a large untacked rip in the carpet. She fell hard to the floor, hitting her head on the corner of a nearby table. She suffered a concussion, broken facial bones, and skin lacerations. As a result she had continuing headaches, dizziness, and facial pain.

Community residents came to the local courthouse, read one of the two cases, and then deliberated in groups to decide on the negligence of the defendant and the contributory fault, if any, of the woman who fell. The striking finding that is relevant to our consideration of victim blame lies in how mock jurors saw the contributory fault of the plaintiff. When Ms. Brown tripped over a torn carpet in a private home, she was given a larger share of the blame than when she tripped in the store. Those who evaluated liability for the accident in the home were much more likely to see the plaintiff as somewhat or very responsible herself for the accident, while the mock jurors who assessed the store accident were comparatively more apt to judge the plaintiff as slightly or not at all responsible (Figure 2-2). Out of the twelve mock juries who deliberated the case of an injury occurring in a private home, every single one found that the plaintiff was at least somewhat at fault. In percentage terms, the plaintiff was attributed an average of 53% of the fault. When the injury occurred in the furniture store, ten of the twelve mock juries again found the plaintiff at least somewhat at fault. However, the average amount of fault dropped to 23%, less than half the fault that she was given for her fall in the private home. The organizational context changed the meaning of her fall—from one that was predominantly her fault to one that was largely the store's responsibility.

The videotaped mock jury deliberations provide a glimpse into how the jurors in the two conditions discussed the plaintiff. In a practice consistent with the juror

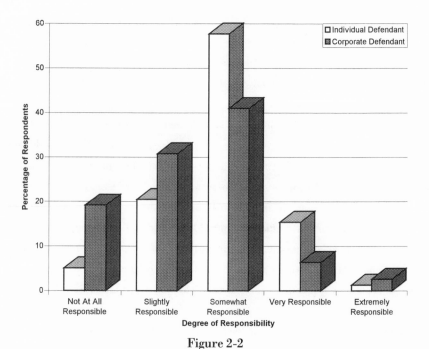

Figure 2-2

Mock jurors' judgments of the plaintiff's responsibility for her own accident.

interviews, mock jurors in *both* experimental conditions spent a good deal of time discussing issues relating to the plaintiff's own role in her injury. They castigated her for reading the newspaper while walking and thus, in their view, contributing to her own accident.

In groups deliberating about the injury that occurred in the private home, mock jurors often argued that the plaintiff bore the responsibility for her own injury. They occasionally displayed some harsh judgments, calling the plaintiff "stupid" and "not very bright":

> She was looking at the paper; she's just as much at fault. (Group 16, J1)
> If I'm in a strange home, I'm careful where I walk and what I do. (Group 12, J6)
> She could have prevented this if she would have been looking. (Group 12, J2)
> She was plain careless, that was not very bright . . . would a reasonable
> person walk around not watching where you were going? (Group 22, J1)
> I can't imagine anybody being so stupid walking around the house reading a
> newspaper. (Group 23, J4)
> You can't go into someone's home with blinders on, you have responsibility
> for yourself, you don't go through life with a blindfold on. (Group 24, J4)

I figure if you go in somebody's house and they got a gun sitting there and you pick it up and shoot yourself in the foot, is that person responsible? (Group 31, J4)

Their comments also reflected doubts about the legitimacy of her claim:

She had headaches before, how do we know how much worse they are? It's like, "Ow, my neck!" I think she's taking advantage. (Group 16, J2)
Our insurance today is out of this world! This lady should have taken some care, she shouldn't have expected the owner to be responsible. (Group 24, J4)
She previously had headaches, she's either a hypochondriac and looking for trouble or she's a born litigator and maybe she was glad and maybe she even fell on purpose. (Group 16, J4)
O.K., let's give her enough money to hire a driver so she can go looking for somebody else to sue. (Group 21, J6)

Even though they concluded that the plaintiff was only somewhat responsible for her injury in the store, the mock jurors who deliberated about the injury in the store made similar comments about the plaintiff:

A reasonable person knows that you can't depend on your path being cleared . . . you shouldn't be walking along especially in a strange place reading a newspaper. (Group 14, J4)
If it's a large rip, you should see it but she was looking at the paper, she's at fault. (Group 18, J4)
That lady was responsible for her own well-being. (Group 19, J2)
What a fall, she must have been a klutz! (Group 20, J2)
It was unfamiliar territory where she was walking, she should have stopped to look. (Group 30, J5)
A customer also has the responsibility, you go into the supermarket and somebody has knocked over a jar of pickled beets and it's lying on the floor and you're the one who sees it, you have the responsibility to inform someone, an employee of the store. If you walk by and don't say anything and someone comes behind you not paying attention, this is really not negligence on the part of the store but negligence on the part of the customer. (Group 18, J2)

In this study, then, although virtually all of the mock jurors considered the potential fault of the plaintiff whether she sued an individual or a business, the plaintiff was ascribed less responsibility for falling in a store.

45

Recall that I chose a narrow way to examine the role of the business in this mock jury study, by locating the place of the injury in a commercial setting. The phenomenon of lower blame for plaintiffs injured in corporate environments is not universal. It could depend on how the alleged injury or violation relates to the business context. In two other experimental studies based on a scenario involving harm to workers injured while clearing a lot owned by either an individual or a corporation, the responsibility of the workers was seen as about the same in both situations.[35] A third study by another researcher who used a variety of cases also showed no consistent reduction in plaintiff responsibility in corporate settings.[36] Therefore, it is important to point out that whether a plaintiff's responsibility is lessened in a corporate environment, or is reduced by the presence of corporate actors, may be affected by a variety of other factors yet to be determined.

The Facts of the Case Matter

Whether the corporate context modifies victim blame, and the extent of victim blame, are clearly affected by the facts of the case. In an auto-accident case in the juror interview study, the driver of a company van who caused the accident ran a red light. He did not see the motorcycle driven by the plaintiff because he was driving, talking with a coworker, and trying to read a map all at the same time. The fault of the defendant was straightforward, and the jurors engaged in very little victim blame.

In general, situations that allow a substantial amount of control by the victims, whether they are workers or consumers, should create expectations that the victims are at least partly responsible for their own injuries. Instances in which there is little control should discourage the attribution of blame to injured victims.[37]

Consider, for example, the very different ways that smokers and those affected by secondhand smoke are likely to be perceived in litigation. Until the late 1990s, tobacco companies had been largely successful in defending themselves against lawsuits brought by smokers and their families who asked for compensation for injuries and deaths caused by smoking. Interviews with jurors from some of the earlier trials showed that they were reluctant to hold tobacco companies responsible when smokers had chosen to use the product and knew, or should have known, that it was dangerous.[38]

In contrast, the prospects of lawsuits by plaintiffs affected by secondhand smoke over which they had no control (such as flight attendants on an airline) are not as amenable to the defense that the injured person exercised personal choice. (A different problem affects the secondhand-smoke lawsuits: the plaintiffs need to establish a causal link between exposure to others' smoke and their health problems.) Advances made by state attorneys general in forging settlement agreements with tobacco companies for recovery of state medical expenses associated with tobacco illnesses and death have been possible partly because not all of those who stand to recover are smokers, who are widely perceived by the public as responsible for their own medical problems.[39]

Finally, some scholars have hypothesized that plaintiffs in tort cases are regarded more harshly than plaintiffs who sue over a contract. At least in terms of responses to the question about the general legitimacy of plaintiff claims, however, there were no significant differences between jurors who decided tort and contract cases in my study of jurors.

Judgments about the Plaintiff's Responsibility for Injuries in Places of Business

Reactions to those injured by corporate conduct are often complex and multifaceted. Jurors begin their task with substantial skepticism about the plaintiff. In assessing the merits of a lawsuit, they routinely consider matters of assumption of risk, the plaintiff's conduct, contributory fault, and individual responsibility. In his book *Total Justice*, historian Lawrence Friedman argues that, in contrast to the past, our contemporary legal culture has as a basic tenet that innocent victims of injury should receive compensation.[40] If that is true, the urge to compensate innocent victims is balanced by jurors against their beliefs that plaintiffs often try to capitalize on sympathy and receive compensation that is not rightfully theirs. It is the juror's perceived role to determine whether the victim is indeed innocent.

Many citizens continue to espouse an ethic of individual responsibility, emphasizing an individual's ability to choose and behave independent of outside forces.[41] Responsibility resides in the individual for freely chosen behavior, such as *choosing* to stay in a job despite asbestos dust, or *choosing* to smoke cigarettes even though they are known to be harmful. Analyses of early litigation against the tobacco companies for compensation for cigarette smokers' injuries and deaths show that plaintiffs' claims were stymied because the freedom-of-choice defense resounded so well with juries.[42] Some jurors appear to be concerned about the consequences of lessening individual responsibility. If people cannot be held accountable for their actions, will they behave even more carelessly? Will a lessening of personal responsibility undermine the fabric of our society?

Yet at the same time, crosscutting these themes is the recognition of limits on individual choice and autonomy posed by powerful businesses. The world is increasingly dominated by large governments, institutions, and corporations.[43] The dramatic changes in liability of business corporations discussed in Chapter 1 have raised questions about the boundaries of individual responsibility. Just what role we as individuals will continue to play—and the responsibilities that we will continue to hold—is the subject of intense debate.

In February and March 1999, the Philip Morris tobacco company was hit with two mammoth jury judgments against it. A San Francisco jury awarded $51.5 million ($1.5 million in compensatory damages and $50 million in punitive damages) to Patricia Henley, a former Marlboro smoker with inoperable lung cancer.[44] Henley, who pledged to donate the money to educate youth about the dangers of smoking, had argued that Philip Morris had covered up scientific evidence about the effects of smoking on health. The following month, a Portland, Oregon, jury awarded $81 million to the family of another Marlboro smoker who died of lung cancer.[45] Attorneys for the Portland plaintiff argued that the tobacco company had hidden information about the negative health consequences of smoking. Why did the plaintiffs prevail in these two cases, when the tobacco companies had almost always been able to convince juries in prior cases that smokers were personally responsible for smoking? I believe that the internal company documents identified during the discovery phase of ongoing litigation against the tobacco companies, which were subsequently made public, were key. Some of these documents can be read as supporting the coverup claims of the plaintiffs. Because the company acted to withhold information from smokers and potential smokers, the act of smoking came to be perceived not exclusively as a personal and individual choice but as an act that was at least partly determined by the company's behavior.

Given differences in perspective about the continuing significance of individual responsibility, it is not surprising that under some circumstances jurors take the organizational context into account, or disagree among themselves about whether an individual should remain completely responsible for the consequences of his or her actions. Some jurors in the paint-store case, for instance, observed that the clerk, not the customer, had better knowledge about the potential hazards in the store. Others stated that the clerk should have anticipated potential problems with customers' children and arranged the store's merchandise accordingly. Recognizing the injured sports player's assumption of risk in participating in a high school team sport, jurors nevertheless also saw responsibility residing in coaches, schools, and equipment manufacturers. Mock jurors took the business location into account in reducing the responsibility of the plaintiff for her own injury, again acknowledging the significance of organizational context.

In sum, there is a clear tension in views about the responsibility of the individual and that of the business. The tension exists in the minds of individual jurors, as each one struggles to evaluate a plaintiff's behavior in its corporate context. The tension can also erupt in the jury room if jurors disagree about how to allocate individual and business responsibility. Where do we, as jurors or as a society, draw the line? In the next chapter, I put these views about plaintiffs in a broader context.

3

"SUE-CRAZY": CITIZENS'
ATTITUDES ABOUT CIVIL LITIGATION

A recurring theme in the comments jurors made during their interviews was that there is far too much litigation in the United States. People are "sue-crazy," jurors claim, and the practice of turning seemingly every dispute into a legal action threatens to endanger the central institutions of our society. As one juror I interviewed put it: "I am not one for lawsuits. I think it's ridiculous. I was involved in an accident; it wasn't my fault by any means. I probably could have cleaned up on it, I know I could have cleaned up on it. Everybody from my parents . . . my wife was the only one on my side. I still hear what a fool I was, how rich I could be. I went in there [to the jury trial I sat on] with a sour attitude toward lawsuits. Everybody sues everybody for everything. I don't buy it" (C10-J4). The purpose of this chapter is to explore in more detail these general views about litigation, especially predominant beliefs that many citizens bring worthless lawsuits, that legal judgments are out of line, and that we are in the midst of a litigation crisis.

Litigation Horror Stories

In 1992 an elderly woman named Stella Liebeck bought a cup of coffee at the drive-in window at a McDonald's in Albuquerque, New Mexico. Sitting in the passenger seat of her grandson's car, with the Styrofoam coffee cup between her legs, she tried to take off the coffee lid so she could add cream and sugar. In the attempt, she accidentally spilled the hot coffee on herself, causing third-degree burns. The burns were extensive, requiring skin grafts and a week-long stay in the hospital. Ms. Liebeck later sued McDonald's for negligence on the grounds that their coffee was dangerously hot. An Albuquerque jury awarded her $160,000 in compensatory damages (reduced from $200,000 because the jury found that she was 20% at fault) and $2.7 million in punitive damages.[1]

The multi-million-dollar award sent shockwaves around the country. Immediately after the verdict, newspapers nationwide featured the high award, and editorials denounced the jury's decision.[2] In these news stories, relatively few details were presented about the context, issues, and evidence in the McDonald's trial. The jury's action was quickly characterized as a $3 million award for a cup of spilled coffee. For many citizens, the award seemed to confirm their worst fears that the civil justice system was out of control. Even a classic American institution like McDonald's was not immune from what appeared to be exceedingly frivolous litigation. To many Americans, the McDonald's coffee-spill case seemed to illustrate perfectly the outrageous demands that American consumers routinely make in lawsuits against business, and the equally scandalous response of civil juries to these illegitimate claims.

Some writers and policy makers argue that cases like the McDonald's trial are part of a larger pattern of a highly litigious populace and spiraling awards, which have combined to produce a state of so-called litigation crisis.[3] In a congressional debate over tort reform, Representative Ron Packard of California used Stella Liebeck as a "poster child" to argue in favor of reform: "Our courts have become a lucrative feeding ground for unscrupulous lawyers and greedy plaintiffs who abuse the system. Litigation is spinning out of control when a woman can file suit over spilt coffee and walk away millions richer. Republicans will work to curb this lucrative feeding frenzy by passing a commonsense product liability and legal reform bill."[4]

Stella Liebeck was not the only plaintiff to start the presses rolling. Litigation horror stories of all stripes abound. By now, many readers have probably heard about the burglar who fell through the skylight and sued the building owner; the fat man with a history of coronary disease who suffered a heart attack while mowing the lawn and subsequently sued the lawnmower manufacturer; or the workman who set his ladder in a pile of manure and who, after injuring himself when the ladder slipped, sued the ladder manufacturer for failing to warn about the dangers of setting the ladder up in slippery stuff like manure.[5] These and other classic litigation horror stories have been widely disseminated through speeches and industry articles about tort case excesses.

Many contemporary examples can be found on the Internet. A visit to the Web site of the American Tort Reform Association (ATRA), a leading organization that promotes reforming the civil justice system, yielded "Stories That Show a Legal System That's Out of Control." Among them was the tale of a man who sued the dairy industry because a lifetime of drinking whole milk had led to his clogged arteries; and the story of a woman who sued her credit card companies over $70,000 in online gambling debts she had racked up. Also featured was the story of a man who sued a rock group and the theater after attending a rock concert that he says caused permanent hearing damage.[6] Another fascinating Web site that advances similar themes is sponsored by Citizens Against Lawsuit Abuse (CALA). One of their "Looney Lawsuit of the Month" Awards went to a California woman buying a blender. Four boxes containing blenders were stacked on a high shelf. When she attempted to remove the bottom box, the boxes fell, allegedly causing her injuries, including carpal tunnel syndrome and neck, shoulder, and back pain. She sued the store for its failure to warn customers and for unsafe stacking of the boxes.[7] Although the jury decided unanimously in favor of the defendant, the very fact that a woman could and would sue under these conditions was enough to generate a press release from CALA's executive director.

Of the horror stories listed on the two sites, most described lawsuits against businesses, government, or educational institutions. For example, of the eleven stories of out-of-control litigation listed on the ATRA site on May 12, 1999, ten were lawsuits against businesses and the other one described prisoner litigation against the state. The CALA stories were more diverse, with a disgruntled woman suing her former fiancé over the breakup of their engagement and a surfer suing another surfer for stealing his wave. Still, on the three days I visited the site, more than half of the "Believe It or Not" stories included business, government, or educational defendants. Although the exact numbers may change from time to time, litigation horror stories about lawsuits against business often garner substantial attention. In addition to their intrinsic interest in this issue, groups like ATRA and CALA receive funding from business organizations, which in turn may encourage their focus on business litigation.

Indeed, many business and professional groups have their own especially tailored set of litigation horror stories. The American Consulting Engineers Council undertakes an annual liability survey in which they solicit their members' experiences with litigation. Individual stories about putatively frivolous lawsuits are then used to show "the government and the media how the threat of liability hurts our country's innovation, construction and development, and our infrastructure."[8]

The Academic and Policy Debate over the "Litigation Crisis"

In contrast to the thrust of the horror stories, however, many scholars who conduct systematic research on the civil justice system question whether there has been a general explosion of litigation. Their evidence and arguments have been thoroughly presented elsewhere, but it is important to summarize their major conclusions here because they bear directly on the central issues in this book.[9]

First of all, researchers have provided more detail about some of the litigation horror stories that have circulated in speeches about the litigation crisis. These fuller descriptions often make the plaintiff's claim more credible and the court's decision more understandable than they appeared at first blush. Take the case of the burglar who fell through the skylight and sued a school. Professor Michael Saks has provided some context: "The 'burglar' who fell through the skylight was a teenager who climbed onto the roof of his former high school to get a floodlight. The fall rendered him a quadriplegic. A similar accident at a neighboring school had killed a student eight months earlier. School officials already had contracted to have the skylights boarded over so as to 'solve . . . a safety problem.' The payments [that the teen received] were the result of a settlement; the case did not go to trial."[10]

With these details, our image of an avaricious burglar trying to milk the system is replaced by the face of a foolhardy teen whose life and mobility were seriously and tragically affected by his own dumb stunt, in combination with the actions of the school officials who recognized a safety problem but had not yet remedied it. As for the fat man with heart disease, the plaintiff was a thirty-two-year old medical doctor with no prior history of heart disease; the jury in his case found that the lawnmower was defective. The verdict in the case involving a ladder set up in a pile of manure had, it turns out, nothing to do with the manure. Less amusingly, the ladder, which was safety rated for 1,000 pounds, broke under a weight of less than 450 pounds.[11]

In addition to debunking some of the litigation horror stories, researchers have moved beyond anecdote to cast serious doubt on the representativeness of such tales. The stories are meant to demonstrate that citizens sue over just about anything, and that as a result civil lawsuits have skyrocketed. By examining the empirical evidence about the extent of claims over injuries and lawsuit filings, scholars have raised questions about whether citizens are indeed "sue-crazy," and about whether civil litigation has increased as dramatically as is claimed.

Are Americans "Sue-Crazy"? To begin with, there is substantial doubt about the foundational claim that Americans are overly litigious. The whole notion of a litigation explosion is based on the view that citizens are eager to bring lawsuits at the drop of a hat. Thus, the argument is that Americans are psychologically predisposed to be aggressive in pursuing claims when they have been injured (and even sometimes when they have not). If this is true, then we should expect that a substantial proportion of potential claims are converted into lawsuits.

In fact, however, research examining the extent of injuries, potential lawsuits, and actual claims demonstrates that only a small number of grievances ever result in legal action. One of the best-known studies of this phenomenon is the Civil Litigation Research Project (CLRP), which in 1980 administered a detailed telephone survey to 5,148 households across five jurisdictions.[12] The researchers asked the respondents to report whether anyone in their household had experienced any of a long list of specific problems during the prior three years, and if so, whether and how the problem was resolved. The researchers focused on grievances that involved at least one thousand dollars in estimated monetary losses, because these kinds of problems were potentially the ones that might be resolved through the legal system.

Approximately 40% of the households in the survey indicated that they had experienced one or more of the listed problems costing at least one thousand dollars during the past three years. This figure indicates that many households experience significant grievances that could be transformed into litigation. The researchers then asked those who had experienced such grievances what they had done about them. Had they asked the person or company responsible for some sort of compensation? Had they consulted a lawyer or filed a lawsuit? The results provide some interesting evidence about the litigiousness of the population. In about seven out of ten grievances, people made some sort of request of, or claim to, the offending party. So, for example, if the new car didn't work properly, the purchaser might return to the dealership for assistance; or, if hit by a careless driver, the injured party might contact the offender's insurance company. Roughly two-thirds of these claims were rejected completely or partially by the alleged offending party. Even though many of the individuals who made some sort of initial request of the offending party did not receive full satisfaction, relatively few contacted a lawyer or filed a lawsuit. Overall, about one in ten of those households that experienced a grievance contacted a lawyer, and about one in twenty went so far as to file a lawsuit. The significant dropouts at successive stages formed a disputing pyramid, with many grievances on the bottom and progressively fewer individuals proceeding to claims, disputes, lawyers, and court filings.[13] Notably, whether or not the opposing party was an organization significantly influenced both the likelihood and the success of the claim. When a household member had a grievance with an organization as opposed to another individual, the grievance was more likely to result in a claim;[14] however, claims against organizations were less likely to be successful than claims against individuals.[15]

A national study undertaken by the Rand Corporation, published in 1991, also found that the vast majority of potential plaintiffs do not bring lawsuits. In that study, eighty-seven out of every one hundred people who were accidentally injured took no action to try to obtain compensation for the injury.[16] Of the thirteen of one hundred who took some action, two spoke directly with the party who had allegedly caused the injury, four dealt with an insurance company, and seven contacted a lawyer. Of the seven who contacted a lawyer, four retained the lawyer, and two eventually filed a lawsuit. Again, one can observe the pyramid pattern: there were many injuries, but few of those injured invoked the legal system.

The pyramid pattern is also apparent in the ratio of actual medical negligence to medical malpractice litigation. Several large-scale studies of medical malpractice demonstrate that many more patients suffer injury as a result of medical negligence than seek compensation and file lawsuits. In a 1990 report, the Harvard Medical Practice study concluded that in its sample of New York cases, there was an eight-to-one ratio between the number of patients who suffered an injury from medical negligence (as assessed by a team of medical experts) and the number who filed a malpractice claim.[17] A comparable study in California, done in the late 1970s, also concluded that the number of lawsuits for medical malpractice amounted to only a fraction of the injuries caused by medical negligence.[18]

Speculating on the reasons why so many potential plaintiffs stay away from the courts, Professor Saks suggests that many of those who are injured lack the knowledge to pursue their claims. They may be unaware that negligence has occurred (consider the complexities in assessing medical negligence, for example), or they may not have sufficient savvy to retain a lawyer and file a suit. In addition, they may calculate the costs of embarking on a lawsuit (both monetary and nonmonetary, including, for example, the stigma of being a plaintiff or the continuing connection with the defendant necessitated by the lawsuit) and conclude that these costs outweigh the potential benefits of successful litigation.[19] Their own comfort level with conflict may play a role; people with a high degree of "claims consciousness," who describe themselves as assertive, aggressive, and willing to complain, tend to be more likely to pursue their claims than those who are more passive.[20] Finally, even if they have the gumption to contact an attorney, plaintiffs' attorneys working on a contingent-fee basis may refuse to take their cases, acting as gatekeepers to the civil justice system.[21]

The fact that many are injured but few choose to litigate raises a difficult question: What is the optimal ratio of lawsuits to injuries? If everyone who was injured by another's negligence attempted to receive compensation through the civil justice system, the result would be a staggering increase in lawsuit filings. Current empirical data cannot really address the question of how many lawsuits are optimal. Answering the question depends on the litigation rate's impact on the range of functions of the civil justice system, including compensation, deterrence, and the promotion of safety. However, the low ratio of claims to lawsuits at least casts some serious doubt on the notion that Americans litigate at the drop of a hat. More commonly, we do nothing, or we try to resolve a problem outside the legal system.

This fact—that many citizens have suffered an injury that could have been the subject of a lawsuit but decided either to ignore it or to resolve the problem without litigation—has some implications for the jury. Many (perhaps most) jurors will have had some personal experiences with injury caused by another's negligence, yet they will have chosen other routes to resolution. Having experienced a similar kind of injury may lead a juror to understand a plaintiff's pain and suffering, but if a juror has suffered without asserting a claim, he or she may be critical of the plaintiff who brings a lawsuit.

Have Litigation Rates Increased Dramatically? Public opinion surveys suggest that there is close to universal consensus that litigation rates have skyrocketed in recent decades and continue to explode. This charge has been carefully assessed through an analysis of court filings from the 1960s to the 1990s. In contrast to an expected pattern of dramatic overall increases resulting from expanding litigiousness, however, these analyses of court filings show that increases over time are generally limited to particular types of such high-profile cases as product liability, that increases can often be explained by such other factors as population expansion or government actions, and that some categories of cases have actually decreased. All these factors suggest no overall explosion of litigation.

Starting in the early 1980s, Professor Marc Galanter of the University of Wisconsin Law School has written a series of influential articles debunking common assumptions of "litigation crisis" in the courts. In his first article in the series, entitled "Reading the Landscape of Disputes: What We Know and Don't Know (and Think We Know) about Our Allegedly Contentious and Litigious Society," Galanter challenged assertions that we were in the midst of a caseload and lawsuit crisis.[22] Acknowledging that lawsuits had increased substantially in some areas, Galanter showed how the pattern of increases was inconsistent with a broad shift in litigiousness. Instead, it

appeared to be better explained by population increases, changes in the behavior of
the government with regard to certain types of claims, and the passage through the
system of specific product liability cases, such as asbestos litigation. Subsequent
articles with more recent data have confirmed his basic thesis that charges of skyrocketing litigation are overblown.[23]

Looking at trends over time in state court filings, we see that although filings have
risen in American courts since the 1960s, the major increases in caseloads in the
state court are in criminal and domestic relations cases. In the state courts, tort case
filings reached a high point in the late 1980s and have been decreasing or have held
steady since then.[24] And even in the 1980s, it was primarily cases that involved
automobile tort claims that increased in number, not other kinds of torts. If people are
increasingly litigious, then their litigiousness appears to be limited to the arena of
automobile accidents rather than other types of cases.

The federal courts hear only a small proportion of all the tort claims nationwide—
by Galanter's estimate, less than 5%. Nevertheless, the federal courts are often the
venue for such highly visible types of cases as product liability and class-action
lawsuits. These specialized sorts of cases could have a disproportionate impact on
public policy as well as public and corporate opinion. Galanter's 1996 analysis of
federal court tort filings shows that product liability claims have fluctuated a good
deal and now constitute a much larger portion of the federal court tort caseload than
they did a decade ago.

Product liability cases have a marked but predictable effect on case filing statistics. As injuries connected with a specific product begin to be translated into case
filings, the numbers are low but soon grow and peak, presenting a challenge to the
courts and looking for all the world like an explosion of litigation. Once the bulk of
product injury claims are processed, however, the numbers begin to drop back down.
In earlier decades, black lung cases followed this pattern of increase, peak, and
decrease. During the years 1984–1995, asbestos claims numbered 2,788 in the
federal courts in 1984, peaked at 16,038 cases in 1990, and by 1995 had dropped to
6,821 cases. Currently, claims relating to breast implants are beginning to contribute
significantly to the caseloads in the federal courts.[25] Although recent data show no
general increases in run-of-the-mill tort cases in the federal courts, and product
liability cases in the federal courts account for less than 2% of tort cases nationwide,
the product liability cases are highly salient to the business community and have
gotten a good deal of attention.[26] Furthermore, commercial litigation, particularly

business-to-business contract disputes, has also increased significantly from the 1970s to the 1990s, undoubtedly amplifying the business community's concern over heightened litigation.[27]

In sum, the academic research on the civil justice system does not, on the whole, support the picture of an out-of-control and highly litigious population that is conjured up by the litigation horror stories. Relatively few people who are entitled to bring claims in the civil justice system do so, and litigation patterns in the civil courts show that some kinds of cases have increased in number, while others have decreased or stayed about the same. Many of the litigation horror stories are less outrageous (and admittedly less fun) when we learn more details about them. But the most significant point in contrasting litigation statistics and litigation horror stories is that the stories present a misleading picture of what goes on in the civil courts.

Public Attitudes toward Litigation

Whatever the state of academic knowledge, litigation horror stories and other factors have clearly led many Americans to think that our civil justice system is in serious trouble. Public opinion polls show that most Americans believe that a litigation crisis exists.[28] In a 1986 national poll conducted by Louis Harris and Associates on behalf of Aetna Life and Casualty, many participants agreed that more people bring lawsuits than should, that over the previous decade the number of personal injury lawsuits grew faster than the population, and that the size of awards had increased faster than inflation.[29] Forty-five percent of the national poll respondents stated that the size of most awards in personal injury cases was "excessive," 28% believed that their size was "about right," and just 16% believed that the amounts were "not enough." The jury consulting firm Metricus found similar responses in its 1991 national poll. Two-thirds of their respondents agreed that "juries today are awarding too much money."[30] In a 1993 national poll conducted for the *National Law Journal*, three-fourths of the participants agreed that the amount of litigation was undermining the nation's economic recovery. They placed the blame on lawyers and consumers, as well as manufacturers and insurers, for the excessive litigation.[31] Similarly, in a 1993 survey of Californians that was distributed by Citizens Against Lawsuit Abuse, at least 70% of the populace agreed that frivolous lawsuits have led to higher taxes and higher insurance premiums, and have cost California jobs by causing businesses to leave the state or go out of business. Seven out of ten respondents also reported fearing that one day they or someone in their family would be the victim of a frivolous lawsuit.[32]

The attitudes of business executives also reflect the view that we are suffering from a litigation explosion that has negative effects on the economy. Eight out of ten senior corporate executives in one survey said that the fear of lawsuits has more impact on company decision making now than it did ten years ago, and six out of ten agreed that the U.S. civil justice system significantly hampers the ability of U.S. companies to compete effectively with Japanese and European companies.[33] Similarly, a survey of medical doctors in South Carolina showed that many doctors thought there was a crisis in the tort system. When their views were compared with data from South Carolina tort cases, the doctors were shown to have overestimated the average tort award in medical malpractice and product liability cases to a significant degree.[34]

So why, if such views are not borne out by research, do they seem so ubiquitous? To flesh out and help to explain these persistent beliefs in a litigation crisis, I examined the content and correlates of citizens' attitudes toward civil litigation in detail, taking advantage of juror interviews, taped mock jury deliberations, and the quantitative data from my three samples of 269 civil jurors, 216 mock jurors, and 450 state poll respondents. A number of questions relating to the legitimacy of civil litigation were asked in the three studies. Some analyses determined how participants responded to these questions, and others explored the demographic and attitudinal correlates of views about litigation.

In all three studies, responses to the questionnaire items about the legitimacy of civil lawsuits showed considerable skepticism toward plaintiffs and civil litigation. Furthermore, comments by jurors and mock jurors provided qualitative confirmation that citizens are often skeptical about the merits of civil lawsuits.

Figure 3-1 and Table 3-1 display the results to several key questions about the frequency and legitimacy of civil lawsuits. Approximately four out of every five jurors and mock jurors, and nine out of ten state poll respondents, agreed that "there are far too many frivolous lawsuits today." There is a striking lack of disagreement with this statement in all three studies; no more than 6% of the participants in any study ventured to disagree that there were too many frivolous lawsuits. All the same, state poll respondents voiced the most criticism of civil litigation.

Moreover, the perception is widespread that both the rate of litigation and the level of court awards have recently climbed dramatically. Participants in the mock jury study and the state poll were asked to estimate whether the number of personal injury lawsuits had grown faster, slower, or at about the same rate as the population had grown over the last ten years. Majorities in both studies perceived the growth rate of

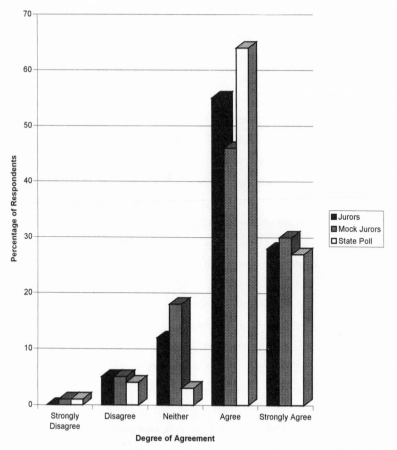

Figure 3-1

Responses to the statement "There are far too many
frivolous lawsuits today."

personal injury lawsuits as faster (56% of mock jurors and 61% of state poll respondents). Similarly, respondents in the two studies were asked whether the size of court awards had outpaced, trailed, or had risen at about the same rate as inflation. Majorities (58% of mock jurors and 65% of poll respondents) saw awards rising faster than inflation. These findings are consistent with the Aetna national poll conducted in the mid-1980s.[35] A widespread perception of growing lawsuit numbers and awards appears to have persisted over this time period.

Comments by jurors and mock jurors gave voice to concerns about excessive litigation. Because I included questions about jurors' general views of civil litigation on a questionnaire, I did not ask a specific question about overall views of civil litigation as part of the standard juror interview schedule. On occasion, though, jurors volunteered general comments about the state of the civil justice system. Several jurors spoke about excessive litigation and high awards. One juror told us: "Basically, I feel that people are too quick to sue nowadays. They're looking for the big pockets. Unfortunately in my line of work, I work in technical service, and my company gets sued a lot for the things they really have no control over other than the fact that they just manufacture the chemicals that somebody may have gotten" (C32-J4).

This person's jury rendered a defense verdict, after the first vote revealed an 11–1 split in favor of the company. Speculating on the reason behind the dissenting juror's views, this juror opined: "I think he just felt sorry for her and just wanted to give her some money. Like I said, people have a tendency to want to do that and therein may lie the big corporation. If it had been you and I that was getting sued, he very well may not have felt that way at all, and not given it any consideration. He did not indicate that that was the reason, I'm just assuming that that may have been the reason for him to feel that way" (C32-J4).

A juror in a medical malpractice case, asked about a spouse's claim for loss of consortium, observed: "Well, some of these awards, I think, are way out of line. This should be something, I guess. But I can't get terribly upset about awards for that" (C12-J9).

The mock jurors debating the case of the woman who slipped and fell in a store (or a private home) often used the case as a springboard for general discussion about the litigation explosion:

> It's so sue-crazy. (Group 22, J4)
> Nowadays they'll sue you for just about anything, you have to watch yourself.
> (Group 16, J1)
> In this day and age everybody wants to sue. (Group 28, J6)
> They sue because there are all kinds of reasons, the garden hose is across
> the lawn. (Group 28, J5)
> There's too much litigation going on all over other things. (Group 16, J4)
> There are a lot of people who file lawsuits and are not that injured. (Group 20,
> J4)
> Things happen to people and it's never their fault, it's always someone else's
> fault. (Group 23, J4)
> Definitely sue-happy, that's why we have big delays in our courts,
> everybody's gonna sue somebody else. (Group 21, J5)

Table 3-1. Attitudes toward Civil Lawsuits

Item	SA	A	N	D	SD
There are far too many frivolous lawsuits today.					
Jurors	28	55	12	5	0
Mock Jurors	30	46	18	5	1
State Poll Respondents	27	64	3	4	1
People are too quick to sue, rather than trying to solve disputes in some way.					
Jurors	18	62	13	6	1
Mock Jurors	17	57	16	10	1
State Poll Respondents	23	67	3	6	0
The large number of lawsuits shows that our society is breaking down.					
Jurors	3	27	31	35	5
Mock Jurors	7	31	27	31	4
State Poll Respondents	10	59	8	22	1
The money awards that juries are awarding in civil cases are too large.					
Jurors	8	29	39	21	3
Mock Jurors	11	30	36	21	2
State Poll Respondents	13	51	20	16	1
Most people who sue others in court have legitimate grievances.					
Jurors	2	33	36	29	1
Mock Jurors	2	49	28	20	1
State Poll Respondents	3	46	12	37	2

Table 3-1. *Continued*

Item	SA	A	N	D	SD
By making it easier to sue, the courts have made this a safer society.					
Jurors	1	6	23	58	12
Mock Jurors	2	14	19	54	11
State Poll Respondents	0	19	8	67	6
Juries do a good job determining the outcomes of lawsuits and assessing damages.					
Jurors	5	56	24	14	2
Mock Jurors	3	48	31	17	1
State Poll Respondents	1	46	19	30	4

Note: Numbers represent the percentages of 269 jurors, 216 mock jurors, and 450 state poll respondents giving each response. Responses are: Strongly Agree (SA), Agree (A), Neither agree nor disagree (N), Disagree (D), and Strongly Disagree (SD).

> That's what's wrong with our system, nowadays so many people out there make a career out of it. That makes people like us sit here and say she's probably just looking for a big award. (Group 32, J3)

A number of mock jurors commented about their own personal experiences, usually instances when they could have sued but did not, to cast a negative light on others who filed lawsuits. For instance, one juror related that "I fell in front of the Museum of Natural History, and I almost died. I could have said there was something in front of me" (Group 25, J4). This jury decided in favor of the individual defendant, in part because they were not convinced that the plaintiff was really injured by the defendant's actions. As one juror explained their stance: "God forbid one of us got some sue-happy person who wanted to sue you, for example, for something and the jury said, 'I don't know she was hurt but . . . '" (Group 25, J4). Another explained why she decided against pursuing a claim: "It's happened to me, but I just didn't feel like being bothered with major lawsuits. Courts are cluttered up enough" (Group 20, J4).

Other mock jurors voiced personal experiences that illustrated how easy it would be to bring a false claim: "I've been in many situations where I've been in a store, not the best store in the world, where a wooden board is sticking up or a nail, but since you didn't get injured you go, oh well, but you think to yourself, if I feel like it I could sue this guy" (Group 28, J5). Similarly: "I could have sued the hospital for malpractice when I fell, but I wanted my health, that's my feeling. Everybody when something happens to them they look for somebody who's responsible" (Group 23, J1).

These comments underscore the point, evident from research studies, that many citizens are injured but do not bring legal claims. When they are faced with deciding the merits of another's claim, they sometimes consider their own personal experiences and prior decision to refrain from litigation. In essence, they may line up the claim before them with their own past: Is this claim worthy of a finding of liability and award, when I did not seek or obtain compensation?

Several items on the questionnaires addressed the issue of why the frequency of lawsuits might be higher than warranted. Many participants laid the blame at the feet of the plaintiffs, who in their view were overeager to sue. Media coverage of the courts also was cited, with 57% of the poll subjects but only 34% of the mock jurors agreeing that "the media exaggerate the number of high jury awards."

One of the jurors from the juror interview study cited the existence of insurance as part of the reason for excessive litigation and awards: "I think if it had to come out of his [the doctor's] own pocket that all of these malpractice suits would, I don't know what would happen to them. They couldn't possibly do it. . . . I'm all against this malpractice insurance. I think it's dreadful" (C12-J9). This juror favored a much lower award than the jury actually reached, but ultimately compromised. Her explanation of the other jurors' reasons for wanting a higher award was as follows: "Because they felt that [the plaintiff] had been put through unnecessary procedures, and the fact that he couldn't do the many things that he used to do, and they just felt that he should get more. I think they were colored also by some of these other cases that have received tremendously high compensations. I think the whole country is doing this" (C12-J9).

Lawyers came in for their share of censure. Majorities in two studies agreed that "lawyers encourage people to file unnecessary lawsuits" (58% of the mock jurors and a whopping 79% of the poll respondents) and that "lawyers ask for twice as much in damages as is warranted" (56% of the mock jurors and 84% of the state poll). Overall confidence in lawyers was relatively low among both mock jurors and state poll participants. These comments about the role of lawyers in encouraging meritless lawsuits and exaggerating claims are consistent with the study participants' general views of lawyers. Other polls show that respect for the legal profession is declining, and that a significant number of citizens believe that lawyers are too interested in money and file too many unnecessary lawsuits. The popular image of lawyers as ambulance chasers undoubtedly contributes to the perception of lawyers as a factor in a litigation explosion.[36]

Mock jurors also spoke negatively about the high expenses and charges of lawyers: "My word, you just think about how the lawyer is getting so much money out of this. . . . The lawyers are going to sap this thing. . . . This makes me feel that there should be limitations on how much money lawyers can land. . . . [It's] obscene for lawyers to make $400,000 on another woman's injury. I do think that's really inappropriate" (Group 20, J2). Similarly: "That's what's costing so much money, the lawyers!" (Group 20, J3). Another group of mock jurors discussed their views that lawyers make out like bandits, that they "take your money and run" (Group 27, J3), and that attorneys' fees are "ridiculous" (Group 27, J4). Nonetheless, jurors and mock jurors often considered attorneys' fees when they decided on a plaintiff's award (see Chapter 7).

As for the impact of civil litigation, study participants saw a number of consequences flowing from the perceived high frequency of litigation. In terms of its impact on the fabric of society, only a minority of jurors (30%) and mock jurors (32%) asserted that "the large number of lawsuits show that our society is breaking down." By way of contrast, fully 69% of the poll respondents thought that the existence of lawsuits was evidence of societal breakdown.

A number of jurors were concerned that high litigation rates and high awards could harm the business community. One of the jurors in a contract case that involved punitive damages reported his reaction when other jurors argued that the award against the big corporation should be higher: "Well, the way I look at it is a big corporation is made up of a bunch of people, and if you take this money from this corporation it's bound to suffer somewhere. Someone invariably is gonna lose their job and that's the way I look at it from my perspective as a working person. In the court system nowadays, it is a completely opposite scene with some of the judgments that go on. It's stupid, there's no reason for some of the judgments that I've seen today" (C11-J1). This juror reported that during deliberation, he resisted agreeing to a verdict for the plaintiff and only reluctantly agreed to an award.

Similarly, a major theme in the mock jury discussions was the presumed impact of excessive litigation at both the societal and personal levels. Litigation was seen as putting the country in bad shape and limiting business opportunities:

> I believe people suing other people for exorbitant amounts of money is what has got our country in the bad shape that it is today. (Group 11, J1)
> Nowadays, I wouldn't want to open a business, the liability. (Group 22, J2)
> In this country we're just suing ourselves out of business. We were just recently trying to go horseback riding, and we couldn't find anyone because of so many lawsuits. If you go riding you know you may get thrown off your horse. (Group 14, J5)

Strikingly large percentages agreed that "high jury awards lead to increased insurance premiums." Fully 85% of the mock jurors and 91% of the poll participants believed that high awards would increase insurance costs. In line with these figures, comments by jurors and mock jurors revealed that one of the most significant aspects of the societal impact of litigation was that it took money out of the pockets of the jurors themselves and their fellow citizens, both because of increased prices that businesses charge to cover the costs of lawsuits and because of higher insurance rates.

> These awards, we all end up paying. (Group 22, J1)
> We pay for this. (Group 14, J4)
> Their insurance rate is going up, and you're going to pay for it the next time you go in to buy. (Group 27, J3)
> You have to understand that every time the store pays one of these claims, you're paying for it because the prices go up. (Group 18, J2)
> You read a lot about people suing, what that does to insurance companies, that's why insurance rates are so high today. (Group 21, J2)
> That's why we're paying the premiums we are. (Group 21, J1)
> This is part of the reason the insurance companies get outrageous, because the money has to come from somewhere. (Group 14, J3)

In one deeply split group, some mock jurors assumed that both the store and the plaintiff carried insurance. However, as one juror pointed out in arguing for an award limited to the medical bills alone, "I say the medical bills, I don't want to pay any more on my insurance" (Group 30, J2). Another jury discussed insurance coverage and the litigation explosion and how it affects society: "That's why you hear in the news so much that medicals are astronomical" (Group 12, J4).

One of the major purposes of the civil litigation system is to encourage general deterrence, creating a safer environment. Yet few of the study participants saw such benefits stemming from the greater ability to make claims in the courts. Jurors strongly disagreed, by a ten-to-one ratio, that "by making it easier to sue, the courts have made this a safer society." Similarly, just 16% of the mock jurors and 19% of the poll participants agreed that making it easier to sue had enhanced general safety. Consistent with the predominant view, jurors and mock jurors rarely volunteered comments about the underlying safety justifications of the civil justice system.

In contrast to their predominantly negative views about civil litigation, study participants reflected greater support for the civil jury, although concerns about high jury awards were frequently expressed. Pluralities in all three studies generally endorsed the civil jury, with most agreeing that "juries do a good job determining the outcomes of lawsuits and assessing damages" (Figure 3-2). The jurors themselves, perhaps not surprisingly, were the most enthusiastic group. They have had the benefit of direct jury experience and need not respond in the abstract, as may have been the case for the other study participants, particularly the state poll respondents. Two-thirds of the state poll subjects (64%) and 41% of the mock jurors also maintained that "the money awards that juries are awarding in civil cases are too large" (see Table 3-1). Even among jurors, a significant minority (37%) expressed some concern that jury damage awards were too high.

Analyzing Views of a Litigation Crisis

Seven items about civil litigation were asked in all three studies. Responses were coded so that high scores on each item indicated greater belief in a litigation crisis. They were then formed into a seven-item Litigation Crisis scale for use in subsequent analyses.[37]

The Litigation Crisis scale was subjected to factor analysis to determine if one or more independent factors contributed to views on the litigation crisis. For jurors, beliefs that people are too quick to sue, that there are too many frivolous lawsuits, and that the rise in lawsuits has not increased societal safety were all associated strongly with one dimension, entitled Excessive Litigation. Two items associated with a second dimension, labeled Jury Criticism, both related to the jury's soundness in reaching verdicts and deciding damage awards.[38] The results of a factor analysis were similar for the state poll respondents, with two factors emerging: one, also labeled Excessive Litigation, included the beliefs that people were too quick to sue, that there

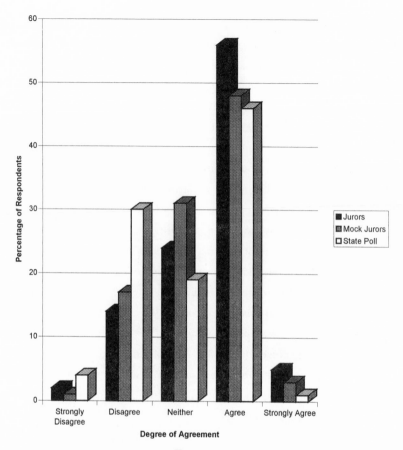

Figure 3-2

Responses to the statement "Juries do a good job determining the
outcomes of lawsuits and assessing damages."

were too many frivolous lawsuits, and that lawsuits showed that society was breaking
down. The two jury items, and an item about legitimacy of grievances, were associated with a second factor, labeled Jury Criticism. Thus, independent perceptions of
the worth of litigation and the ability of the jury both contributed to jurors' and poll
respondents' judgments about the litigation crisis. In contrast, the Litigation Crisis
scale for mock jurors included only the single factor of Excessive Litigation.

Although beliefs in a litigation crisis were widely shared, there were some differences among study participants as a function of certain demographic characteristics
and other attitudes. Data analysis revealed that a number of personal characteristics
were related to views on civil justice. Jurors who were more likely to believe in a

litigation crisis were also more apt to possess a low belief in a just world and a high degree of claims consciousness, describing themselves as assertive and willing to complain. They were more likely to have a low sense of political efficacy (the view that they could make a difference in the world through voting and other public participation).[39] These jurors also were more likely to be white, Protestant, and older. For mock jurors, a low sense of political efficacy and Protestant religion were also more likely to be found among jurors with a sense of litigation crisis.

Comparing the two juror samples with the state poll participants was difficult. Some of the scales (including the Political Efficacy and the Locus of Control scales) were not included in the opinion survey because of the time limitations associated with a telephone poll. In the state poll, conservatives, whites, those with more education, and those with authoritarian views were more likely to assert that we were in the midst of a litigation crisis. Thus, somewhat different factors were linked to litigation crisis views in the survey than in the two jury samples. The fact that the political efficacy scale was not given to poll respondents but was a factor in the jury samples may be partly responsible for the different results in my three samples. Then, too, poll respondents answered questions about litigation in the abstract, without the more personal experience of considering a real or hypothetical civil case in a group with others. Poll respondents may have answered in a more symbolic fashion, considering civil lawsuits as attacks on the status quo, whereas the jury samples may have been more affected by the cases they decided.

One interesting finding is that a participant's income was completely unrelated to his or her views about the problems of the civil justice system. This suggests that a favorable (or unfavorable) position in the nation's economy does not by itself affect the perception that civil litigation is out of control. A psychological predisposition of mistrust and alienation, rather than the objective reality of financial privilege or disadvantage, seems to create perceptions of litigation crisis. Jurors who are disgruntled with the world and who feel that they are not getting a fair shake themselves see additional reason for anger in the supposed excesses of the civil justice system. In my study, the jurors who felt disenfranchised from government and low in their sense of political efficacy, those who had little belief that the world is just, and those who were aggressive in pursuing their own claims all were more likely to question the legitimacy of civil litigation.

Protestants, compared to other religious groups and to those who reported no religious affiliation, were slightly more likely to question the civil justice system. A few other studies have discovered a relationship between people's religiosity and their willingness to derogate suffering victims[40] or make harsh judgments about litigation.[41] In a study of a Georgia community, Professor Carol Greenhouse discovered that Baptists in the town believed that disputing was unchristian. They considered "disputing and litigation as defining characteristics of the unsaved."[42]

In the jury study (but not the other two samples), older participants were more likely to express concerns about civil litigation. Other studies have also found that older people are more likely to perceive a litigation crisis.[43] In his book *Total Justice*, Professor Lawrence Friedman argues that over time people have become more likely to expect full and fair compensation for injustice.[44] If his argument is correct, then it is reasonable to find that younger jurors would see current litigation practice as more consistent with their expectations, while older jurors would see it as more of a violation of the social norms of their day.

One important point must be emphasized. The correlations between Litigation Crisis attitudes and the other variables were generally moderate, and the total percentage of variance accounted for in the regression analyses was modest (multiple correlations, or r's, were .36, .27, and .30 for the juror, mock juror, and state poll samples). That means that between 7% and 13% of the difference in litigation crisis views could be accounted for by all of the demographic and attitudinal factors put together. Even though some people in the population express stronger condemnation of civil litigation, beliefs that the civil justice system is in trouble are widespread and endorsed by majorities of all demographic groups. It is common for jurors and the populace to have concerns about plaintiffs getting something for nothing, or requesting compensation for what are perceived as minor, contrived, or self-inflicted injuries. This set of views, questioning the legitimacy of plaintiff claims and doubting the efficacy of the civil litigation system, is a widely endorsed aspect of our individualistic ethic, not the exclusive province of particular subgroups. It is an agreed-upon part of contemporary legal culture.

Media and Advertising Accounts of Civil Litigation

A number of scholars have attempted to determine why people continue to believe that litigation is out of control, if the actual court statistics do not paint such a dire picture. They have identified two potential culprits: first, media reporting of civil lawsuits, and second, advertising campaigns, sponsored by business and insurance groups, about the civil litigation system.

Few citizens have direct information about what goes on in the nation's courts. In fact, national polls show that the public's knowledge about the courts is minimal.[45] People must rely on newspapers, television, magazines, and other media to convey the most important courtroom proceedings. One well-known finding about media reporting of criminal justice matters is that it significantly overrepresents serious and violent criminal offenses.[46] The reason is that crime sells newspapers and draws viewers. Editors assume, with good reason, that people are more interested in learning about such serious criminal offenses as murder and rape than about graffiti and traffic violations. Thus, many readers and viewers receive an exaggerated picture of the rate of violent and serious crime, and tend to overestimate the extent of such crime and of violent victimization.

A parallel phenomenon exists in reporting of civil litigation. Just what types of civil lawsuits are considered newsworthy? Editors may well judge that lawsuits involving multiple individuals, lawsuits with the potential for broad impact (such as class-action lawsuits), and lawsuits involving claims against high-profile individuals and companies are likely to grab attention. Big monetary awards are likely to be titillating as well. Furthermore, the tedious details of litigation may be deemed unworthy of news coverage, leading to a focus in news stories on the prominent stages of a case, such as the verdict.

Researchers at the University of Washington and the University of Puget Sound followed the media coverage of the McDonald's coffee-spill case and discovered that although the verdict generated tremendous interest, after the initial story was reported there was spotty and incomplete follow-up coverage.[47] Many details about the case became available within the first few weeks after the verdict, and these details placed the trial in context, provided more information about the evidence before the jury, and on the whole made the jury's award more understandable. Despite front-page coverage in one major newspaper, most other papers did not provide the fuller account of the lawsuit.

Within two weeks of the McDonald's verdict, the *Wall Street Journal* ran a front-page story that reported interviews with the jurors who decided the coffee-spill case.[48] Initially, the jurors themselves didn't see why they "needed to be there to settle a coffee spill." Yet the evidence led them to decide in favor of the plaintiff. The jurors were surprised at the severity of Ms. Liebeck's burns from the coffee. Another key to their decision was evidence that McDonald's had handled at least seven hundred complaints of coffee burns during the prior decade and had settled many of them, some for substantial amounts. Jurors told the *Wall Street Journal* reporter that McDonald's executives had hurt the company with their testimony that McDonald's was aware of the potential burns from its coffee but had not consulted burn experts and did not plan to warn its customers about the possibility of serious burns. Furthermore, the executives indicated that they had no plans to change the temperature of their coffee, as consumers like their coffee to be hot. McDonald's pointed the finger at Ms. Liebeck, arguing that she was responsible for her own injury in that she had held the cup of hot coffee between her legs and had not removed her clothes immediately after the spill, which contributed to the severity of the injury. They added that Ms. Liebeck's burns were probably worse than a younger person's would have been because older skin is thinner and more susceptible to injury. The jurors concluded on the basis of the company's actions and representations that "the facts were so overwhelmingly against the company" that "they were not taking care of their consumers" and that they showed "callous disregard for the safety of the people."[49]

But how did the jury arrive at its figure for punitive damages? The plaintiff's attorney had recommended that they penalize McDonald's for one or two days' worth of coffee sales, which he guessed to be about $1.35 million per day. The jury decided on two days' worth of sales as adequate punishment, leading them to a punitive damage award of $2.7 million.

After reading the *Wall Street Journal* article, even if one disagreed with the verdict and award, one at least had a sense about the reasons behind the verdict and the rationale for the specific punitive damage award. The analysis of newspaper coverage of the case, however, showed that few of these explanatory details ever made it into subsequent stories about the case in other newspapers.[50] Furthermore, later stages in the case, in which the punitive damage award was reduced by the trial judge,[51] the reduction was appealed, and the parties ultimately settled for an undisclosed amount,[52] were covered by progressively fewer news organizations. The researchers who analyzed the news coverage observed that "a caricature of the case soon displaced details that would have made Stella's story less outrageous and the jury's judgment more understandable."[53] The coffee-spill case became a "legend," and a politically effective one at that.[54] For many readers, Stella Liebeck will forever be the woman who became a millionaire by spilling coffee on herself. The researchers concluded that the same kinds of reporting characteristics (covering a case only when a verdict is announced and failing to provide much detail or context) were likely to be present in the media coverage of other cases in the civil justice system.

Confirmation of this point was obtained by researchers Daniel Bailis and Robert MacCoun, who undertook a systematic analysis of media coverage of tort litigation. Analyzing articles about civil litigation appearing in popular national magazines, they calculated the frequency of discussion of different types of tort cases, the plaintiff win rate, and the award amounts reported in the articles.[55] They then compared the media "rates" with data from national studies of the civil justice system on the rates of occurrence of case type, win ratios, and mean and median award amounts. Consistent with expectations, they found that the magazines devoted more attention to product liability and medical malpractice cases than to the more common fender-benders that make up the bulk of the state civil court docket. Furthermore, the media overrepresented plaintiff win rates and award amounts. The news magazines' sample of jury awards was dramatically out of sync with the national studies. For instance, the median jury award discussed in the magazine articles was $1,750,000, whereas in the court studies, the median ranged from a low of $51,000 to a high of $318,000.[56] If citizens and corporate executives derive information about the frequency and outcomes of civil litigation primarily from such media sources as these national news magazines, it is clear that they could develop a distorted picture of what goes on in the nation's courthouses.

Scholars have also identified a second source of potentially misleading information about the civil justice system: a continuing advertising campaign sponsored by the business and insurance industry about the alleged excesses of the system. Stephen Daniels and Joanne Martin have written about efforts on the part of business and insurance corporations to affirm that litigation is out of control, that we all pay for high awards, and that tort reform that makes it more difficult to bring lawsuits is essential to the health of the economy.[57] In their analysis, advertising campaigns by the insurance industry have fingered the litigation explosion as the cause of increased insurance costs and reduced availability of business and medical insurance.[58] And the opinions of jurors and other citizens, as illustrated by the quotations from participants from my studies presented in this chapter, are often consistent with the themes of the advertising campaigns.

In a more direct illustration of the effects of the advertisements, Professor Elizabeth Loftus conducted an experiment to determine whether exposure to insurance company advertising about the negative impact of high awards could affect jury judgments.[59] She used a mock juror paradigm, in which some mock jurors were exposed to the advertising while others were not. Those who read the advertising awarded less money for pain and suffering to a hypothetical plaintiff, compared to mock jurors who had not read the advertising. Loftus demonstrated in the laboratory that the right kind of insurance advertising could translate into lower awards.

The assumption that advertising can make a difference in jury trials is the basis for a novel, and contested, advertising strategy on the part of some businesses facing litigation. In the spring of 1997, a few weeks before it was scheduled to stand trial in New Orleans over silicone breast implants, the Dow Chemical Company embarked on an advertising campaign in New Orleans that promoted its corporate citizenship.[60] Another advertisement that aired was produced by the American Tort Reform Association (a group that includes Dow Chemical) and emphasized the positive side of silicone, illustrated by a young girl with a silicone shunt in her brain, whose mother pronounces: "Silicone is not the problem. The personal-injury lawyers and their greed is the problem."[61] The advertising campaign became the subject of dispute between the sides. A plaintiff's attorney charged that Dow Chemical was attempting to "pollute" the jury, while a spokesperson for the company maintained that the ads were designed simply to "rectify the damage to our public image" as a result of the implant cases.[62]

Whether such efforts influence the way juries decide particular cases involving specific companies, advertising and media coverage are likely to have a more widespread effect by influencing the perception that the courts are full of frivolous litigation. Psychologists have documented a phenomenon they label the availability heuristic.[63] In estimating the frequency of an event, people rely in part on the ease with which examples of that event are recalled. They use the quickness with which they come up with examples as a heuristic, a tool for estimating frequency. If one remembers an example very readily, then one is more likely to judge the event as one that commonly occurs. Thus, in forming an opinion about whether there are a large number of frivolous lawsuits, people are strongly affected by the easy recollection of such lawsuits. Media reporting and advertising campaigns together promote the easy recall of the Stella Liebecks (at least the legendary versions), not the vast majority of us who quietly cope when we are injured.

How Belief in a Litigation Crisis Affects Jury Decision Making

How do the ubiquitous perceptions of litigation crisis affect the outcomes of civil lawsuits? Professor Albert Alschuler hypothesizes that the emotions of an actual trial, especially one in which the plaintiff's suffering is substantial and the defendant's pockets are deep, might overcome broad concerns expressed by the public about the impact of jury awards on the strength of the American economy.[64] Whether or not this is so, the empirical research demonstrates that general attitudes about civil litigation appear to have a significant influence on decision making by civil juries. A few mock juror studies indicate that those who support tort reform are more likely to be more negative toward the plaintiff's case.[65] To explore the question further, I examined the relationship of Litigation Crisis attitudes to decision making in all three of the studies in my research project.

The Juror Sample. In our interviews, jurors who were most insistent in assertions about meritless lawsuits and the litigation explosion seemed to be more likely to favor the defense, or, if their jury reached a plaintiff's verdict, to say that they argued for low awards. The juror sample, though of great interest, posed the biggest challenge to the effort to assess statistically the relationship of Litigation Crisis attitudes to case judgments. We interviewed only a subset (albeit a large subset) of the jurors from each of the cases, so the attitudes toward litigation of a significant percentage of jurors who decided a case are unknown. In addition, although jurors often talked about how they were leaning in the case before deliberation, I was not able to collect systematic information about their predeliberation preferences for verdicts and awards. Many jurors said that they had not considered specific award amounts before the jury deliberation. Because jurors decide in a group, we had available for analysis only the *jury's* decision and award in the case. Therefore, to test for an association between litigation attitudes and case judgments, it was necessary to use the jury, rather than the individual juror, as the unit of analysis. That reduced the number of data points considerably.

To obtain a summary score of each jury's attitudes toward civil litigation, I calculated mean Litigation Crisis scale scores for each of the juries separately, by summing the individual jurors' responses on each jury and dividing by the total number of jurors we had interviewed on each jury. I then correlated these mean judgments with the final jury awards in each of the cases, counting defense verdicts as zero awards. The relationship was statistically significant.[66] The more strongly a jury collectively perceives a litigation explosion, the lower the jury award in the case.

The correlation is open to several interpretations. Jurors who begin a case with some predispositions about the overall merits of plaintiff claims may interpret the trial evidence in a manner consistent with their early views. But the causal arrow may point in the other direction. Serving on a meritorious lawsuit with plaintiffs who deserved and received a high award may affect the jurors' general perceptions of the soundness of litigation.

The State Poll and the Mock Jury Study. Because the state poll and mock jury data included individual judgments of liability and award, it was easier to test for the significance of attitudes concerning a litigation crisis. In the public opinion survey, two case scenario judgments—the assessment of negligence and the recommended award—and the Litigation Crisis scale were used in the analysis. Litigation crisis views were significantly related to both negligence and award judgments in the overall sample, and were significantly related to either negligence or award or both in each of the three experimental conditions (which varied as to whether the defendant was an individual, a nonprofit corporation, or a for-profit corporation).[67] The more likely people were to perceive a litigation system out of control, the less likely they were to judge the defendant negligent or to recommend a high award. In the mock jury study, the Litigation Crisis scale was significantly correlated with case judgments overall and within each of the two scenarios (which differed only as to whether the defendant was a business or an individual).[68]

In the public opinion study, questions about litigation were asked *before* respondents made judgments about a specific case. Yet litigation attitudes and case judgments were still significantly related. This fact helps to rule out the alternative explanation for such a relationship that is present in the juror study, namely, that hearing about a particular case affects litigation crisis judgments rather than the other way around. It seems more likely that attitudes toward civil litigation help to shape the approach a person takes to interpreting evidence and deciding a lawsuit.[69]

Why Do People Believe in a Litigation Crisis?

The attitudes of respondents in all three of the studies reflect widespread belief in a litigation explosion and acute concern about the legitimacy of civil lawsuits. The omnipresence of these attitudes is remarkable. The assumption of litigation crisis pervades all sectors of society and consistently influences judgments in civil cases.

Why is it that virtually everyone shares a belief in the litigation crisis? The existence of unrepresentative media reporting and business advertising campaigns tells only part of the story. To say that the media and advertising present a biased view of civil litigation and that our knowledge and beliefs may be influenced by these stories doesn't address the more fundamental issue. What makes these stories so attractive to us—and hence to the media—in the first place? The media oblige us with litigation horror stories in part because our appetite for them is substantial. The advertising campaigns work because they resonate with the way many Americans are drawn to the underlying themes of the advertisements. An interesting question is why we become so outraged by certain claims—such as those of the McDonald's coffee lady, Stella Liebeck, or the burglar who fell through the skylight—that they become icons and symbols rather than actual cases.

I believe that citizens show considerable antagonism toward litigation in part because lawsuits (particularly ones that stretch the boundaries of responsibility) are seen as violating central and deeply cherished values. Each lawsuit that challenges a prime value can be seen as a lesson about the integrity of our social world. Professor Robert Hayden, for example, argues that when a plaintiff uses the courts to obtain compensation for personal injury, the plaintiff may be seen as violating the important social values relating to personal responsibility, equality, and redistribution of wealth.[70]

In my view, the most significant value implicated in civil litigation against business is that of the plaintiff's individual responsibility. Plaintiffs often argue against the ethic of personal responsibility, maintaining that businesses, organizations, or other individuals are to blame for their injuries. Many jurors resist the expansion of responsibility to business and corporate entities, insisting that plaintiffs be held accountable for the ways their own actions may have contributed to their injuries. A plaintiff whose lawsuit threatens a commonly accepted aspect of personal responsibility, such as Stella Liebeck's claim over spilled coffee, is seen as an indication that rules of personal responsibility are in decline. Collective outrage about the deviant nature of Stella's claim, at least the mythical media depiction of it, functions to reassert and reinforce the traditional boundaries of personal responsibility for the community.[71] In a time of transition such as ours, when the lines between personal and collective or organizational responsibility are being tested and redrawn, we can expect controversy over the shifting sands of personal versus business responsibility.

In addition, Professor Hayden points out that individual litigants marshal the state's resources in bringing a lawsuit, thus undermining the formal equality between the parties. If a plaintiff prevails in a lawsuit, the jury's monetary damage award will compensate the plaintiff even though he or she has not earned the money in the traditional way, by working. Americans are hostile to others whom they see as getting something for nothing, particularly at taxpayer or government expense. Consider, for example, the scorn heaped on welfare recipients, the widespread enthusiasm for having welfare mothers work outside the home, and the radical restructuring of the federal welfare system in the 1990s. When plaintiffs sue businesses, lawsuits can be seen as attacks on authority and threats to the integrity and the strength of the business community, which in turn are central to the continued health of the economy and society.

4

THE PERSONHOOD
OF THE CORPORATION

Moving from a focus on plaintiffs and the merits of their claims, I turn to an examination of how jurors judge the responsibility—and civil liability—of a business corporation. The century-long expansion of business liability has created many opportunities for the lay public to judge corporations, but in fact we know little about how jurors approach their task, how they consider the causal roles and responsibilities of corporate actors and business corporations.

I draw on the interviews with jurors, as well as the results of several experiments, to present a picture of what jurors do when they attempt to determine whether a business corporation should be held liable. The examination of how jurors talk about the corporation and its responsibilities in the context of specific trials provides a fascinating glimpse into an issue that has plagued scholars for many years: What precisely do people do when they are asked to reflect on a group entity such as a business corporation? How do they determine whether a group has intent or responsibility when those very terms are usually associated with individual, sentient human beings? And does it makes any sense to sanction an organization for the actions of individuals who work within the organization? Policy makers and scholars of corporate crime have long struggled with the difficulties in conceptualizing, analyzing, and punishing such groups as corporations, because our justice system is organized chiefly around individual persons. There's an often-quoted observation that it is hard to punish corporations because they have "no soul to damn, no body to kick."[1] Therefore, seeing what jurors do with their concrete task of assessing the civil liability of a business corporation can shed some light on strategies for dealing with the amorphous group nature of the corporation.

The Origins of the American Corporation

There is a lively debate among academic scholars, lawyers, and policy makers about the optimal legal liabilities for business corporations. Some argue that business has a special set of responsibilities to the community, its workforce, and its customers, and that liability rules should reflect those great responsibilities.[2] Others maintain that the corporation is a "person" in the eyes of the law, with essentially the same rights and duties as individual persons, and should be treated accordingly. To insist on higher standards for corporations would unnecessarily interfere with the development of American business. Finally, at least one aspect of corporation law describes a *lower* level of responsibility for corporate entities. The corporate form constitutes a legal entity with limited liability. The limitation on liability with co-investors makes it more attractive to invest capital in business corporations.[3]

Ideas about the roles, responsibilities, and even the nature of the corporation have changed over time.[4] The corporation itself, certainly in its modern form, is a relatively recent invention. Before 1800, American corporations were few and far between, and very different from today's corporate entities, not only in size but, more significantly, in purpose. Virtually none of the corporations in colonial times were businesses. More often, governments granted corporate charters to cities, churches, and charities; the charters specifically designated their powers, privileges, and obligations.[5] After the American Revolution, localities awarded corporate charters for the undertaking of collective projects that would benefit the community. For example, they were granted to banks and insurance companies for the provision of financial services, and given to companies organized for the purpose of building bridges and roads or providing other services typically seen as functions of the government. Frequently these grants were monopolies. Because these early corporate charters still specified the particular purposes and duties to be fulfilled by the corporation, and often limited the length and terms of the corporate enterprise, the state exerted significant control over corporate activity, at least in theory.

Change came during the nineteenth century, as the industrial revolution and capital expansion produced a dramatic increase in requests for corporate charters for commercial activity. The demand outstripped the ability of legislatures to adequately craft, vote on, and supervise each and every charter. In addition, the business community complained that the special charter system was an inefficient and awkward method for organizing economic activity. Mounting pressures for standardized corporate charters eventually led to the development of general corporation law, forever changing the characteristics of the typical corporation. As legal historian Lawrence Friedman writes: "Between 1800 and 1850, the essential nature of the corporation changed. No longer was the business corporation a unique, *ad hoc* creation, vesting exclusive control over a public asset or natural resource in one group of favorites or investors. Rather, it was becoming a general form for organizing a business, legally open to all, and with few real restrictions on entry, duration, and management. Business practice led the way. The living law on proxy voting, general and special meetings, inspection of books, and the transfer of stock, gradually created demands (which were granted) for standard clauses in corporate charters; and ultimately these norms were embodied in the statute and case law of corporations."[6]

Thus, the early corporate charters, with their expectations that corporations would fulfill significant public functions and goals, were replaced by a general vehicle whose purpose was to facilitate private business enterprise. In line with prevailing sentiment that what was good for business was good for the economy and society, the shift toward general corporation law reinforced the law's predominant role in the nineteenth century of facilitating the development of the capitalist economy.[7] It is hard to get a clear picture of the public's view of the rise of the business corporation. Although historian James Willard Hurst has concluded that public opinion supported the legal, and societal, deference to industry,[8] other evidence (particularly from the history of labor struggles) indicates that there were great concerns about dangerous working conditions and other serious problems of the industrial order.[9]

Today, the corporate form is the predominant means of organizing economic activity. Although corporation law specifies the fiduciary requirements of corporate managers and directors and a corporation's internal organization, specific duties to the public good have been all but eliminated from formal corporate charters. Corporate actors may have a general sense of duty to improve their communities, or they may perceive strong economic benefits in being a good citizen. Business leaders and academic commentators often discuss the social and community obligations of the business corporation, yet these obligations are diffuse, optional rather than required, no longer part and parcel of the corporate charter. As for the legal duties of the business corporation, the law adopted the individualistic framework of existing law, based on individual persons' rights and responsibilities, and applied it to such organizational entities as corporations. In the legal world, the corporation became a "person."

The "Personhood" of the Corporation

A striking development in corporate law, which helped to set boundaries on responsibilities of corporations, was a decision by the U.S. Supreme Court in 1886 in the *Santa Clara* case. In that case, the Justices held that in the eyes of the law, a corporation is a "person" that possesses essentially the same constitutional protections, rights, and duties as individuals.[10] This remarkable conclusion came at the start of oral argument in the case. Dismissing debate on the matter in just two sentences, the Justices asserted their unanimous view: "The court does not wish to hear argument on the question whether the provision in the Fourteenth Amendment to the Constitution, which forbids a State to deny to any person within its jurisdiction the equal protection of the laws, applies to these corporations. We are all of the opinion that it does."[11]

The case and its progeny invigorated an ongoing debate in the second half of the nineteenth century over the nature of the corporation. Was it best to follow the traditional notion, derived from the fact that corporate charters granted by legislatures created the corporation, that the corporation was an artificial entity created by positive law? Alternatively, was the corporation better conceived of as a partnership, the result of free contracting among individuals? Or, as the *Santa Clara* case came to symbolize, was it best to think of the corporation as a natural entity, a private being like a person, rather than a construction of the state? Morton Horwitz has questioned whether the *Santa Clara* case holding was derived from a theory that the corporation was essentially no different from the individual in its constitutional status.[12] Nevertheless, Horwitz acknowledges the importance of the *Santa Clara* case in encouraging the development of the natural-entity theory of corporations, which in turn had a strong influence on the shape of corporate law.

In some ways, the equation of personhood and corporate identity fit well with the prevailing legal rules, which were organized around categories governing individual activity. It was difficult to insert a collectivity into a law embedded with individualistic rules and conceptions. The notion of corporate personhood provided a convenient means to do so. Furthermore, as Horwitz argues, other views of the corporation (such as the partnership analogy) were seen as containing the seeds of destruction of special corporate privileges, particularly the all-important benefit of limited shareholder liability. The natural-entity, or personhood, theory prevailed.

There are many critics of the notion that the corporation is a person within the meaning of the law. Economist Warren J. Samuels notes the irony that the personhood theory of the corporation developed during a period when business corporations increased dramatically in size, scope, and impact, becoming more distinct from individuals than ever before.[13] Other scholars denounce the equivalence of corporations and persons in constitutional law on a variety of grounds. Some argue that it inappropriately increased the corporation's immunity from governmental control.[14] Others maintain that the structure and complexities of modern corporations make an analogy to the person no longer appropriate, if it ever was.[15] Scholars also point to the ways the legal equivalence of individuals and corporations does not capture the reality of collective decision making[16] and the governing power of large corporations.[17]

In spite of its critics, the individualistic paradigm in law is alive and well. Although numerous laws regulate business activity, elements of the personhood conception continue to play a significant role in shaping legal treatment of the corporation. The paradigm is even apparent in jury trials. In many civil cases involving corporations, judges give the following legal instruction to jurors: "In the case, [one of] the plaintiff(s) (or defendant[s]) is a corporation. The mere fact that one of the parties is a corporation does not mean it is entitled to any lesser consideration by you. All persons are equal before the law, and corporations, big or small, are entitled to the same fair consideration that you would give any other individual party."[18] American law asserts, for some purposes at least, the constitutional equality of persons and corporations. This leads to the inference contained in the judicial instruction that corporations should be treated similarly to individual persons, judged by the same standards, and evaluated within the same framework.

There is, then, considerable discussion in the academy and in the legal community about the appropriate standards for corporate liability. Despite the specific rules regulating large arenas of business conduct, the individualistic thrust of the law encourages corporations to be treated the same as individual persons. As Meir Dan-Cohen observes: "The individual human being remains the paradigmatic legal actor, in whose image the law is shaped and then applied to corporations and other collective entities."[19]

What does the public think about the idea that corporations are persons in the eyes of the law? Do jurors' judgments about corporate entities suggest that they are seen as equivalent to individual persons, or do those judgments instead sharply demarcate between business corporations and individuals?[20] Let's turn to the evidence.

Jurors' Judgments of the Corporation as Ghost

I begin my analysis by considering the general and specific comments that jurors made during their interviews, as they reflected on how they assessed corporate liability. Given that a prime interest of mine was to determine how jurors considered the corporate parties, it came as a surprise (and at first a disturbing one, because it was contrary to my expectations) that many jurors reported no particularly strong views about the corporate parties in their cases. Recall that in Chapter 2, I described the considerable analysis of motives and overall skepticism that jurors displayed in talking about personal injury plaintiffs. In contrast, when jurors talked about the corporate parties in their interviews, it was unusual for them to report such vigorous scrutiny of the motives and credibility of the corporation. The ways jurors talked about businesses were much less *concrete* than the ways they evaluated plaintiffs. Furthermore, even though jurors in most cases in the study concluded that corporate actors should be held liable, most jurors expressed neutral or even positive views of the business litigants.

I was initially puzzled by the striking asymmetry in the types of comments about business corporations and plaintiffs. Yet, in a significant number of cases in the sample, no individual representative of the corporation presented trial testimony. In my study, in many cases, those who actually owned the business were rarely present. Even business managers were infrequent visitors. Of course, the corporation itself, as a legal fiction rather than a real person, could not testify! Often, the defense attorney was the only personal representative of the business in court. The absence of business representatives in many cases may have been due to the moderate stakes of many of the cases in my sample. Corporate attorneys have told me that it is typical practice in high-stakes cases to have a high-ranking official of the business corporation attend the jury trial.

On the one hand, the absence of corporate representatives led jurors to question where these people were. On the other hand, it also meant that jurors had little basis on which to generate detailed evaluations and inferences about their behavior and character, which were so obvious in jurors' assessments of the plaintiffs. As one of the jurors in a worker injury case observed: "When it's a corporation, you get a little bit more impersonal. You don't have one person, it's not like you have a person to focus on. . . . It surprised me that there wasn't someone else [besides the defense attorney] there. Yet, I realize that as far as this case, it wasn't, you know, they really weren't asking millions and millions of dollars" (C14-J1). In a sense, then, the corporation is often a "ghost" in the courtroom. The absence of a corporeal body appears to shape the ways civil jurors consider the corporation and its liability.

Research on memory also points to a reason why people may recall information about individuals and groups in a different manner. People tend to be able to recall more information about individuals than about groups. Psychologists believe that this discrepancy is due to different expectations of, and different processing of information about, the two types of entities. We expect that an individual will have a stable personality, and as we listen to him or her speak we work to form an integrated, global judgment about what that person is like. In contrast, most of us do not expect that individuals who are part of a group (such as a business corporation) are going to behave in consistent ways, and therefore we are less motivated to form a global impression of the group as a whole.[21]

Jurors seemed to focus on the specific individuals and their evidence rather than on the missing corporate "person." In a number of instances, jurors described cases in which individuals sued corporations as essentially a dispute between two individuals—the plaintiff and an individual with some connection to the corporation. In a worker injury trial, jurors focused on specific individuals rather than corporate entities in the course of deciding liability: "It didn't really affect my thinking at all because they were so removed from the process and that may have been a deliberate strategy on their part" (C15-J3). Similarly, another juror from the same worker injury case reported: "It seemed to be [a dispute between two individuals] pretty much anyway, even though [the company] was named in the suit, because it was not there and because all of the testimony kind of revolved around [the two workers]" (C15-J6).

My sample of trials included a fair number of automobile accident cases, in which a person in the conduct of his or her employment had been involved in an accident with the plaintiff. These cases often displayed the greatest degree of ghostliness for the company. The corporate defendant usually was represented only by the attorney and by the driver of the business vehicle. Comments by jurors in one auto accident case suggest just how invisible the corporation was. Although most of them knew that the truck involved in the accident was the property of a company, most did not know the nature or identity of the business (a local roofing contractor). In their words, "that really was immaterial to the case" (C2-J1) and "that didn't enter my mind at all" (C2-J3). Similarly, in a case in which a company truck had hit a driver's parked car, a juror reported: "I didn't think of the company. I kept thinking of [the two drivers]. I didn't know the company. The only thing I can remember is that it was over in [a neighboring state]" (C18-J4). Another juror from that case pointed out that "it was basically two cars, the truck was a little larger than the car, but not much" (C18-J8). Therefore, he reported that the jury considered the case as involving two individuals. He concluded that if the situation had had the potential for greater damage, such as the Exxon Valdez tanker accident, then their views might have been different.

Medical malpractice cases were also ones in which the corporate identity of the parties remained in the background. Typically, doctors were sued both individually and as part of their own medical corporations, but jurors tended to focus exclusively on the doctor and not the corporation. In fact, when we initially asked medical malpractice jurors how they were affected by the presence of a corporation in the case, many looked at us blankly. They reported that they were unaware that the corporation was a named party in the lawsuit. As one juror put it, "Whether [the doctor] was part of a corporation, that thought never came to my mind, nor was it made clear to us at the time, that I recall" (C12-J7). One juror in a dental malpractice case asked what it meant to be incorporated, saying that she had not been told and did not learn that the doctor was a member of a medical corporation (C16-J1).

Corporate actors did appear to have more presence in certain trials. Asbestos trials stood out in this regard (see Chapter 6). In asbestos litigation, a substantial amount of evidence revolves around historical information about how asbestos companies dealt with the potential health consequences of asbestos use, so the corporation tends to be highly visible. In two other cases that generated a substantial degree of scrutiny of the motives of corporate representatives, the business was a small, owner-operated, local concern. The owner's testimony allowed jurors to focus on a live individual rather than a nameless corporate ghost.

Did Jurors Give the Corporation the
Same Treatment as an Individual?

One way of assessing whether jurors treat corporations as "persons" is to ask whether the case would have been different if it had been a dispute between individuals. I was very interested in determining whether jurors thought they were affected by the corporate identity of the defendant in the case. Not only would their answers speak to issues about corporate personhood, but they might also provide a window into the jurors' evaluation process. Therefore, I asked jurors to reflect on how they were affected by the fact that one of the parties in the case was a corporation. I also asked, as a follow-up question, whether they would have thought about the case any differently if the defendant had been an individual rather than a corporation (and if all the other circumstances were the same).

These two questions were challenging to jurors. They required jurors to introspect about the factors in their own decision making. Psychological research indicates that people are often limited in their ability to determine whether certain elements have affected their behavior.[22] The second question was challenging for an additional reason: it required jurors to rearrange the facts of the case so that the defendant was no longer a corporation but an individual. The facts in some cases facilitated this thought experiment. It was easier for jurors to imagine the absence of a corporation in a car accident case, for example, than in an asbestos trial. A further complication is that judges and attorneys had often admonished jurors to treat corporations as they would individuals. Thus, jurors often knew what the legally approved answer to these questions would be.

Nevertheless, their replies, and the reasons they gave for them, are interesting. When jurors were asked explicitly how they were affected by the presence of a corporation in their case, many jurors replied that they were not influenced. Sixty-eight percent of the jurors said that it did not affect their decision making, while nineteen percent said that it did. The remaining jurors gave ambiguous answers that could not be coded as yes or no. Some jurors apparently considered the question to be probing for anti-corporate bias, as reflected in this juror's response: "It didn't really affect me. I try to be fair with people" (C14-J2). In line with several of the jurors' comments quoted earlier, other jurors stated that they focused on the individuals in the case: "It didn't matter whether it was an individual or a corporation. I was more interested in the exact testimony that was presented" (C4-J5). As one juror from an auto accident case observed: "I really wasn't thinking on the fact of it being a company. Mostly what I was personally thinking was the fact of which one was negligent in the case. . . . I don't remember us even talking about it" (C18-J10).

A juror in a case against a landscaping company, when asked if he was influenced by the presence of a business corporation, replied: "No, basically I saw the business as being [the individual who was the owner]. . . . It wasn't really a corporation that we were dealing with, it was really one man's kind of operation. [I considered the company] only to the extent that he was responsible for the work that was done even though he was not intimately involved in the laying of the sod initially or later on. He still bore the responsibility of the work that was done" (C8-J3). One juror thought:

It may have affected my initial thinking, in other words, I might have thought, "Oh here they are being wronged by a business," and I might have gotten that initial impression. However, as the case went on I really feel that I would have been objective in trying to determine who was right and who was wrong and that in this particular instance to me the business man appeared to be the person of less integrity, the person who hedged more, who didn't have facts written down and I think who had done the wrong thing. If it had been the other way around, and he had had facts to back what he had done and he had had a secretary who answered the phone and said she had gotten messages from [the plaintiff] or that sort of thing, you know I really feel that I could have been objective. I just think that in this case being objective meant that I really felt he was not maybe being completely truthful and [the plaintiff] was. (C8-J6)

One juror in a contract dispute, when asked whether he was affected by the fact that the case involved corporations, replied: "Not particularly. My father owns his own business so to me it's no big deal that a guy owns a company. You know, you're liable for it because it's yours, so to me, it didn't really make much of a difference. A company is a company and the guy that owns it is the guy that owns it, but it's his company, it's his responsibility" (C13-J2).

In the follow-up question, similar results were obtained. We pressed jurors about whether they would have decided the case differently if there had been no corporation—if the dispute had been between individuals. Most jurors—a total of 64%—said that they would have decided the case just the same. Nearly a quarter of the jurors (23%) said that if the case had included only individuals, their thinking would have changed. The remainder of the jurors gave ambiguous answers that could not be definitively coded one way or the other.

The type of case that jurors had decided clearly influenced their statements about whether the corporation made a difference in the case. Jurors in contract cases, worker injury trials, and asbestos cases were more likely than jurors in auto accident cases and cases involving injuries in a place of business to say that the identity of the corporation had an impact, or that the case would have been different if it had included only individual litigants.

Those jurors who claimed that the corporate party had not influenced them made a number of points. Some appeared to be affected by the corporation's literal absence from the courtroom, leaving them to focus on individual parties who testified in the case rather than on the corporation. Jurors are also inclined to look at the individual representatives of a corporate entity. Recall the paint-store case described in Chapter 2: when some jurors expressed their view that the store had partial responsibility for the boy's injury, they talked about the clerk and his presumed knowledge of the danger spots in the paint store. As one juror explained: "Businesses and corporations are made up of individuals. They don't act as a body that has no mind or anything. They are individuals, and it's kind of a fallacy for me to think that a business [is different from] the people who make up the business. . . . They are the people. It's a contradictory statement to make" (C2-J2). Similarly, one juror in a case involving a worker injured in an auto plant, when asked about her general views about auto companies, emphasized that companies are made up of individuals: "Some car companies make bad cars, and some of them make good cars, but then again I don't think it's the company that's doing it. I think it's the people that's doing the job that they have in the company. I don't think you should blame the company because of it. Because some people go to work just to say they've got a job. They'd do anything. You know, that's that. I don't think you should really blame the company" (C14-J9).

In the medical malpractice cases, we eventually abandoned asking jurors about the impact of the medical corporation in the case because most were unaware that a corporate party was named. They tended to focus on the actions of the doctor and the patient. "I just thought it was one man against another," as one juror put it (C16-J7). We did, however, ask a number of jurors to speculate whether the medical context for the injury made a difference to them. Consider the following exchange:

Interviewer: How do you think this case might have differed had it involved an injury that wasn't part of a medical injury? If, for example, somebody had the same kind of injury but caused by a different mechanism, such as a car accident or a fight? How did the medical nature of it affect your thinking?
Juror: I don't know. I do expect a medical professional to know what he's doing and to take responsibility for his actions and perhaps that's a bias that was there. If it had happened in some other way, we would have had to look at what did cause it and see how that related. (C16-J2)

A significant minority of jurors did say that they were affected by the presence of the corporation and would have treated a case involving two individuals differently. Among the reasons provided were that corporations were composed of more people, that corporate actions could affect a greater number of people, and that corporations should act with a higher standard of care. I describe these and other reasons for differential treatment in detail in Chapter 5.

Jurors embody the individual thrust of the law as they focus on the individual actors who are present in the courtroom. The ghostliness and diffuse nature of the corporate entity makes it difficult to conceptualize that entity as an actor. The plaintiffs are always in the courtroom, are always easily identified, and always have a financial interest in the case. What is intriguing is that the financial interests of the corporate defendants do not appear to be as salient. The literal presence of the plaintiff and the absence of the corporation, as well as the jurors' predilection for individual-level reasoning, seem to shift attention toward the plaintiffs who sue corporations.

An Individual Template for Corporate Responsibility

A second aspect of jurors' decision making also speaks to the issue of corporations as legal persons. In deciding on corporate responsibility, jurors frequently invoked an individual template for assessing corporate responsibility. That is, in trying to decide whether they should hold a corporation liable, they often considered whether an individual person in similar circumstances would be liable for the same behavior. They did not always apply the identical standard to individual and corporate behavior, but the reasoning process was similar. Consider some of the analogies provided by jurors between individuals and corporations. One juror from the paint-store case stated: "I thought of it in the same way I would treat my premises. I would not want somebody to be injured on my premises, and I see a store owner as having a similar obligation, just from a safety standpoint" (C20-J2). One of the asbestos jurors made an analogy between the asbestos companies and individual behavior: "It's just like me trying to give you a bottle of poison and say here, and I don't tell you what it's gonna do to you and you use it or take it and you get sick or die, that's not right. And that's what these people are doing" (C22-J9). In another case, a worker had been injured on the job in a plant owned by a particular company, and because the worker had been hired by another contractor, the company did not fully investigate the accident. One juror protested, using the analogy to a private home: "If somebody's working in your house, I would feel that you would be responsible if something happened to that person, and with people working for [the defendant company], I felt that they do have some responsibility, maybe not total, but the conditions are safe and coordinated so that people can work safely" (C14-J1).

In a workplace accident case, the jury engaged in a discussion during deliberation about the comparability of people who slip and fall in a private home, and in the work setting. One juror reported: "If he had fallen in somebody's house . . . that's kind of hard to relate this to this situation, because he wouldn't be up on a conveyor. Actually, we got into a discussion about that, but I thought that it was unfair that if somebody slips in your house inadvertently, and you did nothing to cause it, that you could be sued. And we got into a big discussion about that. And I said that I'm not going to have anyone come over to my house, because if they fall, I'll get sued. I felt that the law was really unfair, the law for individuals, if that's what it is" (C14-J6).

In one of the asbestos cases, jurors had difficulty differentiating among the legal standards of negligence, recklessness, and willfulness. The foreman distinguished among them in a colloquial fashion:

> Now I have a very large dog. The dog is in my yard, and the dog is running around the yard and somebody happens to wander in my yard, and the dog bites him. Well, I have a big dog, I knew there was a chance the dog might bite somebody, and it bit somebody, you know, I didn't post any kind of a "beware of dog" sign or anything on there, so I was negligent. A year later, the same dog, same situation. Somebody comes in there, and they get bit by that dog again. Well, I already knew the dog would bite, and it bit somebody in the past, and I still hadn't posted a warning sign. That's reckless. Now willful, if I open the gate up and sent him after somebody, that's willful. So that was the example that I had given to some of the other jurors on the difference between negligent, reckless, and willful. Now, how accurate it is, I don't know, I can't say, I'm not an attorney, but that's the best I could do in giving an example to the other jurors. (C22-J7)

In this reasoning process, the foreman tried to think of a human equivalent of a corporation.

In their search for appropriate human analogies to the corporation, jurors sometimes invoked the relationship of a parent to a child (or an owner to a dog), reflecting a perceived asymmetry between the corporate defendant and the plaintiff. Recall that one of the paint-store jurors, a grandfather himself, likened the store's responsibility to that taken by his wife when their grandchildren came to visit ("My wife would check right away to make sure she doesn't have anything out for the kids to hurt themselves on"). Another juror complained that no one from the corporation had attended the trial: "I really think somebody should have been there from [the corporation]." He likened the head of the company to a parent with a son: "If my son went out and injured somebody, I wouldn't go take a lawyer, and send a lawyer into court, leaving my son there, and a lawyer, in court, and say, 'have at it,' and whatever happens, happens. I feel that that's me, that's my name. I'm directly involved as anybody, and I'm responsible as anybody" (C21-J4). Both the parent-child and corporation-worker (or corporation-consumer) relationships constitute hierarchical pairings, with the parent and corporation at the top of the hierarchy and the child and worker or customer at the bottom. People tend to attribute greater responsibility to parties at the top of such hierarchies, and the jurors' analogies between parent and corporation may reflect this tendency.[23]

The Complexity of Determining Corporate Responsibility

Even though jurors seem to prefer an individually based approach to corporate liability, in some circumstances they cannot use such an approach. The corporate nature of the case can complicate attribution of responsibility because of the complexity of determining who is responsible in a group setting. The classic tort case of *Summers v. Tice* nicely illustrates the problem.[24] In this case, two hunters simultaneously fired their weapons, and one of them wounded the victim. No one can figure out which hunter is at fault. Should neither of them, one of them, or both of them be held responsible? The California Supreme Court concluded that both of them acted negligently, and because the injury had come from one or the other of them, both could be held liable for the injury. It was incumbent upon each hunter to prove he was not at fault, rather than on the plaintiff to prove that a particular hunter *was* at fault.

Summers v. Tice included two actors who could have caused the harm. In a business and corporate setting, decision making includes many inputs and actors. If harm results from a group decision, what is the appropriate method of determining who is liable? Group decision making is quite different from individual decision making, and responsibility may change accordingly.[25]

A number of cases in our sample involved incidents in which there were multiple potentially liable parties, and multiple individuals within the corporation whose responsibility had to be determined. Some jurors expressed the view that the corporate setting made it difficult to figure out what had happened. They imagined that simpler scenarios would occur in cases with individual parties. This was highly salient to jurors in one worker injury case, which involved a man working on one floor who was knocked from a ladder apparently because a worker on another floor started a conveyor belt. One juror from the case discussed the jury's struggle to understand what had occurred: "I guess it would be different if it was just a person in a home. . . . Hopefully you would have more explicit information and would know what the heck was going on rather than everybody hinting at this is what happened or that is what happened and nobody having an accident report. . . . At least if you have the testimony of somebody that actually was there, if it was within your home you'd be there, and you would have maybe seen or been right there or something" (C14-J1). Another juror from the same case concurred: "I think if it was at home, someone would know exactly what happened. But this was sort of a mystery" (C14-J2).

In another case involving a complex international transaction, with diametrically opposed testimony about a disputed shipment of goods, one of the jurors observed that there were multiple parties to consider as prime actors, including contractors, subcontractors, a freight company, and the end user of the goods. The corporation included employees, managers, and stockholders. Finally, two different court systems handled the case. "So you have to hire attorneys here to hire attorneys there to defend you. And nobody knows what they're doing because everything gets lost in the shuffle" (C13-J6). These remarks point to the challenge of determining responsibility when considering the behavior of different members of a group.

Special Legal Rules of Business Liability

Another challenge facing jurors in applying an individual template of responsibility is that some business cases are governed by rules of liability that go significantly beyond the responsibility of individuals directly involved in an act. Social psychologists who have studied lay judgments of responsibility have discovered that individual judgments about responsibility are linked to the intentions, the knowledge, and the proximity of the defendant. Defendants are most likely to be held responsible for an injury if they intended to injure, knew about the likelihood of injury, and were in a position of proximal, or immediate, causation. Modern rules of business responsibility, including strict liability, joint and several liability, and respondeat superior, go beyond the straightforward, fault-based, and individually based conceptions of responsibility. For example, in the doctrine of respondeat superior, a superior or a corporate entity can be held responsible for actions by those at lower levels in a corporate hierarchy. The notion of strict liability, in which a business may be found liable even if it was not negligent but nevertheless caused an injury, is also at odds with much traditional law and social attitudes regarding individual responsibility. These rules, then, may seem foreign to jurors.

Furthermore, there is always the danger that a group setting can produce a diffusion of responsibility, where no one is attributed responsibility because it is distributed or diffused among the group members. A good deal of research by social psychologists has documented the phenomenon of diffusion of responsibility. Whether we take charge in an emergency, help others, or even tip our fair share can all be affected by the presence of others. One of the classic research studies, for example, showed that when bystanders were present, people were less likely to help apparently injured or needy persons.[26] The presence of multiple people, any one of whom could act to help, decreases the onus felt by each one to take responsibility.

By the same token, an individual who is acting along with others in a group may be attributed less blame if something goes wrong.[27] Adding to the problem of diffusion of responsibility is the fact that many people in work settings are collaborating with others and responding to orders from supervisors and thus do not see themselves as fully responsible for the outcome of their joint projects.

A number of cases presented the opportunity to explore how jurors reacted to legal rules holding businesses responsible for actions of their employees or their sub-contractors. One issue confronted in several worker injury cases was that the immediate employer or supervisor of the injured worker was not named in the lawsuit, usually because of workers' compensation rules. Instead, a supplier, manufacturer, or contractor was the defendant. During the case's presentation in the courtroom, jurors did not always learn that worker's compensation provides compensatory benefits but prohibits lawsuits against the employer unless extreme negligence can be demonstrated. In other cases, key defendants settled before or during trial, leaving more peripheral defendants in the lawsuit. Recall the paint-store case, where the doctor who mishandled the boy's injury was absent from court, leaving only the store as the defendant. Jurors were at times perplexed about the choices that plaintiffs made to sue particular defendants. It sometimes seemed to them that the wrong party was being sued, or alternatively, that the chain of responsibility was stretched too far. Nevertheless, they tried to follow the legal rules that permitted recovery from these more remote parties under certain circumstances.

One juror complained about the difficulties they faced when defendants were eliminated from the case during the progress of the trial: "Two of these attorneys dropped out part way through the trial. Now this is one of the things that was very upsetting to me. We would be sent out of the courtroom to the jury room. And you'd come back, and that attorney would be gone. . . . We don't know what happened to them. They just were out of the court when we went back in, and the judge said: 'Just ignore anything that they had said up to this point, because they are no longer concerned with this portion of the trial.' And that was it. . . . They didn't give the jury the common courtesy of saying, 'Well, they have settled or they are willing to put up with what happens later in the trial.' They give you no credit for having any intelligence at all" (C22-J1).

In the conveyor-belt accident case, jurors felt that the defendant company, which owned the facility used by the contractor who had hired the injured worker, was not really responsible. As one juror told us, in this state it is illegal to sue your employer, so the plaintiff was forced to sue the contracting firm. "I think it would have been a better case against his employer. It seemed like he had to lay blame on somebody for actually starting the equipment, the actual safety of the employees. It all seemed to point toward the contractor as being more responsible for their employees than [the defendant company]. [The defendant company] didn't even report the case. They didn't even do an injury report on a contractor injury. Which is kind of strange. I work for [a large corporation]. And it doesn't matter if it's a contractor or not" (C14-J4).

In spite of concerns about the chain of responsibility being stretched, one juror maintained: "The case was decided according to the law. That's how we decided it. Everybody felt the opposite of what we decided in their hearts. In their minds and in their gut, they felt that [the company] was thoroughly innocent. [The company] was not responsible for the injury. But the law said they were, so they were" (C14-J4). Another juror from the same case concurred, saying: "My feeling before we deliberated was that [the defendant company] wasn't the one who should have been paying any money—the contracting company should have been the one. . . . And it was just basically the way we read the law and the way that we interpreted it . . . that's what persuaded the whole group to say [the defendant company] was liable. Because they were owners, they owned the facility, they contracted these people, and they were ultimately responsible for the overseeing of the happenings and work on their premises" (C14-J6).

The first juror commented: "The law is weird, I guess. That fact that you can't sue your employer in this state, that's what set up [the defendant company]. That's the whole thing that set them up. We all agreed that he should have sued [his employer]. He shouldn't have sued [the defendant company], but he couldn't sue [his employer] so he went after [the defendant company]. The next best thing, I guess. Or the next person in line to sue. I don't know who or why they wrote the laws, for industry and business. But they obviously wanted to make them responsible and according to the law it did. They made them responsible. Whether they were physically responsible or not, they had an obligation" (C14-J4).

A key issue in the conveyor-belt case was the extent to which the defendant company, which had hired the contracting company, was an active co-coordinator in the work being done by the contracting company. There was considerable dispute about what level of supervision would satisfy the definition of active co-coordination. As one juror put it: "My theory of a co-coordinator, what I felt they meant by co-coordinator, was that they actually went out and told the contractor how to do their job. Not just say we would like it done this way, or we want it done this way, but actually go out and tell them 'you go over here and do that or you go over here and do this' " (C14-J4). The issue reportedly became the subject of lively debate on the jury, and the jurors requested that the judge re-read them the relevant judicial instructions. As this juror reported:

> I thought a co-coordinator was directly responsible for the workers. That's how I would make them liable, if they were directly responsible for the workers. But we went back and had the law read again to us. And that's not what it said. It said they had to have an active hand in the project, telling them how to do their job. And someone brought up a point, remember when so-and-so [one of the witnesses for the plaintiff] said . . . the cross-struts they were putting on were bolted. Every time they put in a conveyor belt, this company, they bolted these bars, these cross-supports. And [the defendant company] wanted them welded, so they made them take all the bolts out and weld them. Now that's an active hand in planning of the project, or actively coordinating. Plus, [the defendant company] had the ability to request anyone be taken off the job from that company—any contract worker, any supervisor, anybody. We read, we had a copy of the contract agreement between [the two companies], and reading through that, [the defendant company] had more than their fair share of control on the project as to how the project was run, who worked on the project, what tools they used, how they did it, which made them a co-coordinator, plus the fact that [the defendant company's] engineers oversaw this. (C14-J4)

Another relevant rule, which came up in the asbestos cases, is that a company that buys out a second company is generally responsible for wrongdoing on the part of the second company. Responding to the argument that the first company was not entirely responsible because it did not know the extent of the suppression of information by the second company, one juror concluded: "It didn't do anything for me at all. I think if they were going to invest and purchase this company as being their own they should have investigated to see what was going on, and since that was happening, yes it was covered up, but whatever they get, they get it all" (C22-J10).

As this quotation indicates, some jurors were willing to follow responsibility rules that held the business owner and the corporation liable. For example, we asked some jurors whether they thought that specific individuals within a company, rather than a business corporation, should have been held responsible for damages. Although some jurors wanted to see the individual held solely liable, several others thought differently, as indicated by a juror in the landscaping case involving improperly laid grass sod:

96

Interviewer: Did you personally ever think that somebody inside this business, the owner or maybe one of the people putting down the sloppy yard or something like that, that somebody within the business should be held personally liable as opposed to the business as a whole?

Juror: No. I think the business, I think that when you go into business you have a responsibility to see that the business is run properly and you've got to just see that that's done, and I just feel that even for example if the people who did the sloppy job did the sloppy job, it's not just those people who are responsible for doing that, they obviously were not supervised well or the owner didn't require them to do a good job to begin with so therefore it's his business who's at fault and not the man. The people who did the sloppy job may not know any better, they may not know how to do a good job, so if you have a business you're responsible to see that the business is run properly. (C8-J6)

This comment suggests that at least some jurors see the value of suing a group entity (or, at least, the business owner) for wrongs committed by those who are members of that group. Another reason for this practice could be that the business corporation has money. One juror from a worker injury trial resisted the inclusion of the individual coworker, along with the company as a whole, as one of the defendants in the lawsuit. She complained: "I don't understand why [the individual] was being sued. Why wasn't [the plaintiff] against [the company alone]? I can't imagine me being at work and something happening and going to court and it reading Fancy Foods Products and Elizabeth Smith.[28] I mean, what do I have that somebody would want to sue me for? I mean, who would pay whatever money that they were gonna go after, who was gonna pay this? [The coworker] evidently didn't have that kind of money, I mean he's working for a company so I thought the company was liable. I didn't know why his name was on there to begin with" (C15-J4).

In sum, certain configurations of defendant parties, the result of worker's compensation rules or settlements with particular defendants, can present a perplexing situation to jurors. Some business cases challenge the traditional view of individuals as the primary social actors, and fault and causation rules patterned on individual wrongdoing. Jurors may be ordered to disregard the central roles of certain actors who are not parties in the case, and are most likely not even told the outcomes of other litigation. Jurors do try to make sense of the absence of key parties, and to assess responsibility of the parties in the lawsuit. But their predilection for employing individual, fault-based templates no doubt makes certain cases baffling.

Going beyond Juror Interviews

The comments that jurors made in their interviews are fascinating, but they have their limitations. Requiring jurors to introspect about the impact of various factors may be a difficult task. In addition, most jurors report deciding cases involving businesses and corporations in a manner that is generally similar to how cases with individual parties are decided. They state that they focus on the testimony presented in the courtroom. However, the legally enunciated desirability of treating corporations the same as individuals may have affected the jurors' willingness to report any differential treatment. Thus, it is important to supplement the juror interviews with other means of determining how and why jurors respond to corporate litigants.

The laboratory experiment provides another way to explore the issue. In 1986, M. David Ermann and I developed an experimental study to explore the potential for differential treatment of corporate litigants.[29] Using University of Delaware students, we conducted an experiment in which we varied the defendant's identity in a personal injury lawsuit but kept everything else about the scenario the same. Subjects read a scenario in which some workers were harmed by clearing debris from an empty lot. The debris was later found to contain toxic waste. Subjects then evaluated the negligence of the key actors in the scenario and decided on an appropriate award for the injured workers. Half the subjects learned that a "Mr. Jones" had hired the workers, while the other half read that the "Jones Corporation" had done so. Thus, the mock juror experiment that we conducted was very much like the thought experiment I asked the jurors to perform.

The results of this study were striking. Compared to the subjects in the Mr. Jones condition, subjects in the Jones Corporation condition were significantly more likely to hold the defendant morally and legally responsible for the workers' injuries from clearing the toxic waste. Respondents saw the corporation as more reckless, more likely to have known beforehand that the workers might be harmed, and more blameworthy. Furthermore, compensatory awards to the workers injured by the actions of the Jones Corporation were significantly higher than those to the workers injured by Mr. Jones. Statistical analyses found that judgments of corporate culpability and recommendations of awards were linked most strongly to perceptions of the Jones Corporation's recklessness, not its perceived financial resources. This suggested that rather than responding to deep versus empty pockets, respondents applied different standards of recklessness to the corporation and the individual.

This study had some limitations, however. The subjects were college students, whose attitudes about business might be quite different from those of the population as a whole. Furthermore, they did not discuss the case with other individuals, as members of a real jury might do. Therefore, I decided to undertake additional experiments to examine the question of differential treatment in a more realistic manner and to test several explanations that could account for differential treatment of the corporation.

The Mock Jury Study

The mock jury study tested in a more realistic setting whether people would treat a corporate defendant differently. Mock jurors came to the courthouse and were randomly assigned to read either the Mr. Wilson case or the Wilson Corporation case. They then reviewed a description of the evidence and legal instructions in the slip-and-fall civil case. In the Mr. Wilson case, the plaintiff slipped on a rip in the carpet at the home of Mr. Wilson during a garage sale. In the other experimental condition, the slip occurred in the store of the Wilson Furniture Corporation. During the trial, Mr. Wilson (or an employee of the Wilson Furniture Corporation) denied prior knowledge of the rip in the carpet.[30] In both stories, it was conceded that Elaine Brown had tripped on a rip in the carpet, but the defense attorney argued that Ms. Brown was contributorily negligent because she was reading while walking and not watching her step. General legal instructions on negligence were provided, and they were the same in both conditions. No specific instructions about the liability of a homeowner or a business were included, because the purpose of the experiment was to gain insight into lay norms of responsibility in these two different contexts.

The defendant's identity as an individual or a corporation proved to be a significant factor in shaping judgments about the case. Although there was a good deal of overlap in the study participants' responses to the two scenarios, some statistically significant differences emerged. In their initial, individual reactions to the case, those people evaluating the Wilson Corporation scenario were significantly more likely to see the defendant as negligent.[31] Four out of every five of the study participants who read the Wilson Corporation scenario initially thought that the corporation was probably or definitely negligent, compared to about half of the study participants reading the Mr. Wilson scenario (Figure 4-1). Twice as many participants in the Wilson Corporation case as in the Mr. Wilson case selected the "definitely negligent" option, reflecting their certainty that the defendant had negligently caused Ms. Brown's injury. In contrast, more than a third of the readers of the Mr. Wilson scenario leaned toward a finding of no negligence on Mr. Wilson's part. Thus, these initial judgments, made

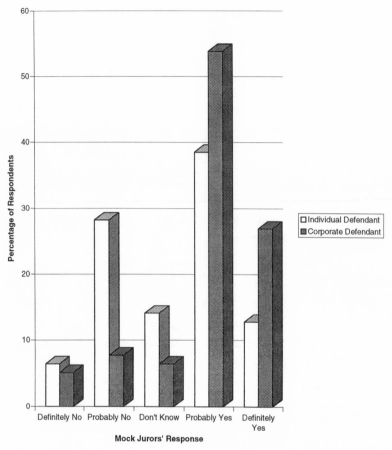

Figure 4-1

Mock jurors' judgments of the defendant's negligence.

before the participants deliberated in mock juries, show a similar pattern to the judgments of students who evaluated the Jones worker injury experiment: greater negligence for the corporation.

The mock juries' group verdicts about the negligence of the defendant were not significantly different: most groups in both conditions concluded that Wilson was negligent (nine out of twelve of the Mr. Wilson mock juries, and eleven out of twelve of the Wilson Corporation mock juries). However, the final percentages of fault attributed to the defendant were significantly different (Figure 4-2). In the Wilson Corporation scenario, most groups concluded that the store bore the brunt of liability for the plaintiff's fall. Eight out of the twelve mock juries discussing the store scenario

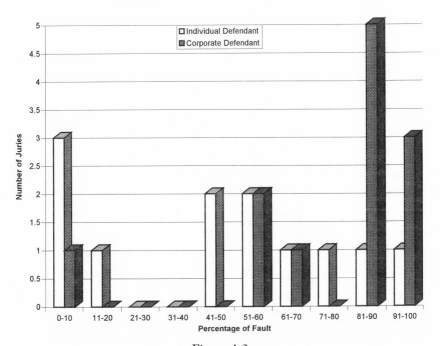

Figure 4-2

Percentage of fault attributed to the defendant by mock juries.

allocated a very substantial portion of the negligence (from 81% to 100%) to the defendant. Indeed, all but one of the mock juries using the store scenario found the defendant more than 50% at fault. In contrast, mock jurors discussing the negligence of Mr. Wilson were less likely to find the defendant the primary responsible actor. Half the groups allocated the defendant less than 50% of the fault. In a number of jurisdictions, if the defendant is less than 50% at fault, the plaintiff cannot collect damages.

The awards were also quite different. Even before deducting any amount for plaintiff fault, which would make the awards even more disparate, the average award in the Wilson Corporation condition was $1,180,000, more than twice the average award of $500,000 from the Mr. Wilson juries.[32] Most striking was that just three of the twelve Mr. Wilson juries awarded the plaintiff any amount over the claimed medical expenses, whereas ten of the twelve Wilson Corporation juries did so. Although they concluded that negligence had occurred and merited an award, most juries felt reluctant to award money for pain and suffering to one individual when the award would be paid by another individual. They did not show a similar reluctance when a corporation would pay.

The videotaped mock jury deliberations allowed us to listen in on jurors as they debated the determination of negligence and awards. Two research assistants, undertaking a qualitative analysis of the jury deliberations, watched each of the deliberations several times, taking notes on mock jurors' key points and statements, particularly those relating to the defendant's negligence and the plaintiff's fault. Then, one of the research assistants summarized their joint observations in a written account, including relevant quotations from the mock jurors.

Most of the deliberations began in the same way: the foreman or forewoman (the research assistants assigned a mock juror to fill this role) usually read the list of questions that had to be answered. They included whether the defendant was negligent, whether the plaintiff was negligent, the percentage (if any) of fault to be attributed to the plaintiff, and the total amount to be awarded to the plaintiff before any reductions were made due to the fault of the plaintiff. The wording of these questions was based on those used in cases in the juror interview study. There were also copies of medical records that the mock jurors often passed around at the beginning of the deliberation. The structure of the deliberations often followed the ordering of the questions on the interrogatory form.[33] The bulk of the deliberations was spent in discussing competing perspectives on the responsibilities of the defendant and the plaintiff.

Comments made by jurors in the Wilson Corporation scenario revealed clear expectations that the store should be safe for its customers. Deviations from this safe environment—even if workers and owners were unaware of those deviations—were frowned upon:

Group 4, J6:   If you're gonna have a big sale and you want them to take advantage of your prices, you know they are gonna be doing other things, not looking at the floor.

Group 4, J4:   People who invite the public in like restaurants, they really take a responsibility especially for their floors, things falling down, and overhead, 'cause they have invited that person to come in.

In one group, a mock juror observed: "The store has the responsibility to provide a safe place . . . it is overwhelmingly the store's fault for not providing a safe place" (Group 17, J1). Similarly, in another group, a juror noted: "I think if they're having a sale, they are inviting the public to come in and participate in this sale, that they owe it to the public to have a relatively safe place to walk around in and do their business.

I've personally tripped over twenty carpets. . . . People don't walk looking at their feet" (Group 18, J1). This juror's colleague agreed: "If the rip wasn't there, she wouldn't have tripped. . . . The store is supposed to provide a safe environment" (Group 18, J6). Another group (Group 19) discussed the fact that when stores have sales, they often crowd the aisles with merchandise, creating a hazardous walking situation. Stores also put out flyers for customers to read while they walk around the store.

Most groups agreed relatively quickly that the store was primarily negligent. Group 20, for example, decided that the plaintiff bore a small share of the fault but attributed most of the fault to the store:

J1:   Is the store responsible for the maintenance of their property? Yes, they are.
J2:   The employee didn't observe the rip, so maybe he wasn't doing his job.
J3:   She tripped over the carpet, the store is negligent, you shouldn't have to worry where you put your feet.
J4:   I don't think if I go to K-Mart I have to watch where I'm going. . . . They have a responsibility because they have a flow of traffic through there to maintain the carpetings and the aisleways, but this doesn't occur.
J5:   It's always on a business person, you have to keep your sidewalks and all that.

In contrast, Group 29, which allocated just 60% of the fault to the defendant, hotly debated the responsibility of a store owner. Although J3 pointed out that "the store has the burden of responsibility to have a safe floor" and that "it's their job, they let people come in, they are responsible," J4 countered that her father owned a store and that he couldn't "check everything. . . . They can't be God, they can't watch everything." In this debate, jurors made up scenarios, putting themselves in the shoes of either the defendant or the plaintiff. They were split over whether the majority of the responsibility lay with the customer or the store.

The defendant's negligence was more frequently contested in the Mr. Wilson scenario. Some jurors appeared to identify with the defendant: "Nowadays I wouldn't want to open a business, the liability" (Group 22, J2). They thought of ways the rip could have occurred without his knowledge: "Maybe somebody carried out furniture and ripped it earlier" (Group 24, J3). Some juries also debated whether the rip was really there or simply alleged to be there. Jurors questioned Mr. Wilson's liability: "I don't think it was Mr. Wilson's fault at all, I've been to many yard sales" (Group 16, J5). "If it was his fault, then how come he didn't fall?" (Group 16, J4).

In trying to assess whether Mr. Wilson could be held responsible for the plaintiff's injuries, mock jurors drew on their own knowledge of the legal and moral duties of a person who owns property and invites others in. Their comments sometimes reflected a "strict-liability" approach:

> Whenever you have a friend come over, you're putting liability on yourself. (Group 15, J5)
> When you invite people into your home, you have a responsibility. (Group 21, J3)
> It is his responsibility to know about it. He opens up his house to the public, he better make it safe. (Group 21, J6)
> He may have been unintentionally negligent, but nonetheless he invited everyone and their dog into his home. (Group 15, J1)
> This is why homeowners . . . that even if they put a fence around a pool and some neighbor's child climbs over the fence and goes into the pool, they're responsible. . . . Don't you think he [Mr. Wilson] has the responsibility to see where people are moving furniture, he's got to be watchful. (Group 22, J1)
> When you have a crack in your sidewalk, mailman breaks foot, you're responsible. (Group 24, J5)

In comparing the discussions of liability, I was fascinated to discover that mock jurors tended to use similar arguments in favor of defendant liability in the two conditions. Even though the mock jurors were exposed to only one experimental condition, some spontaneously employed the other condition as an analogy. Quite consistent with the tendency of the jurors I interviewed to rely on individual templates for assessing corporate behavior, the mock jurors showed an interesting habit of intertwining individual and corporate models. They often made comparisons between the liability of the home owner and the store owner. For example, in Group 15, jurors discussing the responsibility of Mr. Wilson argued that he should be responsible just as a business would be, and they made many analogies between home ownership and owning a restaurant or a furniture store. A pro-plaintiff juror in Group 21, in the Mr. Wilson scenario, observed: "You're walking through a shopping center and Mr. Janitor mops the floor, he puts a sign up, someone slips, the store is still liable" (J6). In Group 25, the mock jurors compared the plaintiff in the Wilson residence to a hypothetical department or grocery store: "When you go into a department store you look at the items, not the ground" (J2). Referring to Ms. Brown's reading while walking, this juror claims: "All of us have done this—in the grocery store, paper."

Jurors in several groups concluded that although there is an analogy between stores and private homes, they expect different levels of care from the store. In Group 32, which discussed the Mr. Wilson scenario, a difference of opinion about the appropriate level of care emerged:

J5:   It was his own residence, it wasn't like it was a store. If it was a store, the public . . .

J1:   Then there would be a higher degree of care.

J5:   If he was a regular businessman, he really would be responsible.

J1:   The scene at his house was like a store because he was selling items.

J5:   I don't think you should expect as much responsibility for a private, it was kind of like a garage sale.

J3:   When you invite people into your house to buy something in your home, you're responsible just like if you have a business in your house and someone comes and trips.

Similarly, Group 31 jurors, in the Mr. Wilson scenario, discussed how the case would look to them if the accident had taken place not in a home but in a store. One juror believed that it would be easier to conclude that the store is liable: "That wasn't a public place, like a store [names local grocery store], and there's a rip in the store. I don't think we'd have any question to say it was their fault, even if it might have occurred an hour before" (J5). Thus, although the mock jurors used the individual-store analogy in reasoning about responsibility, they apparently concluded that the store's level of responsibility was greater than that of an individual—even an individual holding a garage sale.

These studies indicate that although there is a good deal of overlap in the way people judge individual and corporate liability, when differences occur people tend to expect more from a corporation. The mock jurors regularly emphasized that businesses invite the public into their store and as a result have a duty to make it safe for the public. Inviting a person into one's home or place of business seemed particularly significant to mock jurors in both the conditions of the experiment, but they appeared to hold the home owner to a lesser standard of care.

There is an interesting parallel between the mock jurors' apparent standards for the two locations of store and home and legal standards pertaining to two categories of visitors. The law has developed different duties of care for business invitees (visitors who enter the premises for the purpose of doing business) and for licensees (visitors who have permission to enter the premises but who come for their own reasons).[34] The law

THE PERSONHOOD OF THE CORPORATION

applies a higher duty of care for the invitee than for the licensee. There is an affirmative duty to protect the invitee, but the licensee has to look out for himself or herself.

The Scenario Experiment in the State Poll

A scenario experiment, conducted as part of the state poll, was designed to shed more light on why people might treat corporations differently. People could be responding distinctively to business corporations and applying different standards of care for a host of reasons. First, jurors may be prejudiced against business, leading them to more findings of liability against business corporations. Second, the corporation is a for-profit enterprise, and there may be particular expectations of a commercial enterprise that are linked to higher responsibility (see Chapter 5). Third, a business corporation usually consists of a group of people, some with specialized skills. The fact that it is a group, rather than a sole individual, may produce greater liability.

To try to disentangle these reasons for differential treatment, in this experiment the defendant to a personal injury claim was described as either an individual, a nonprofit corporation or association, or a for-profit business corporation. These three conditions allowed me to examine separately the impact of the commercial business identity and the group identity of the corporation. If the fact that a corporation is a business is important (perhaps because people are anti-business or because they have certain expectations of profit-making enterprises), then we would expect respondents to distinguish between the business corporation, on the one hand, and the nonprofit corporation and the individual, on the other. If instead the individual or group nature of the defendant is important, then both the group defendants—the business and the nonprofit organization—should be treated comparably, and the judgments of group defendants should be significantly different from those of the individual defendant.[35]

In the state poll, respondents first gave their views of civil litigation, business, and other social attitudes, then heard a single scenario description and answered questions about their evaluations of the incident described by the scenario. Some respondents decided a slip-and-fall case based on the Wilson fact pattern used in the mock jury study, whereas others responded to a case description of worker injury from clearing toxic waste, similar to the Jones case used in the earlier Hans and Ermann research. In the individual defendant conditions, the defendant was described as either Mr. John Wilson (the slip-and-fall case) or Mr. Jones (the worker injury). For the business corporation conditions, the defendant was described as either the Wilson Furniture Corporation or the Jones Corporation.

For the nonprofit organization conditions, we decided to use two somewhat different types of nonprofit organizations in the two cases. In the Wilson case, the nonprofit was named the Wilson United Charities Corporation and identified as a nonprofit corporation, while in the Jones case, it was the Jones Civic Association and described as a nonprofit neighborhood group. Thus, the nonprofit organizations differed along two dimensions: their activities, and whether they were explicitly labeled as a corporation or as an association.

Here are two examples of the facts presented to the study respondents:

1. Mrs. Brown, a thirty-five-year-old woman, went to a store owned by the Wilson Furniture Corporation, where they were having a furniture sale. Walking in the Wilson Furniture Corporation's showroom, she tripped over a large rip in the carpet and fell, suffering a cranial concussion. As a result of the fall, she has severe headaches, slight memory loss, and must undergo plastic surgery to correct some scarring on her face. Mrs. Brown sued the Wilson Furniture Corporation on the grounds of negligence for failing to correct the rip in the carpet. (Wilson scenario, corporate defendant)

2. Mr. Jones hired five workers to clear debris from a newly purchased lot next to his home. While clearing the lot, the workers complained to Mr. Jones about feeling lightheaded and dizzy. Mr. Jones told them to continue working but to let him know if they felt worse. Within a week, three of the workers had to be hospitalized for severe respiratory problems, and suffered permanent lung damage. Toxic waste was discovered on the lot. The five workers sued Mr. Jones for negligence, on the grounds that he was reckless for failing to check the debris and for sending the workers back after they complained. Mr. Jones said that he had no idea that the lot contained toxic waste, and pointed out that the workers who suffered the most lung damage were cigarette smokers. (Jones scenario, individual defendant)

It may be useful at this point for the reader to undertake a thought experiment: Would the situations seem different if Mrs. Brown had fallen in Mr. Wilson's living room, or the Jones Corporation had hired the workers? Whatever the reader's

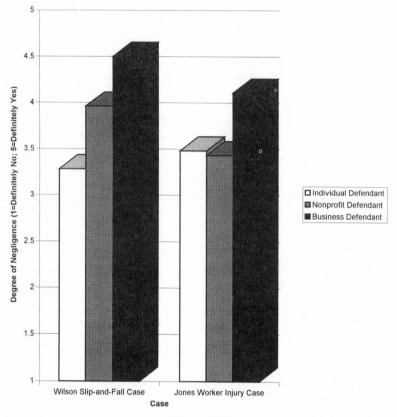

Figure 4-3
State poll participants' judgments of the defendant's negligence.

response, the participants in the study reacted differently to the cases depending on the identity of the defendant. As in the other studies discussed in this chapter, the defendant's identity had a consistent effect on respondents' judgments of negligence and recklessness. The subjects found the least negligence and recklessness for the individual defendant and the most for the business corporation defendant, with responses to the nonprofit group falling in between.[36] Thus, the pattern of results supports the importance of both identity as a business and as a group in shaping evaluations of litigants.

In respondents' judgments of negligence, there was a statistically significant interaction between defendant identity and the case (that is, either the slip-and-fall case or the worker injury case).[37] Although respondents who read the Wilson slip-and-fall case and those who read the Jones worker injury case rated the negligence of the individual as less than the negligence of the corporation in both instances, they evaluated the nonprofit organization in the two cases differently (Figure 4-3). In the Wilson slip-and-fall case, in which the nonprofit was described as the Wilson United Charities Corporation, a nonprofit corporation, the nonprofit's negligence was perceived to be less than the corporation's but more than the individual's, the same pattern as the overall results described above. However, in the worker injury case, in which the nonprofit was labeled the Jones Civic Association, a nonprofit group, the negligence of the nonprofit was the same as the individual and both of them were perceived to be less negligent than the business corporation. Therefore, the more organized nonprofit entity, and the one with the corporate label, is treated more like a business corporation, while the less organized association is seen more as an individual, at least from the perspective of legal negligence. This suggests that distinctive treatment of nonprofit entities could stem from several sources. First is the nature of the work that they do; second is their degree of organization. The type of case could also be a significant factor. In a worker injury case, one might tend to distinguish more sharply between an individual and a group, whereas in a slip-and-fall case, there might be more of a continuum.

Confirmation of a Corporate Identity Effect

The basic finding that people differentiate between individuals and corporations has been replicated by other scholars. Robert MacCoun had citizens from a California jury pool evaluate six different personal injury cases. The participants read stories that varied whether the defendant was a poor individual, a rich individual, or a corporation. Most of the stories involved injuries occurring in a business context. For example, in a slip-and-fall case, the poor defendant was Mr. Brock, the operator and owner of Chowdown Palace, a small take-out food stand (representing a Mom-and-Pop type of business). The rich defendant was also described as Mr. Brock, again the operator and owner of Chowdown Palace, but now the business was identified as a chain of take-out food stands. Finally, the corporate defendant was described as Chowdown Food Enterprises, which owned the Chowdown Palace, a chain of take-out restaurants.[38] This comparison was quite different from the Wilson slip-and-fall case, for example, where the injury occurred in a private home or a store, depending on the identity of the defendant. Nevertheless, MacCoun found that people differentiated between the individual and corporate defendants. Although there were no differences in the judgments of liability for the poor and rich individuals, there were significant differences in the judgments of liability for the individuals versus the corporation. The corporation was more likely to be held liable than either the rich or the poor individual.

Other differences in perceptions of individual versus corporate actors have been uncovered by researchers V. Lee Hamilton and Joseph Sanders and their colleagues, who conducted public opinion surveys in the United States, Japan, and Russia for the purpose of examining how citizens of these countries treat corporate wrongdoing. In their surveys, they presented vignettes describing acts of wrongdoing in corporate settings. One of the stories was similar to the Hans and Ermann worker injury scenario, in which either an individual or a corporate actor caused workers to be injured by permitting them to work in an area that had toxic waste. Some vignettes portrayed the actor as stopping the work when alerted of the potential harm (a relatively low level of negligence), while other versions portrayed the actor as behaving more recklessly by instructing the workers to continue working near the potentially toxic waste. Looking at the Japanese and American data, the researchers found that their participants differentiated between individual and corporate actors primarily in the low-negligence vignettes. When actors behaved recklessly, both individuals and corporate actors were treated similarly and held to high levels of responsibility. But when the degree of negligence was lower, respondents thought that the corporation was in a better position than the individual to have anticipated and avoided the injury to the workers.[39] In sum, these investigations confirm the existence of what we can label a corporate identity effect.

From the perspective of the lay public, including jurors, there is something quite attractive about the notion of the corporation as a person. Just as the legal world found it beneficial to integrate corporations into the highly individualistic framework of the law, so too do jurors readily use individual analogies in reasoning about corporate responsibility. Many jurors appear to judge the corporations in their cases along the same lines that individual actors would be evaluated.

Yet the notion of the personhood of the corporation, roundly criticized by many scholars, can also be problematic in the jury room. Some corporate cases cannot be easily analogized to an individual equivalent. The presence of multiple actors with different agendas, the complexities of group decision making, and inefficiencies in organization and communication all challenge the application of an individual template to corporate deliberations and actions. My experimental studies could actually

THE PERSONHOOD OF THE CORPORATION

be understating the problem of nonequivalence, in that I tried to use situations, such as a slip-and-fall case, that could be readily described as occurring in either an individual or a corporate environment. Finally, it may be inappropriate to treat corporations and individuals the same. Inequalities of power and resources can be ignored through such a practice.

The experimental studies that I have conducted and the ones that have extended the basic finding of the corporate identity effect suggest that in a number of diverse situations, people respond distinctively to a business corporation. There are also some hints (from the reactions to the nonprofit defendants in the Wilson and Jones scenarios and from the MacCoun study that varied Mom-and-Pop operations and chains) that the greater the degree of organization, the greater the amount of liability that jurors will attribute. This may help to explain why many jurors whom I interviewed report that they paid little attention to the fact that the defendant in the case was a business corporation, because many of the corporate defendants were local or regional businesses rather than big national or multinational corporations.

But the question remains: Why do people treat corporations differently? Is it true that they are prejudiced against businesses or want to tap the deep pockets of the corporation? Or are there other aspects of a business corporation that citizens find important in judging responsibility? The next three chapters take up this question in some detail.

5

A DIFFERENT STANDARD
FOR CORPORATIONS

I now turn from the theme of similarity—that is, how corporations are like individuals—to consider more explicitly how corporations are distinctive entities that deserve unique and differential treatment. This chapter explores citizens' beliefs about the standards that are appropriate for the evaluation of corporate conduct, and presents the reasons people give for treating business corporations differently than individual defendants in the courtroom.

Some sociologists believe that the distinctive nature of the corporation requires unique treatment. Perhaps the most influential scholar to espouse this view is James Coleman, whose book *The Asymmetric Society* presents evidence of the dominance of the corporation in contemporary society. Coleman observes striking asymmetries between natural persons and corporate actors, not only in the type of actor but also in the typical resources each possesses. These asymmetries have significant consequences: "The corporate actor nearly always controls most of the conditions surrounding the relation. The corporate actor controls much of the information relevant to the interaction. . . . The end result is that two parties beginning with nominally equal rights in a relation, but coming to it with vastly different resources, end with very different actual rights in the relation."[1]

The greater dependency of individuals on organizations is associated with increased pressure to hold the organizations responsible when individuals suffer misfortune.[2] The distinctive nature of corporate deviance has led many criminologists to call for different types of sanctions for corporate than for individual wrongdoing.[3] In this chapter, I shall examine how citizens' views compare to those of the sociologists.

The Lemon Law Case

What exactly does it mean to believe that corporations should adhere to a higher standard than individuals? How does such an expectation affect the specific tasks that are part of a jury's decision making? A look inside the jury's decision making in a lemon law case provides some insights into how jurors link standards of business conduct to corporate responsibility.

It's every car owner's nightmare—buying a lemon. And the plaintiff in this lemon law case seemed to have purchased a doozy. The polite, soft-spoken engineer worked at a job that required him to drive a great number of miles. He had a lot of respect for, and good experience with, a certain car manufacturer—in fact, his wife owned one of the company's cars.[4] So when the car manufacturer offered a two-year, unlimited mileage warranty, he bought the car that became the subject of the lawsuit.

Right from the start, there were problems. As he drove the car out of the showroom the first evening, he noticed that the car's gears did not shift easily. He also observed that his brand-new car had four hundred miles on the odometer. The next day, he went back to the dealership, reported the gear-shifting problem, and asked about the four hundred miles, which no one had mentioned to him during the car sale. The car dealer responded that a new car's gears are often stiff, that it would all work itself out, and that he should come back at the 1,500-mile checkup. As for the four hundred miles, the car was a dealer trade and had been driven from the other dealer's showroom in a different state. That fact was buried in the sheaf of papers that the new owner had signed during the car purchase.

Yet despite the reassuring response to his initial complaints, the plaintiff's problems with the car continued to grow, as he reported years later on the witness stand. He began to notice a ticking sound, especially when he drove the car frequently. Shifting gears became more and more difficult. One dealer concluded that the problem was with a constant velocity joint, and the plaintiff brought the car in to the dealer to replace the joint while he was at work. The invoice, which the jurors reviewed during deliberation, stated "replaced cv joint" and gave a labor time of 110 minutes. There was no reason for the plaintiff to suspect, and he was not told at the dealership, that the cv joint had not been replaced. The repairman had ordered the wrong part and therefore did not replace it as planned. (The dealer stated on the witness stand that they tried to contact him later for a follow-up appointment but could not reach him.) Thereafter, the problems grew worse; the clicking became louder and louder, and the driver had to keep his hand constantly on the gear shift or the car would slip out of gear. As one juror described it: "Apparently it had gotten so stiff that it took all of a man's strength to put it into gear and then you had to hold it, you had to steer with your left hand to hold the gear shift with your right or it would bounce around into different gears" (C25-J4).

Over the year and a half that he drove the car, he made (by his own count) thirty calls and seven visits to car dealers to try to correct the escalating problems. The calls were not returned, and the visits failed to correct the problems with the car.

After a year and a half, he attempted to follow the clause in his warranty that set up arbitration if the customer was not satisfied with the repair service. He met a dead end: the area office informed him that he now had too many miles on the car to be covered by the arbitration process. Finally, after a call to the Better Business Bureau, in which he told the bureau that he believed the car was a lemon and that he wanted to give it back, area representatives of the car manufacturer met with him. A manager took a test drive in the car and concluded that there did seem to be something wrong with the transmission, although the manager was unwilling to call it a bad transmission. Nevertheless, he stated that the company would replace it right away. The plaintiff agreed to the plan and called his workplace, telling them he was going to take the rest of the day off work and wait to have his new transmission put in. He was then informed, however, that the dealer did not have the transmission in stock at the moment. In the words of one juror, the dealer called "all up and down the east coast, and nobody had transmissions that fit this car, so they said well it's gonna take a while, a few days, a week, whatever, but eventually we'll get you a new transmission" (C25-J4). Fed up and completely devoid of confidence, the plaintiff stated that he "wasn't gonna fool with it any longer" (C25-J4). If they did not take the car, he was going to sue them under the lemon law.

The plaintiff had his day in court, and the jury saw it his way, concluding under the state's lemon law that the plaintiff had indeed purchased a lemon. Their interviews describing how they decided the case reveal that the public expects a high level of business conduct and responsiveness to consumers.

We asked jurors whether they thought it was appropriate to hold corporations to a different standard than individuals. As is often the case in corporate litigation, the judge in the lemon law case instructed the jurors that they should treat the corporation just as they would an individual defendant. Nevertheless, six of the eight jurors we interviewed from the lemon law case believed that it was quite appropriate to hold the corporation to a higher degree of care.

The wife of an independent businessman observed: "I know what my husband goes through to be licensed to sell in the state. I think when you make a profit from the people of the state, certainly you would expect that there isn't fraud in their advertising" (C25-J1). Another juror agreed that a car dealer has more responsibility than an individual selling a used car to another individual: "Number one, they supposedly have the sophisticated equipment to check out an automobile. They have lifts that they can get up under, they can look. Supposedly they have service people that go to these courses that can pinpoint things, and we don't have that, at least I don't" (C25-J3). She went on: "You're trying to tell the people, we'll stand behind our product and this was a pure example that they didn't. This was one case, and they'd rather go bring it to court than solve the man's problem" (C25-J3).

Another juror noted the resources of the corporation: "I always think of a corporation as having a lot of resources behind it. They pay top money for engineers to do the job correctly, and supposedly they have quality control and things like that so that when the product reaches the consumer, the consumer should have some satisfaction that he's buying a product that's going to work for him. I don't expect as much of going out and buying a hundred-dollar television set as I would if I were buying a fifteen-thousand- or sixteen-thousand-dollar automobile. I always felt that the automobile dealers in particular should be held more accountable for safety reasons, and the fact that you're investing so much money in something that has just a short life" (C25-J5).

One of the few jurors in this case to argue for the same standard for individuals and corporations had a good deal of personal experience as a business partner, which affected her thinking: "I've seen both sides of it, not just as an owner but also on the consumer side of our projects. . . . Individuals run the corporations. So, they make mistakes, they do things wrong, they represent the corporation. I think we all, as individuals, have responsibility" (C25-J8).

There was disagreement between the parties over whether the plaintiff had met the terms of the lemon law, which required that the plaintiff request a reasonable number of times that a specific problem be repaired before declaring the car a lemon. The car dealer argued during the trial that the plaintiff had not specifically mentioned that it was the transmission that was causing him problems during his multiple visits. But there was evidence that the repairmen had not written down the exact words that the plaintiff had used to describe his problems when he brought the car in, and several invoices had errors or words scratched out, leading jurors to speculate that the correct or covered information might have been unfavorable to the defendant. In addition, some jurors saw the identification of the car's problems as residing in the dealership— as part of the dealer's job, not the customer's: "He was trying to get them to just fix it, whatever may be wrong with it, you're the people that built the car, you're the one that services it, you're the one that's guaranteeing my warranty, I want you to fix it. But what the dealer was saying during the whole trial was well you didn't tell us that it was exactly the transmission so therefore we didn't know to fix it. And my feeling was well they're the ones that, you know, if I took my car in and diagnosed it, why would I need a dealer? They're the ones that are supposed to be able to diagnose the car and repair it, and I think they were trying to place all the blame on him because he wasn't able to tell them exactly what was wrong with the car" (C25-J5).

Even though most jurors in the lemon law case endorsed a higher standard for corporations, they were not initially unanimous. According to the juror interviews, the first vote they took was nine to three in favor of the plaintiff. A number of jurors noted that the plaintiff was soft-spoken and not very aggressive. Although the jurors thought that this helped to explain why the car dealer took advantage of him, those in the minority argued that it was the plaintiff's responsibility to have been more vocal and insistent about the problems early on. In a statement reminiscent of the victim-blaming comments presented in Chapter 2, one juror confessed: "I'm an assertive person, so with that I was very angry that he didn't go in and say, 'Here, keep this car; I'm not gonna take it.' I would do those things, but I'm not like all people; there are some people who get taken advantage of. They're shy and they're not assertive, and I think I've seen that in him. They played with him for a little while, I guess" (C25-J8).

In addition, a juror voting in the minority voiced the principle of *caveat emptor* (let the buyer beware): "[The plaintiff] bought a car and it was no good. And when you get a car that's no good, you pay it off and get a new car. He kept on to that bad car for five years, which I thought was pretty stupid, but I give him credit for being persistent. . . . Everyone knows when you buy a car you take a chance. So, it wasn't the car manufacturer's fault that it was a lemon. They can't test drive every car that they make. And let's be real. If all the car dealers got sued for all the lemons, they wouldn't be producing any cars. . . . They don't do it on purpose; they have these guys putting these cars together on the assembly line. They should guarantee it; they should stand behind it. But they can't guarantee it's gonna be one hundred percent perfect. Things do slip through the cracks" (C25-J6).

This juror's expectations and standards pertaining to business were crucial to her judgment of whether the defendant did anything wrong. She had a negative assessment of the standard operating procedure for car manufacturers, which in her view frequently produced lemons. She talked about her own recent experience in buying a new car, which she had to take in for repairs because there was a defect on the hood. But rather than making her sympathize with the plaintiff, her situation seemingly led her to normalize the defective car as a predictable if unfortunate part of the manufacturing process.[5] In a pattern similar to the victim-blaming approach of jurors in other cases, she placed the onus on the customer to make sure that the company stood behind its warranty: "You've got to put your foot down and tell them this is what you want. It's under warranty, they're gonna fix it. And he was a nice person, whereas I wasn't, and that's the difference" (C25-J6). She also adopted a stringent definition of a defective car, disagreeing that the plaintiff's car was a total lemon: "It's not a lemon, because when you drive a car, things go wrong. When you drive it ten miles a day, it's not gonna go bad, but when you [are] putting thirty, fifty miles on the car in one day, you can't expect the car to be in tip-top shape after a year" (C25-J6).

In debating the damages, the jurors in the minority asserted that the car dealer should be compensated for the substantial mileage that the plaintiff had already put on the car. The idea was to deduct a certain amount from the compensatory damage award in recognition of this use. Although they lost their bid for a specific deduction for the mileage, the minority jurors were successful in limiting the amount of overall compensatory and punitive damages.

In sum, the jurors' standards and expectations about the car manufacturer and dealer played key roles in their assessment of the reasonableness of the company's actions. One of the jurors in the minority endorsed a similar standard for corporations and individuals, while another reported low expectations of car manufacturers. Those in the majority argued that car manufacturers should be held to high safety and quality standards because it was their duty to the public and it was integral to their business.

Role Responsibility for the Corporation

As the lemon law case illustrates, the public often considers it highly appropriate to hold higher expectations of business corporations. Even the most vigorous supporters of the constitutional equivalence of individuals and corporations would not maintain that individuals and corporations should always be treated identically. Certainly the wide variety of legal regulations of the business community, of which lemon laws are one example, is evidence enough that the government exerts control over business corporations that it does not attempt to exert over individuals. Workplace regulations, employment laws, pure food-and-drug acts, consumer fraud statutes, occupational health and safety rules, trade practices, and many other laws have been developed to regulate specific business activity. Many of these laws control particular asymmetric relationships, such as those between employer and employee, producer and consumer, and govern instances in which the business and the individual have widely varying levels of power, control, and knowledge.

Role responsibility, that is, the obligations and expectations that are linked to different tasks and roles, is a significant dimension of responsibility.[6] In public opinion studies of the importance of roles to judgments of responsibility, Professor V. Lee Hamilton and her colleagues have found that roles are a highly significant aspect of judgments of responsibility.[7] The public attaches obligations to specific roles. Persons in positions of authority over others, such as bosses or parents, are seen as incurring certain general obligations not only for their own behavior but also for the behavior of subordinates or children. Superiors are expected to oversee the activity of others and to anticipate and deal with problems. Role-based responsibility expands the range of an authority's culpability. Therefore, persons in positions of authority are held to higher levels of responsibility compared to equals or subordinates. Often, however, what we expect of authorities can be diffuse. It can be difficult to forge a tangible link between a person in authority and a negligent action by an inferior. The people in charge are often far from the physical chain of causation, and the duties they have to oversee are broad and general, making it hard to pin down violations.[8]

Applying the findings about role responsibility to the issue of corporate responsibility, it is obvious that consumers are highly dependent on manufacturers to provide safe products, and that workers are in a hierarchical relationship with employers. These asymmetrical relationships should carry with them a strong set of obligations—albeit diffuse ones—for the superior party, the business corporation. These characteristics of corporate power and asymmetry should, in theory, lead to greater moral and legal responsibility.[9] But it may often be difficult to determine exactly when a corporation has failed to meet its responsibilities.

More evidence that many citizens believe that corporations should be held to higher standards than individuals is provided in their responses to questions about the desirability of equal treatment of individuals and corporations. To examine the public's view, I asked participants in all three of the studies that I conducted whether they agreed or disagreed with the statement that "corporations should be held to a higher standard of responsibility than individuals" (Figure 5-1).

Jurors were split in their views, with more favoring the same standard than a different standard. A plurality of 48% disagreed and 41% agreed with the statement that corporations should be held to a different standard.[10] The remainder gave ambiguous answers that could not be definitively coded as yes or no. In interpreting these

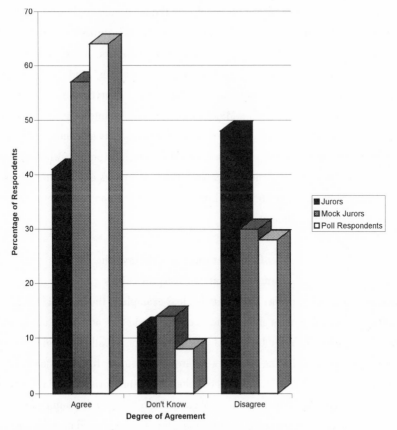

Figure 5-1

Responses to the statement "Corporations should be held to a
higher standard of responsibility than individuals."

percentages, one should bear in mind that it was common for the judges in these cases
to instruct the jurors to treat the corporation the same as the individual. Part of the
standard instruction emphasizes the fairness of jurors' treating corporations just as
they would individual parties.

The type of case that the jurors decided appeared to affect their views about the
appropriateness of a higher standard. Jurors who decided asbestos cases, cases involving worker injury, and contract disputes were more likely to support a higher
standard than jurors who decided cases involving auto accidents and customers
injured in a store. Recall that jurors also acknowledged being affected by the corporate identity of the parties more frequently in the first set of cases.

Respondents in the public opinion poll and the mock jury study were much more apt to support the idea of a higher standard than the civil jurors were. Fully 64% of the poll respondents and 57% of the mock jurors endorsed a higher standard for corporations. These results are consistent with a multinational study on judgments of corporate crime. V. Lee Hamilton and Joseph Sanders surveyed people in Washington, D.C., Tokyo, and Moscow. Majorities in all three countries agreed that corporations have a greater obligation than individual persons to try to avoid accidents, that they expected organizations to be more careful than ordinary persons when they make decisions, and that if companies are careful, they can always avoid doing things that hurt people.[11] In their study, more highly educated respondents were likelier to disagree with these statements.

Why Corporations Should Have the
Same Standard of Responsibility

The lemon law case presents an unusually clear example of the issue of special rules and standards for business. Jurors had to consider whether or not the car manufacturer and dealer had abided by several special rules specifically designed to regulate business conduct, including the rules regarding consumer fraud, lemon laws, and deceptive trade practices. However, the notion of the appropriate standard for corporate conduct is in play in a wide variety of cases. In this section I examine the types of arguments jurors made opposing the idea that corporations should be held to a higher standard of responsibility than individuals, and in the following section I present the arguments they made in favor of a higher standard.

Many jurors said that the presence of a corporation did not influence their decision making (see Chapter 4). When asked whether corporations should be held to a different standard than individual parties, these jurors tended to maintain that corporations should be treated just the same as individual parties.

Jurors who believed in equal treatment often stressed the appropriateness and fairness of treating corporations the same. For example, one of the jurors in an asbestos case observed: "I think it should be the same, if they know that they're harming someone, same as an individual, a company should be responsible" (C26-J2). Another asbestos juror concluded: "No, I think right is right, and it either is or it isn't, and whether it is an individual or a corporation I think you still have a responsibility to do what's right" (C4-J5). Similarly: "I think responsibility is the same for an individual or a corporation, to be honest" (C22-J4). A juror from a case in which a blood bank was charged with negligence argued: "No, I think the standards should be as high as they can be whether it's a corporation or an individual" (C28-J8). Several jurors specifically emphasized the fairness of treating corporations the same:

Interviewer: Do you think corporations should be held to a higher standard than individuals?

Juror: I guess so, but then when you think about that, it's a corporation, but it's just people like us working for them. So they shouldn't be punished for, they can't help it because they're a corporation. I guess I'm trying to say I'm not biased and I would not go in and say "That's a big company, make them pay." That's not fair. (C18-J7)

Likewise: "I don't think there's any basis for that sort of discrimination. I feel that corporations have the same ethical, moral responsibilities that we individuals do, and I think they should be held to those standards. But I don't see any reason for differentiation" (C31-J4).

Several jurors advocating equal treatment emphasized that the role of a corporation was a significant factor in its responsibility, but that if a similarly situated individual adopted the same role, the person should be treated identically. A juror from a case in which a serviceman was injured in a company-owned building argued that corporations and individuals "should both have equal responsibilities. If the company's going to be the owner of a house or the individual, they both should have responsibility of keeping it up, keeping it up to standards. It doesn't matter. If they are going to own the property, they're going to accept the responsibility. They should live up to the responsibilities whether they are an individual or a company" (C10-J8).

Similarly, a juror in a case involving landscaping noted the specific obligations of business regarding product quality and customer service, but declared that businesses should be held to the same standard of responsibility as individuals: "I just think they should be responsible. They should be responsible to their customers and back the product and try to perform a good service. But I don't think that individuals should be any different from them" (C8-J6).

Others who endorsed an identical standard pointed out that the basis for corporate action was individual behavior. Reflecting the perspective of one of the lemon law jurors, jurors from other cases asserted: "No, it goes back to the individual. The corporation is only as good as the individuals that make up the corporation" (C4-J3). "I really wouldn't see why, because the corporation is made up of the individuals, so I really can't see what the difference is" (C5-J1). Similarly: "The actions of corporations are based upon individuals within those corporations. So, whether it's a corporation or an individual, no action is taken unless an individual does it. So to have different standards for corporations and different standards for individuals, I don't think is right, even though there may be more money in the corporation pot to be dealing with. I think if we're not careful, the legal system can start focusing only on the corporations because they feel that's where the money is" (C15-J2).

Therefore, several justifications were offered by the plurality of jurors who believed that it is best to treat corporations the same as individuals. Ideas about fairness, equality, and the avoidance of prejudice are significant, as is the logical problem of holding corporations to higher standards when corporate activity is undertaken by individuals.

Why Corporations Should Have a Higher Standard of Responsibility

Some jurors reported that aspects of the corporation did affect them or other jurors (see Chapter 4). Many of these jurors also thought that corporations, because of their role, status, size, organizational resources, or greater potential impact, *should* be held to a higher standard of responsibility than individuals. It is useful to catalogue these lay views of corporate responsibility, which echo the insistence of the lemon law jurors that corporations stand by their work and their products.

One set of arguments dealt with the nature of the corporate entity. Jurors asserted that a corporation has greater organizational resources than typical individuals, which creates a situation where the corporation has or should have greater knowledge about the potentially harmful effects of its products and workplace. Another set of arguments highlighted the special roles and responsibilities that corporations take toward the public, their workers, and their customers. Also important was the impact or potential impact of a corporation's activity. A corporation's size was seen as relevant both because it enlarged the corporation's resources and because it increased its potential impact.

Organizational Resources and Special Knowledge

In justifying a higher standard, a number of jurors cited the organizational resources typical of business corporations. These organizational resources allow the corporation to hire experts and others who are highly knowledgeable about products and safety. This special expertise residing in the corporation increases the knowledge base that corporate actors may have about potentially dangerous practices and products. Thus, in highlighting the role of organizational resources, jurors point to the factor of knowledge, a central element in lay judgments of responsibility for individual actors as well.[12]

Consider the following justification for higher standards, which links an organization's resources to greater knowledge and expertise: "Because a corporation has a group of people that should be able to handle a situation and may be more knowledgeable about a situation than an individual might be. And I'm talking about a big corporation who has different departments to handle different things. As a safety department would and maybe a law department, an accounting department, and their people are experts in these fields so of course they're gonna know more than maybe just one individual person" (C15-J4).

An asbestos case juror espoused a remarkably similar justification for a higher standard: "Maybe a little higher [standard of responsibility for the company], because of the fact that most big corporations have research departments, they have medical staffs, and all that to test their products and if they label it safe when they start making it, they should be more liable because if a person starts making something, it's just that one person and he has to rely on other information. The corporations have researchers and research departments and medical departments that they should maybe know a little more than the average person" (C26-J7). As a juror in a contract case observed: "An individual is just one person, one bad moment and it's bad. Corporations, you got a whole board you act through and move through, so there should be some reasonable answer there. You could do a lot more damage as a corporation than an individual" (C11-J3).

A juror in a case involving an injury in a blood bank relied on resources to argue for higher standards, because "they do have more resources available to them. For any given situation, you take something like this, you take the environment, you take anything, it's a lot easier for a corporation to get the information that they need to make an intelligent decision than it is for an individual. They also have the resources of capital to make an informed decision. I think they should be held to a set of higher standards" (C28-J2). Resources were also important to another juror in the blood-bank case: "I think we should ask more of them, more of them as an organization, because they definitely have the resources, the expertise to draw from. In a well-run organization, [they] should be capable of protecting themselves" (C28-J6). Even a nonprofit corporation, then, is seen as having advantages that require it to conform to higher standards.

The corporation's knowledge of the potentially harmful effects of its products was significant to one of the jurors in the paint-store case described in Chapter 2: "In this particular case, if the people and the corporation have the same degree of knowledge, then, in other words, the information available to them is the same, then sure, [the corporation and the individual should have] the same degree of responsibility. But if a corporation is involved, if it's a product that may be unsafe, the company made it and they know they have a responsibility to have tested it, whether it's a chemical or an instrument or a product in an automobile, they have a lot more information about how that product can hurt someone, and people don't. So I think the corporation has to accept a higher burden of responsibility" (C20-J2). Substantial resources, then, produce the opportunity to hire experts and specialists, who are expected to anticipate potential problems and dangers for consumers and workers.

Although jurors were deciding cases in which this expertise had apparently failed to prevent injury, they almost never mentioned that the complexities of organizational structure and size could impede the effective use of this expertise. Organizational sociologists have observed that problems in lines of authority and communication within large organizations can set up conditions that encourage carelessness and risky behavior.[13] There was an occasional statement about the challenges of making a business run efficiently, but jurors did not volunteer these organizational problems as excuses for reduced responsibility.

Role and Responsibility

The nature of the corporation, and its specific obligations, were invoked by some jurors who argued for a higher degree of responsibility. A few jurors felt that corporations in general had a privileged status and therefore bore more responsibility. For example: "I think that a corporation enjoys some privileges from a tax point of view and from a liability point of view that individuals don't enjoy, so I think they should also have a responsibility that goes along with that, that they should be held even more accountable for maintaining the letter of the law. Yeah, I believe that" (C27-J2). A black woman juror observed that corporations should be held to a higher standard of responsibility than individuals because it was, in her words, higher and bigger:

"The higher you are and bigger you are, then the more responsible you are for certain things. Even in everyday life. This is just a parable. You in your position [*referring to the interviewer*], they look at you different than they would look at me. Not because I'm black or white. This is the same difference, you know what I'm saying? Because they expect more out of you than they would me" (C14-J9).

The fact that those who work for corporations are representing their companies led another juror to demand more of the individual corporate representative:

Juror:	If the individual is acting on behalf of the corporation, that's one thing. If the individual's acting on his own, that's another. I'm only saying that because of the company I work for.
Interviewer:	So you think that somebody working for a business should take more care because they're representing somebody else?
Juror:	Yes. Well, like you work for the University of Delaware, you're representing U of D, right? So anything that reflects on you also could reflect on the university. (C9-J5)

In justifying different standards, other jurors made specific mention of the type of corporation, its mandate and duties to the public and its workforce, and the nature of its products. One juror felt that a warranty company, which was disputing a claim, should be held responsible: "For them to be the warranty company, to me they have essentially taken the builder off the hook. They have taken, anything the builder does wrong, they have guarantees, they will cover it and they will make it right. To me, it's like an insurance company, it would be like if I have a car and I'm paying my premiums, but the minute I have an accident you drop my insurance and you don't pay me to fix my car" (C3-J3).

In considering whether corporations should be held to higher standards, a juror from an auto accident case differentiated between specific types of corporate actions. She argued that under some circumstances, including the case she had decided, the same level of responsibility was appropriate, whereas in other instances a higher level would be required: "I think it all depends on what you're talking about. If you're talking about an automobile accident or something like this, no. If you're talking about environmental pollution or something like that, yes, because they're affecting everybody. . . . I think a company has a certain right to their employees, and certainly a company has more resources and should be more alert to safety so that if something happens to an employee at work, they have that responsibility to their employees. But if the employee is out driving a truck, and is in a wreck, certainly that company can't be held any more responsible for that wreck than if I am driving a car and run into somebody as an individual" (C6-J1).

A nearly identical perspective was put forth by a juror in another auto accident case, in which the plaintiff had been hit by a company truck: "In this type of a case where you're talking one incident, in particular a traffic-type incident, I think the standards have to be the same. If you're talking about something that is more ethical or you get into toxic waste, things where the scope of the problem becomes so much larger because it is a corporation, I think perhaps it does need to be looked at differently. But I think in something like this, where it is one on one, then it should be the same" (C35-J3). These jurors favor greater responsibility when the injury occurs for a reason that is more centrally related to the corporation's mission.

The notion of the supervisory role of the corporation for acts undertaken by its employees was seen by some jurors as carrying additional responsibility. One of the jurors in the landscaping case argued that because the owner of the corporation had to supervise his workers, he was responsible for their sloppy work. A juror in a workplace accident case argued that we should expect more of companies than individuals because of the special obligations of a supervisor: "Companies, I feel, should have strict guidelines that they're responsible for. Now individuals have to go by guidelines of the company, but the company is the one that has to enforce these rules, so the company should be the more responsible. I mean, because somebody does something wrong, the company is the one that should have been training and supervising if that person has the knowledge in it. If a person did something wrong not knowingly, it's the company's fault. If the person was trained and knew that he was doing it wrong, it's his fault. But a company should be more responsible and more stringent on their policies" (C15-J7).

Jurors' comments about the corporation's role imply that the mission and duties of the corporation are linked to its responsibility. For example, jurors expect a car manufacturer to abide by a high standard in the production of safe vehicles, because producing a sound car is the purpose of the automobile corporation. Jurors appear less concerned about seemingly tangential injuries, such as when an employee driving on business hits another car and causes injury. The jurors seem to be constructing a specific type of role responsibility for the corporation depending on the purpose of the company and the nature of the injury. This approach is consistent with the work by Hamilton and her colleagues on the special obligations incurred by roles.

Taking the idea of role responsibility one step further, we might ask if jurors have a set of role obligations that they assign to actors who are involved in commerce, a theme one can observe in a few jurors' comments. Robert MacCoun attempted to determine whether the commercial nature of an action that led to injury would affect judgments of responsibility. He theorized that if jurors respond to the commercial aspect of corporate conduct, then whether or not individuals are engaging in commerce when they cause an injury should affect liability decisions. To test this idea about the importance of commercial activity, he developed a trial vignette in which individuals or corporations caused an injury as a by-product of commercial activity or, in another version, personal activity. Liability ratings for the corporation were virtually identical in the commercial and personal-use conditions.[14] Taken together with jurors' comments, these results suggest that although commercial activity might contribute to judgments about responsibility, other factors are more important.

Professional Responsibility

The linkage between role and responsibility is strongly reflected in the medical malpractice cases. Jurors who decided these cases often advanced the notion of a higher standard for professional people. Doctors are judged against the standard of medical practice, that is, whether the doctor's actions regarding a patient were in line with the medical practice followed by other doctors with the same specialty in the same community at the same time.[15] The standard is thus the reasonable doctor in contrast to the reasonable person in other tort cases.

When asked whether doctors should be held to a different standard of responsibility than other people, one juror observed: "Well, they take an oath, and we don't, to do what they should do, and nobody's infallible. I'm sure that there are mistakes made by physicians, but I don't think [the doctor who was the defendant in the lawsuit] deliberately didn't do the job right, if it wasn't done right" (C9-J1). Another juror from the same medical malpractice case asserted: "I believe they are held to a different standard, more so than an auto mechanic or something like that. I mean, an auto mechanic's with your car, a doctor's with your body. So I think they are held to a different standard. . . . I believe their standard is higher because of the job they do, and their education, and their responsibility and all, so their standard's got to be higher" (C9-J2). As a juror in another medical malpractice case put it: "It's written right in the doctor's code" that doctors should adhere to a higher standard of responsibility than others (C33-J1). Similarly: "I really think they should be [held to a different standard] because they are responsible for helping well-being, they take the Hippocratic oath and that obligates them to different standards, I believe" (C33-J7). Also: "I think doctors should be held to a higher standard . . . because they hold themselves out to be an expert in that field" (C33-J8).

Jurors argued that there was a responsibility that attached to the nature of the medical profession. Agreeing that doctors should be held to a different standard of responsibility than other individuals, one juror observed: "Well, yes in a sense that that is their business. You know, for their line of work. But, if you're an engineer and the bridge falls down, you have a responsibility there too" (C23-J3). Another juror from the same medical malpractice case agreed: "I think they should be held accountable for what they are supposed to do. In other words, if they are trained, at least doctors here have very skilled surgeons, I think they should be held accountable" (C23-J5). Training was also mentioned by a dental malpractice juror: "I feel that they have a lot more education and a lot more training, so they should be held to a little more standard" (C16-J6).

Another dental malpractice juror argued: "I think professionals should be held to a different standard than nonprofessionals. . . . Because that's what their training is, and that's what you get when you pay for their services, you expect professional services, and you don't get that, there's a problem" (C36-J6). One medical malpractice juror was surprised to learn that the doctor was incorporated, but learning about it made him expect a higher standard: "You think of a doctor as a professional. Being with somebody, something that's incorporated, it's like highly, well-thought-out organizations with morals and things like that of a higher level than what you assume of something that's not incorporated" (C33-J6). In contrast, another juror said that he didn't "see any distinction in my mind between a doctor and a doctor who's incorporated himself. So I don't think a doctor who had incorporated himself should be held to a higher standard than just a doctor" (C33-J8).

Another juror who espoused a higher standard for doctors said: "If they're going to be in that profession, and take somebody's life in their hands, yes, then they are special. I don't think that they're gods and I don't think we can expect them to be. And I think they are going to make mistakes and I think that's human nature, because they still are human. However, they have to be above a lot of other types of professions" (C12-J2). But another juror from the same medical malpractice case disagreed:

Interviewer: Do you think that doctors should be held to different standards than other individuals?

Juror: Personally, no. I don't really, I don't. I realize that they can make some life-altering decisions and stuff, but I think that really they're no different than the rest of us. When it comes right down to it, we make mistakes, we pay for it; if they make mistakes, they should pay for it, basically. (C12-J6)

Several other studies in addition to mine suggest the importance of high standards for professionals. In an experimental study of medical malpractice judgments, Duke Law School professor Neil Vidmar used a sample of people from a jury pool.[16] The study participants often explained their decision to find a doctor liable in terms that evoked the special role and responsibility of the medical professional. One participant observed: "We depend on doctors not to be careless. We are leaving our lives in their hands. Basically, I feel that doctors should not make these kinds of mistakes." In words that echo the jurors in my project, another participant in Vidmar's study wrote: "I think a 46 year old Dr. should have the expertise not to make careless mistakes on human life. That his job is to see that people are helped and treated with care."[17] Even though Vidmar discovered that people have high expectations of doctors, his research also found that overall success rates for medical malpractice are significantly lower than the success rates in other tort cases.[18] Therefore, high expectations do not always lead to harsher treatment in the courtroom.

Potential Impact

Another motive for holding corporations to higher standards of responsibility than individuals involves the potential impact of their actions. Whether more severe consequences for an action will increase imputed responsibility for that action has been the subject of academic research and debate for several decades. An experimental study in 1966 found that when the consequences of a car accident varied (from minimal injuries to severe ones), the perception of responsibility for causing the accident also varied. Study participants attributed greater responsibility to the person who caused a more severe accident. Some researchers have replicated this basic finding, while others have failed to find that people are harsher in judging an action with more severe consequences.[19] The issue of expecting higher standards for actions with more serious potential consequences is somewhat different from the situation confronting people who are judging responsibility for a past action. One is prospective, the other retrospective. However, the central concern is the same: What level of care is appropriate for activities with broad consequences?

Jurors supported the idea that corporations should be held to higher standards because of their potential impact. A juror from a supermarket slip-and-fall case with a verdict in favor of the store claimed: "Of course they've got to exercise a great deal more safety awareness, they've got many more people in there to worry about. Yeah, I think they fall to a higher standard. I think even we were holding them to a higher standard" (C32-J1). This juror concluded, though, that even by this higher standard the supermarket was not negligent. The asbestos case jurors also saw the potential impact of asbestos use as requiring a high standard: "Oh, yeah, I think so, just because they're affecting so many people with their products" (C26-J8). Another juror noted: "Corporations are looking out for thousands of people; an individual doesn't look out for that many people. . . . The effect of the corporation's actions affects more than an individual would other people in society" (C26-J5). Stated a juror in another asbestos case: "They're making, disseminating a product into the environment, or into society that has the potential to harm" (C4-J7). Finally: "An individual has a responsibility to himself, and to a limited amount of people. Where a corporation that's shipping products worldwide has a helluva sight more responsibility than an individual" (C22-J1).

A juror in an auto accident case observed: "Sometimes I think maybe a more stringent responsibility than individuals. . . . [Organizations] can impact people in a more, in a bigger way than an individual can impact another person. Like this thing with the Alaskan oil spill. I mean, now because a big business wants to go cheap, they only have tankers that only have one hull, instead of having the double lining. And just out in California another one runs over its own anchor and it spills oil. So you know, an organization, company, whatever, should, you know, look out for things more because they can impact everybody" (C6-J7).

Another juror in an accident case involving a company truck argued for a higher standard of responsibility: "In an oil company business where there's a truckload of oil, that's dangerous. I think they should have a little bit more priority on how their drivers drive. The guy that drove the truck said that he just learned on the job training. I think if you're carrying fuel oil you should have a little bit more training than that" (C31-J3). In an employment discrimination case, one juror noted that corporations and institutions "should be held to a higher [standard] because they are responsible for more people" (C34-J7).

The greater potential risk in corporate settings was also important to a juror in a worker injury case, but upon reflection she felt some ambivalence about holding corporations to a higher standard: "Yes, that [corporations] would be more account-able. . . . I'm just thinking along the lines of safety, in particular. A corporation has much greater chances of injuries or accidents happening than just one specific individual. And I guess that would depend on who that one specific individual was. I guess if it was a homeowner, there are less chances of accidents or injuries occurring. But then on the other hand, it's not right. I'm not sure which way I think" (C14-J5).

Another juror contrasted the medical malpractice case that she decided with the responsibilities of a large employer: "Not in a case like this. I can think of cases where they should be [held to a higher standard]. If a company has ninety-five employees at one location who suddenly come down with black spots on their legs, and they don't investigate fully, I hold them more accountable in that sense than an individual. I think that they have more responsibility because they have taken on more responsibility by being a corporation. But in a case where a doctor is incorpo-rated as part of a partnership, no, I think the issue is, did this person perform inadequately, or did he do something to injure this person" (C9-J6).

Size

Generally speaking, the public is more negative toward large business corporations and more positive toward small businesses (see Chapter 6 for a detailed discussion of how people's attitudes toward business tend to vary with the size of the business enterprise). In their comments about the appropriateness of treating corporations the same as individuals, jurors sometimes reflected this differentiation between large and small business. The size of a business corporation proved to be relevant partly because it expanded the potential impact of the corporation, and partly because a large corporation was presumed to have more organizational resources. These re-sources in turn lead to a presumption that those in the corporation should know better. In a case involving a man injured in a building that was owned by a family corpora-tion, one juror drew a distinction between the case he decided and one that involved a larger corporation:

Interviewer: Do you think more generally that corporations and businesses should be held to different standards of responsibility than individuals?

Juror: Not on a small scale as I see this case. I think that [names large company] should be more responsible for letting toxic fumes in the air than some guy who is burning leaves in his backyard and throws some plastic on it and that gets fumes in the air.

Interviewer: Why not? Why should [the company] be held to a different standard than the guy who throws the garbage bag on the fire in his backyard?

Juror: It's a larger scale. It's a question of [the company] should know, it does know what they're doing as far as toxic emissions or something like that is dangerous, is illegal. Whereas the guy that's got the backyard and throws plastic on it and puts toxic fumes out there, he probably doesn't realize what he's doing. (C10-J4)

Similarly, an asbestos juror agreed that corporations should be more responsible "because of their size and the damages that can be caused by anything they could be selling, not necessarily asbestos products, but any products that they could be selling. I think that they should be more responsible. That's with all companies, 'cause I, by me working at the bank, there's things that I don't know until later on, so it's rough" (C26-J6).

A juror who worked for a large corporation observed: "I think your bigger corporations have more tendency to push for quality and control of things. Where a small, you know, some corporations are only made up of five people or something. And I really think that there's a tremendous difference in that. . . . The bigger corporation should be held more responsible than just individuals . . . just because they're responsible for so many more people" (C36-J3).

In contrast, one juror saw the size of the corporation as presenting problems for adhering to high standards. This is one of the few comments that explicitly mentioned the difficulties corporations face in coordinating their resources: "It's much more complicated in a corporation. The standards that you should be functioning in a safe environment and they should try to provide the safety and you are liable for what happens applies to everybody whether it's in your home or whether it's in a factory or whatever. It's just that with a corporation, you're taking on responsibility of so many more people and so many more things and machines that it gets really complicated. I just think it's more difficult to carry off because of the size, the number of people involved, just numbers" (C14-J1). In any case, a corporation's size and potential impact appear to be integrally related in the jurors' minds, with large corporations having greater potential for harm and therefore a greater burden of responsibility.

The Effect of Supporting a Higher Standard for Corporations

Theoretically, the notion of a standard against which corporate behavior is judged is distinct from the behavior itself. As the quotations from jurors suggest, however, views about the standards for evaluating corporate behavior are likely to influence their judgments in specific cases. In the juror study, we analyzed the relationship between beliefs in a higher standard for corporations and whether the jurors acknowledged that the corporate party made a difference in their own case. The relationship was a strong one: those jurors who endorsed a higher standard were much more likely to say that the corporation affected them in their own case, or that the case would have been different if it had included only individual parties.[20] Among those who endorsed a higher standard, 48% said that the corporate identity of the parties had made a difference in their case. Of those who asserted that corporations should be treated the same as individuals, just 22% said the corporate identity of the parties had made a difference. Thus jurors who tended to report no impact for the corporation also tended to assert that the same standards should apply to both individuals and corporations.

In the mock jury study and the scenario study, we were able to assess whether there was a statistically significant relationship between respondents' views about corporate standards and their judgments of business negligence. In the mock jury study, the more an individual endorsed a higher standard for the corporation, the more likely that individual was to find the business defendant negligent.[21] In the scenario study, there was a similar result. Judgments of negligence of the for-profit business corporations were positively and significantly related to the respondent's agreement that corporations should be held to a higher standard than individuals.[22] Thus, respondents in both studies asserted their general belief that corporations should be held to higher levels of responsibility than individuals, and their specific evaluations of levels of care in the context of personal injury reflected those beliefs. Although most jurors endorsed the same standard, the jurors who believed in a higher standard were more likely to say that the corporate identity had affected their decision making.

In the multinational study of corporate crime by Hamilton and Sanders, those respondents from the United States who endorsed differential treatment for corporate entities were more likely to hold individual corporate actors responsible for wrongdoing.[23] All these results indicate that just as there is a "reasonable person" test against which jurors and judges evaluate individual recklessness, so there appears to be a distinct standard for a reasonable business enterprise that is an important factor in assessing corporate negligence.

Who Believes in a Higher Standard for Corporations?

Hamilton and Sanders found in their multinational study that highly educated respondents in all three countries they studied were more likely to endorse a similar standard for corporations. The highly educated respondents were more apt to say that the corporation did not need to be more careful and did not have a greater burden to avoid accidents than ordinary individuals. Furthermore, they tended to think that sometimes corporations could not avoid doing things that would hurt people. Hamilton and Sanders offered two potential reasons for their finding: that education brought corporations "down to size" and that more highly educated people might use looser standards because they were more likely to be running corporations.[24]

To determine whether education or other personal factors affected how jurors and other participants in my studies made judgments about corporate standards, I conducted a series of analyses. First, I analyzed the relationship between, on the one hand, judgments about corporate impact and standards and, on the other hand, demographic and attitudinal factors among jurors. There were several statistically significant relationships, although most did not account for much of the variation in responses. The following factors were related to whether the jurors stated that corporations had made a difference in their cases: age, political conservatism, whether the juror belonged to a union, and the juror's job. Younger jurors were more likely to say that the corporate identity of the parties had made a difference to their decision making.[25] Those jurors who held nonmanagerial jobs, including service workers, technicians, household workers, transportation workers, and laborers, were more likely to state that they would have decided differently if their case had had individual rather than corporate parties.[26] Finally, jurors who had never belonged to a union and politically conservative jurors were more likely than others to say that they had been influenced by the presence of a corporation in their cases.[27]

As for the issue of corporate standards, just one factor affected whether jurors said they believed it was right to hold a corporation to a higher standard. Jurors' scores on a Political Efficacy scale, which measured the degree to which they felt politically effective, were linked to beliefs in the same standard. In other words, jurors who felt politically effective were more apt to say that corporations should be held to the same standard as individuals. The degree of political conservatism of jurors, however, did not make a difference. In contrast to the study by Hamilton and Sanders, education did not influence jurors' preferences regarding a corporate standard.[28]

The public opinion survey, though, did provide some support for the work of Hamilton and Sanders. Highly educated respondents in my public opinion poll (the same method used by Hamilton and Sanders) were more likely to state that corporations should be treated the same as individuals. Furthermore, respondents with higher incomes followed the same pattern of endorsing similar treatment for corporations, lending some credence to the suggestion that self-interest may lead people to desire a similar standard for corporations, given that wealthier people are more apt to run corporations or hold stock in them. Whether a poll respondent had been a member of a union was again statistically related to the person's view about corporate standards, but in a direction opposite to that found for the jurors. Poll respondents who had been or were union members were now more likely to favor a higher standard for corporations.[29]

The mock jury study again found a statistically significant link with income: wealthier mock jurors endorsed a similar standard for corporations.[30] Education was only marginally related, but the pattern was similar to those of the poll respondents, with more highly educated mock jurors tending to recommend the same treatment for individuals and corporations.[31] The mock juror's sense of political efficacy was related to beliefs in a higher standard in the same way as for jurors: those who felt politically effective wanted the same treatment for corporations.[32] Minority jurors were more likely than white jurors to endorse a higher standard. Finally, whether the mock jurors had served as civil jurors in an actual case also related to their views about corporate standards: those who had served as civil jurors were more willing to recommend that corporations follow a higher standard of responsibility than those who had never served as civil jurors.[33]

In both the mock jury study and the public opinion poll, as might have been expected, participants who had positive attitudes about business in general were less likely to agree that corporations should be held to a higher standard of responsibility.[34] That was not true of the jurors. A juror's general support for business, confidence in business, or belief that business had too little or too much power were all unrelated to the view about whether corporations should be held to a higher standard.

In summing up, it is worth drawing attention to the similarities and differences in the findings of the three studies. In all three, there is some evidence that those on the "bottom" of societal status hierarchies, including minority jurors, those who do not feel politically effective, those with lower incomes, and those with less education, favor holding corporations to higher standards of responsibility. Perhaps these individuals feel more keenly the disadvantages of corporate power and believe that it is important to insist on high standards for corporate actors. Yet, actually serving as a juror (and, perhaps, hearing the judge exhort the jury to treat corporations as legal persons) appears to affect the juror's views about corporate standards, and even about whether corporate identity has an impact in the jury room.

In conclusion, jurors and others often hold specific, and higher, expectations of corporate entities. These expectations do appear to influence jury decision making and lay perceptions of corporate malfeasance; generally speaking, those with high expectations are most often those who are likely to find corporations negligent.

A number of jurors seem to consider the corporate entity as they might a professional or an individual in a position of authority, and hold them to higher standards because of their special roles and expertise. Generating something akin to a "reasonable corporation" standard, jurors see the business corporation as having substantial organizational resources, being privy to expert advice, and having the ability to know when something it does will cause harm. This kind of standard seems closest to that adopted in professional malpractice cases. Prosser and Keeton's classic torts text contrasts the expectations of the reasonable person with those of the professional: "If a person in fact has knowledge, skill, or even intelligence superior to that of the ordinary person, the law will demand of that person conduct consistent with it. Experienced milk haulers, hockey coaches, expert skiers, construction inspectors, and doctors must all use care which is reasonable in light of their superior learning and experience, and any special skills, knowledge or training they may personally have over and above what is normally possessed by persons in the field."[35]

Tort law is flexible enough to allow the use (conscious or unconscious) of a reasonable corporation standard by jurors.[36] Analogizing the corporation to a professional expert, as some of the jurors appear to do, acknowledges some of the advantages of expertise and specialized information possessed by the business corporation. It can also help to explain the higher standards expected of certain nonprofit and charitable corporations.

At least some jurors acknowledge the distinctive characteristics of the corporation that James Coleman and other scholars have identified. They believe that a different standard of responsibility is appropriate given the asymmetries in resources and potential impact of individual versus corporate action. These jurors, however, encounter others in the jury room who insist on the fairness of treating corporations the same as individuals. These differing perspectives on corporate standards and corporate liability, and the debates they engender in the jury room, reflect our continuing struggle to work out the proper place and standards for corporations in law and society.

6

ARE JURORS
ANTI-BUSINESS?

We can now examine whether the differential treatment of the corporation that I documented in earlier chapters can be traced to anti-business sentiment among jurors.[1] Business leaders often assume the worst about juries: that they are hostile to business corporations and more prone to sympathize with the injured plaintiffs than with the men and women of the corporation. Indeed, many business executives appear to share the views of the veteran business lawyer George McGunnigle, Jr., who argues that jurors' unrealistic expectations of business people, their naivete and lack of experience in the business world, and the good old tradition of sympathy for the underdog lead to significant disadvantages for the corporation in jury trials.[2] In his experience, a corporation faces the most serious problem of juror bias when an individual who asserts that he or she has been "bullied" by the corporation sues it.[3] Advocates who represent a small family business against a large industry possess the same kinds of advantages that the individual possesses when suing a corporation.

Professor John Lande conducted systematic interviews with business executives and attorneys who did a great deal of business litigation, asking them about their views of the court system and alternatives to litigation. He discovered that most executives had negative opinions about the courts in general and the civil jury in particular.[4] A substantial majority of the executives who were interviewed estimated that juries did a good job in determining liability less than half the time. As one executive put it: "Is it any surprise that many commercial contracts these days have a clause where each party waives its right to a jury trial? Doesn't that tell you something? That they are not willing to trust twelve peers off the street with the complexity of their business transaction."[5]

The attorneys, especially attorneys from outside firms, were slightly more positive about jury trials in business cases but nevertheless had concerns about the impact of bias on the jury's decision-making process. One of the general counsel for a corporation observed: "Oh, a plaintiff's lawyer can get [jurors] all riled up on emotion. It's got nothing to do with the law. It's got nothing to do with real liability. It's got nothing to do with real facts. It's got to do with who's the better actor."[6] Similarly: "I think jurors are sometimes willing to do justice . . . because they just view this rule . . . as one that kind of comes up with a harsh result in this case. And those are the cases that maybe will go to a jury more often than not because a plaintiff's lawyer knows that and [thinks], 'God, if I get by this motion for summary judgment and get to a jury, I've got a real chance because that argument about, "Well, the law says X" is just not going to be real persuasive to most folks on the jury.' "[7]

In Chapter 2 I demonstrated that jurors have ambivalent and complex approaches to plaintiffs, assiduously scrutinizing their credibility and often blaming the victim who sues a corporation. But what about the independent claim that juries are by nature hostile to business corporations? The belief in the anti-business prejudice of jurors is widespread, even though there have been few efforts to document it. This chapter examines attitudes about business held by jurors and other citizens, and analyzes the extent to which anti-business prejudice affects decision making. Thus it provides an empirical response to the charge that juries are prejudiced against business.

The Impact of Attitudes in Law

One justification for examining public attitudes about business corporations is that such attitudes are likely to influence legal proceedings against corporations. Public attitudes affect substantive law and legal procedures both directly and indirectly. At the most basic level, legislators take public opinion into account when they create laws, responding to dynamic public attitudes by considering and enacting new legislation.

Attitudes can also influence what cases are brought into the courtroom. A potential plaintiff must first recognize that an injury has occurred, must decide that a company is to blame, and must think it is important or worthwhile to make a claim against the business. Expectations about the responsibility of business and appropriate standards of business conduct are thus critical to the early stages of lawsuit filings. On the criminal justice side, prosecutors consider public attitudes in deciding whether to charge someone with a crime. There are no reliable data on whether prosecutors are similarly sensitive to public opinion in cases of corporate wrongdoing. Nevertheless, perceptions of the legitimacy and fairness of the legal system affect compliance with the law. If the public believes that business interests are favored in the prosecutor's office or in the courtroom, this belief could undermine their support for the entire legal system.

The most obvious way in which public attitudes may affect court outcomes is the jury.[8] A microcosm of the public, the jury directly represents that public in the courtroom. Jurors' attitudes toward business in general and specific business litigants in particular trials have the potential to affect the outcomes of jury trials.

Influential theories of juror decision making give a central role to the individual juror's expectations, perceptions, and world knowledge.[9] There is a good deal of research on the effects of attitudinal differences that jurors hold on the decisions that they make in criminal trials. Controversy exists over just how useful juror attitudes are in predicting decision outcomes, with some scholars and practitioners arguing that they are critically important to juror decisions.[10] Others believe that their significance is overrated.[11]

In the context of criminal justice, general attitudes about crime or personality variables are not very successful in predicting jurors' decisions in cases. For example, researchers have not been able to identify reliably the demographic factors that are associated with conviction-proneness across a wide range of cases.[12] Yet more specific attitudes toward the crime in question, such as attitudes toward rape in sexual assault cases, have been found to relate to juror judgments.[13]

Attitudes toward the death penalty also appear to correlate reliably with criminal case decisions. In the work that Professor Phoebe Ellsworth and her colleagues did on attitudes toward the death penalty, they examined three situations in which attitudes might make a difference: evaluating witness credibility, resolving ambiguous evidence, and deciding on a standard of proof. They found that mock jurors who were opposed to the death penalty were more likely to favor the defense in all three of these intermediate steps. They also made more pro-defense statements during tape-recorded mock jury deliberations. Her results show the different ways attitudes can matter in the jury's decision-making process.[14]

Most of the work examining the impact of attitudes to date has examined criminal trials. This book is one of a relatively small number of efforts to examine in a systematic manner how attitudes toward business and civil litigation influence jury decision making in civil trials.[15] But theory and research done in criminal cases suggest that attitudes toward business could be potentially significant.

Of course, when jurors express positive or negative attitudes toward business, there is no surefire guarantee of a verdict consistent with those attitudes. After all, public opinion surveys have for years documented strong negative assessments of tobacco companies, yet smokers' lawsuits against the companies during the past several decades have produced mainly victories for the tobacco companies. Nevertheless, the work mentioned above suggests that attitudes toward business can influence the evaluation of evidence, the burden of proof, and the perceptions of legal arguments in a lawsuit.

Specific Examples of Jurors' Attitudes toward Business Litigants

It is worthwhile to start our inquiry into attitudes toward business with a look at jurors' remarks about business litigants in the trials they decided. In the interviews, however, jurors' comments about business defendants were often less focused and frequent than comments about the individual plaintiffs in their cases (see Chapter 4). Corporate executives were rarely present in the courtroom, a factor that may have encouraged jurors to focus more on the plaintiffs. And although jurors held corporations to high standards, they often expressed relatively benign interpretations of negligent behavior. The remarks of a juror from the lemon law case described in Chapter 5 were typical: "I think this was a specific thing that happened. In fact I said I don't think that they deliberately went out to do this, I think he fell through the cracks, but the cracks shouldn't have been there" (C25-J2).

In looking for anti-business bias, it makes sense to start with the two types of cases that one might predict would be associated with the greatest degree of anti-business hostility by jurors: punitive damages cases and high-award cases.

Punitive Damages Cases

In punitive damages cases, one might well expect the greatest hostility toward the defendant companies. After all, when plaintiffs request punitive damages, they have assessed that the level of misbehavior of the defendant is intentionally egregious and deserves the most severe civil sanctions. Only three of the thirty-six cases in this group (including the lemon law case) resulted in a punitive damage award. Although punitive damages were requested in all the asbestos cases, they were never awarded. Curiously, even in the two contract cases in which punitive damages were awarded, jurors did not express particularly strong condemnations of the business defendants during the interviews.[16]

One contract case involved two small businesses and an insurance company, all involved in a dispute over an international shipment. Before the trial, none of the jurors had heard of any of the companies involved in the case. Their views of the owner of the plaintiff corporation were positive: "It seemed to be a nice small family-run business" (C13-J3); "totally honorable and admirable" (C13-J4); "a pretty straightforward guy, a little rough at times, but taking into consideration the stuff he'd gone through with the case, I could understand him being a little curt at times with the lawyers" (C13-J2).

Even though the jurors concluded that one of the defendant companies had deliberately withheld a shipment and in doing so had damaged the plaintiff company, meriting punitive damages, jurors did not uniformly voice strong condemnation, as might have been expected. The most negative juror was a man with construction experience who described it as a "travesty" that the entire international operation fell apart because of the actions of the defendant company. He highly valued the cooperation of multiple parties that is necessary to put together a construction project, noting that in this case everybody did their job but the defendant. When the defendant testified that he regretted what he had done and had not meant to hurt the plaintiff, this juror thought "that he told the truth" but "my opinion was, you know, so what, the plaintiff was damaged, it doesn't matter whether it was through malice or stupidity" (C13-J4).

Other jurors took a more generous approach. According to one juror, the defendant "struck me as a rather shrewd businessman, but he didn't have much common sense about it" (C13-J2). In the view of another, the defendant "needed it to try to help his business and it didn't work and it hurt somebody else. I think he was sorry that it hurt somebody else, not that that helps the plaintiff but I think he was sorry" (C13-J3). One juror "felt sorry" for both parties and described his general impressions of both plaintiff and defendant as "favorable" (C13-J5); another juror described her views of both plaintiff and defendant companies as "neutral." She did, however, describe insurance companies negatively: "They write policies to benefit themselves. . . . I think a lot of times, especially when it comes to like this bonding insurance, there were things that could be taken several different ways, if you don't read it just right. Like one clause, even when we were deliberating you had to read it and then reread it and have somebody else reread it and then you have to analyze every single word before you can figure it out" (C13-J6). Similarly, another juror objected to the insurance company: "The other defendant was the insurance company, which, you know their argument goes, well we have these loopholes, you have to read the fine print. . . .

And I was shocked when the attorney for the insurance company did come up and present loopholes" (C13-J4).

Another contract case that resulted in punitive damages involved chemical companies. A brokerage firm that supplied chemicals argued that its agreement with the larger company for a long-term contract to supply a specific chemical had been breached. The case was complex and relatively lengthy, lasting about two weeks. Jurors expressed mostly neutral or positive views of the companies involved in the dispute. When asked what he felt about corporations involved in the chemical industry, one juror characterized his general reaction as neutral, explaining: "I don't think there's any harm involved, to be honest with you" (C11-J2). Another juror drew on his personal experiences with chemical companies: "My brother and my father work for a very large petrochemical company, so course I have a positive feeling for them because that's clothed me, sheltered me, and fed me my whole life. There are a lot of them out there that I'm not particularly fond of because of what they have done to the environment, but other than that they have their purpose, so that's the way I look at it" (C11-J1). Commenting on the specific companies in the lawsuit, the juror saw the broker of chemicals, the middleman, in a more negative light: "That was against them because I see there's no need, a company like that is unnecessary. It's just a waste of time. The [defendant] company could have had someone working for them do the job much better and at a cheaper cost" (C11-J1). He had friends working for the defendant company, and "I've never heard much bad about them and you know they are headquartered here, and just basically I have friends that work for them and like working for them and everything" (C11-J1). In his view, there was "no clear-cut villain" in the case.

One juror, describing her impressions of both the companies as neutral, thought that the good and the bad of chemical companies balanced each other:

Interviewer: Do you have any general feelings about chemical companies?
Juror: Not necessarily. Depends on what you're reading about them, I mean you know they do a lot of good but at the same time there's a lot of bad, so you got to balance out the progress somewhere.
Interviewer: And what kinds of things come to mind when you think of the good that they do?
Juror: Plastics, medicines, I don't know, everything most.
Interviewer: And then what about the bad, what kinds of things come to mind?
Juror: Well, I think Love Canal, pollution, Agent Orange. It balances out somewhere, hopefully. (C11-J3)

Another juror showed a remarkably similar view of chemical companies, discussing concerns about the environment but acknowledging the necessity to "step on some toes" to make money. "It's a tough, tough question. . . . Even back when I was a little kid and everybody was on pollution, blah, blah, blah, blah, and everybody's walking around with their signs and whatnot. But people don't realize, you know, it took markers and paper to write that stuff and they pollute. Big companies make that stuff. People don't realize that" (C11-J5). Another juror "just knew of [the defendant] as a big company and that's it" (C11-J4). But she had critical observations about both companies: the witness who testified from the chemical brokerage company "wasn't believable" and she "didn't get a good impression from him," whereas in the large company, "they were messed up, they didn't have a good sales department, they didn't know what they were talking about between the boss and the one under him, they didn't have any communication at all."

According to jurors' explanations, punitive damages were awarded in addition to compensatory damages to "make it hurt," so that the defendant company could feel it, realize that it did something wrong. One of the jurors who argued unsuccessfully for a larger damage award felt that the amount they arrived at just wasn't enough; the plaintiff company should have had more "for all the trouble and heartache they went through" (C11-J2). But, in the words of one juror: "We wanted to give them something but we really didn't want to, just like a slap on the wrist, just not really penalize them too bad. . . . Basically I figured nobody was really getting hurt by that, it was just like a phone call from the bank when your Visa's due late, you know, it's nothing that's going to kill you" (C11-J5).

Thus, considering that both these business disputes resulted in punitive damages, remarkably little negativity surfaced in the juror interviews.

Large-Award Cases

Another place to look for negative views about business corporations is in the trials that produced extremely large awards. Company executives express fear that a hostile jury could jack up even the compensatory damages out of proportion to the actual injuries suffered by the plaintiff. When we review the few large-award cases in this sample, however, we find that none of them appeared to reflect consistent hostility toward the corporate defendant. Often a juror or two on each case expressed some strong negative opinions about the company, but most jurors we interviewed evaluated the companies in positive or neutral ways.

The largest award in the sample ($8.7 million) was given in the case of a motorcyclist injured in an accident by a company truck. An employee driving the truck admitted that he had been looking at some paperwork as he drove through a red light and hit the motorcyclist, who was severely injured and would require lifelong nursing care. Most jurors had positive comments about both drivers, showing sympathy for the badly injured plaintiff but also for the driver who hit him: "[The defendant driver] was a really compassionate person also. He never had a problem saying he was guilty. He really felt bad for what had happened. It was a suit against the company because of his negligence, but he never argued that he wasn't guilty" (C21-J6). As another juror observed, "It was really a case where you just really felt sorry for both sides" (C21-J7).

This case was a prime illustration of the ghostliness of the corporation. Except for the driver, no one from the company, a regional home-building firm, testified. Jurors did not report observing company representatives in the courtroom. Although several jurors had heard of the company, none of them knew very much about its business practices. It's not surprising, then, that jurors had little to say about the corporation. Some typical quotes include "As far as we were concerned, the company never came up" (C21-J1), "Nobody from the company said a word" (C21-J2), "Well, I really didn't have too much of an opinion, because I've never dealt with them" (C21-J3), "I don't know anything about them, so it's not for me to say" (C21-J5), and "I've heard of them, but I don't know what they do or I don't know what they make or anything" (C21-J6).

Jurors agreed with the principle that the corporation should be liable "because this man was working for the corporation, and to me they were responsible for their drivers, even though they had nothing to do with the accident" (C21-J3). One juror did wonder whether the corporation had pressured the driver to finish his paperwork, or whether he was in a hurry to get the truck back and punch out. This juror would have liked someone from the corporation to address that question as well as the issue of driver training. He thought, "Somebody should have been there from [the corporation]. It's their company, it's their driver" (C21-J4). The jury decided on a record-breaking multi-million-dollar award, but as one of the jurors explained, that was linked to the economic needs of the plaintiff and his family rather than animus against the corporation: "We weren't out really to get [the corporation], you know what I mean, it wasn't really that kind of trial, nor were the other jurors hostile, it was just something that happened" (C21-J7).

It is interesting to speculate about the effect of the ghostliness of the defendant corporation. If the chief executive or managers had testified, or at least had been more visible at the trial, would jurors have reached the same award? Or would that have encouraged them to reflect on the impact of such a high award on the vitality of the business enterprise?

In another high-award case ($3.5 million), the sports injury trial briefly discussed in Chapter 2, the equipment manufacturer who was sued was generally evaluated favorably. We interviewed six jurors from that case, and only one stood out because of his generally negative opinions about the company. Asked about his first reaction to the fact that an individual was suing a corporation, he said: "Well, I figured he was fighting a losing battle, because you get an individual against a corporation who have all these lawyers and so forth for them, that I thought he took on a hell of a challenge. And I'm really, really glad he won" (C1-J3). Convinced by expert evidence about the equipment design that the company could have produced a better piece of equipment that would have lessened the plaintiff's injury, he quickly concluded that the company was "guilty" and the plaintiff deserved a high award. He stuck to his guns throughout the deliberation. But he lambasted other actors, too. In addition to criticizing the other sports player who ran into the plaintiff, he also blamed the school:

> I don't think it's all just the company's fault, because they're just in the business of making sports equipment. You can buy a good piece of equipment, or you can go out and buy a bad piece of equipment. It all depends on how much you want to pay. They [the school district] happened to choose cheap equipment. Then, they put them on the players' heads, and then if they get hurt, well, tough luck, next player. I don't think that's right where a student has to sign away his life in order to participate in a sport. I think that sports are stupid. . . . I can't understand how so many millions of people will sit in the stands and watch guys run back and forth and try to get a ball. Stupid! . . . I don't believe that the players should have to assume the risks. The school wants them to play sports, so the school should take the responsibility if they get hurt. That's why they got coaches and teachers and people to show you how to play the sport in a safe manner. (C1-J3)

In addition, this juror's motivation for granting a high award seemed to be linked more to the plaintiff's situation than to the company's: "I wasn't really trying to give the equipment company a message. I just wanted to try and help the plaintiff, because he needed all the help he could get. As far as the equipment company, I hope they did get a message out of it, I hope they make the best equipment possible and have only that on the market. Then, if somebody does get injured, 'Hey, we did our best' " (C11-J3).

Contrast this juror's views with those of the other five jurors whom we interviewed from the same case. One juror described her general view of sports manufacturing companies as "favorable" (C1-J1). She was asked whether the corporation in her case was best described as a generally careless company or as a company that was generally careful but might have made a mistake in this instance. She chose the second option. Another juror said that he "had no opinion about [sports manufacturing companies]. Even after the case, you can't judge the whole company or field of companies by one company" (C1-J2). Asked his opinion of the corporation, one juror stated that he had never heard of it before, but "I've never heard anything against them. I just took for granted that they were doing a good job, in trying to make equipment safe for players. . . . I think they were a good clean-cut company, I think they were doing the best they could to their ability to make things safe for everybody. But it was just an imperfection, that's part of life itself, and that can't be avoided. . . . Mistakes are made in manufacturing, somebody's bound or liable to make something defective, unintentionally, and it gets out into the public, and it happens to get into the hands of somebody who's physically weaker" (C1-J4).

One juror who also had not heard of the corporation before the trial commented: "I had a favorable opinion of the company. We were given the history of the company, and it's a very old company, and I felt they must have done something right to be in business for as long as they have been in business" (C1-J5). He concluded, though, along with the rest of the jurors, that the defendant company was negligent. His views may have been affected by personal experience. In a prior job, he wrote operators' manuals for heavy equipment. After a particular piece of equipment caused the death of two men, he and others working on the development of that equipment were fired. As he put it: "I had this background, I knew what goes on when you're trying to sell a product, you're in a rush to get it out the door. And you cut corners" (C1-J5).

Another juror also gave positive impressions of the defendant company: "Let's just say they did the best they could and they're a first-class operation, from what I got through their records and data. And comparing it to what we do here [at the juror's own workplace], I've got to say it's first class" (C1-J6). This juror was undecided, leaning toward the corporation, but in the deliberation he concluded, "the corporation knew they could have improved on the equipment and they didn't." That was "good enough for me," but the decision still did not sit well with him. This undecided juror, who had questions about liability, argued for a lower award in the jury deliberations, illustrating the merger of liability and award decisions, which are theoretically supposed to be distinct. In sum, although one juror was quite negative, and another knew from experience that some businesses cut corners, the rest of the jurors expressed positive views of the company and the overall quality of its work even as they awarded the plaintiff a multi-million-dollar judgment.

The third tort case in our sample with a relatively high award ($1.1 million) involved a plaintiff whose lung had been removed unnecessarily by a doctor during an exploratory operation to determine whether the patient had lung cancer. While the operation was going on, the hospital laboratory identified a frozen section of his lung tissue erroneously as cancerous. The doctor then removed about half of one lung. A later biopsy revealed that the lung was not cancerous, and the hospital settled with the patient before the doctor's trial. The key issue in the doctor's trial was whether the standard of care required that he conduct screening tests before surgery to make sure that the surgery was necessary.

Even though the jury concluded that the doctor was negligent and a substantial award was merited, their evaluations of the doctor were fairly positive. At the start of the case, one juror reported being drawn "toward the doctor, because I believe there's so many cases brought up against doctors, as far as malpractice," although by the end of the case her sentiments had shifted to the patient (C12-J1).[17] Her view of the doctor was "neutral. I think he was just a doctor doing his job. And the impression I got from doctors from that whole case is that they do whatever they think is best, and that's what he did, and doctors do that." Another juror observed: "I think he defended himself pretty well. But I think he needed other people to back him up" (C12-J9). Another who described him as "a sound, sound doctor" was unsure at the end of the trial "that we should trash this doctor's career for one, well, not that it would put him out of business, but based on this decision he had made, he was misinformed, no doubt about it" (C12-J4). One juror said that she "kind of liked him" and received the impression that "he's a very good surgeon. . . . My feeling was that he jumped in maybe too quickly on something, and I think he realized that he did that, but it was done. I don't think that should discredit him, but I know anytime you have a malpractice suit up against you, I'm sure that it's not good" (C12-J6). Similarly: "He seemed to be a very professional individual and an individual who I think is a very competent surgeon, and certainly was qualified to do the surgery" (C12-J7). This juror reported that the plaintiff's attorney attempted to insinuate that the doctor derived a good deal of income from surgery and perhaps was overeager to operate, but the juror found this argument unpersuasive: "I don't think anybody would do, really, I don't think any-body's gonna get rich or poor over doing a lot of unnecessary surgeries. I think that they probably are more of a belief that surgery is better because you get the tissue out. I don't think there is any financial incentive to them" (C12-J7).

Perhaps the most negative comment came from a juror who described the doctor as "cold": "I got the impression of the doctor that he felt he was above reproach, he is a doctor, he is far above anyone else" (C12-J2). However, the juror went on to say: "Doctors are there to help you, for the most part that's really what they want to do. I don't think anybody wants to deliberately do harm. I also think at times we expect too much. I mean, they're not gods by any means, they're human beings and they do make mistakes and you have to realize that. But unfortunately, you have to pay for your mistakes" (C12-J2). Similarly, another juror observed: "I was one of the majority who felt he was guilty, and I feel that he goofed. And when you're a surgeon and you're in charge of people's lives, I'm not willing to give much leeway. I wouldn't want a doctor cutting me up without real need" (C12-J3). These comments, though negative, were relatively mild.

Thus, in all the high-award cases, the predominant response of most jurors we interviewed was in the neutral-to-positive range. This might surprise those who believe that high awards to plaintiffs result from animus against business defendants.

Jurors' Negative Views of Business Litigants

In a few cases, jurors did express strong negative views about the business defendant. The negativity appeared to stem primarily from the specific evidence produced at the trial rather than preexisting negative attitudes toward a particular business. One set of cases involved the asbestos companies. Another two cases in which jurors were negative about the business litigants were small-stakes cases involving lawsuits against modestly sized local enterprises.

Asbestos Cases

We interviewed twenty-eight jurors from three asbestos cases. As is typical, each trial included multiple defendants and multiple plaintiffs and lasted about a month. All three found the companies negligent, but the awards were quite different. Two of the cases produced relatively low awards, whereas the third resulted in a comparatively high award.[18] Because my information came exclusively from the juror interviews, I could not determine whether evidentiary or legal issues differed dramatically across the three cases, but there appeared to be substantial overlap in evidence and legal arguments.

Most of the asbestos jurors we interviewed began their trials with little knowledge of the companies that manufactured or distributed asbestos. A pretrial jury selection questionnaire tapped knowledge about the defendant companies and asbestos litigation. It is possible that the unusually extensive jury selection process eliminated jurors with more substantial knowledge or more extreme views. Most jurors did not report strong initial opinions one way or the other about the asbestos companies. Asbestos jurors typically remarked: "I'd heard [asbestos cases] mentioned a few times, but I didn't know anything about it" (C22-J5). Another juror "just recognized the name" of certain companies who were defendants in asbestos cases (C4-J2). "I'd heard generally reading the newspapers that there were a lot of [asbestos cases], but I didn't know of any specifics of what they involved or anything like that. . . . Only when something made a paper, they were going bankrupt, and there was a little bit in the news then. I don't remember a lot of it, just that I knew it was a real problem and there was a whole lot of litigation" (C22-J4). Another juror reported surprise that the case involved the specific companies, "because I had no idea these companies had anything to do with asbestos. I didn't know anything about it, except that they were taking it out of the school that I work in" (C22-J2).

Others couched the expression of their views about asbestos companies in terms that highlighted the plaintiff's rather than the company's responsibilities (see Chapter 2). For example, one juror who didn't "know that much about it," and refrained from expressing a general feeling about the asbestos companies, nevertheless asserted that the plaintiffs retained a good deal of responsibility for their condition (C4-J4). Similarly, a juror from the same case, who gave her reaction to the companies as "neutral" (C4-J1), expressed outrage that the plaintiffs were "out to make a killing from these companies" and said she did not think that the asbestos companies should have to pay the plaintiffs money damages. The theme of plaintiff responsibility was, of course, prevalent in a wide range of cases, including asbestos trials.

In contrast to most of the other cases, a number of asbestos jurors stated that the testimony presented during the trial led them to develop strong negative opinions about the companies. A good deal of testimony in asbestos trials revolved around the knowledge and actions of individuals in the company, albeit at earlier points in the company's history. Information about the health dangers of asbestos, when they were first discovered, and when the manufacturers were likely to have known about these negative health effects, are now standard components of the typical trial in asbestos litigation, introduced through taped depositions and written memoranda from company officials. That was true in all three of the asbestos trials in this study. Although some jurors reported that the admission of documentary evidence was tedious, the information influenced jurors' beliefs about the companies. The most negative jurors were concentrated in Case 22, where the jury decided on a much higher award compared to the other two asbestos cases in the sample: "They were proving that the company knew about this years back from 1935, 1934, all the way that far. And anybody that puts out a product is supposed to investigate it and see what kind of harmful things it does to you. And they did not ever put a warning label on it or tell them how to install it by wearing respirators or suits in which today they do, and they let it go on for years and years and years. That's because if they put on it 'dangerous' or something like that, they're not going to sell the product. . . . The companies had doctors working on it and studies made but they always sidetracked it and it was for the benefit of money, they didn't worry about people's lives" (C22-J9).

Another juror from the same case reported: "There was a number of letters that they read from one company to another and from people they'd actually hired to investigate the dangers, and the letters were presented as evidence. There was even a report brought into evidence from the United States Health Service back in the early 1930s telling them some of the dangers of asbestos. Maybe it wouldn't be common knowledge, but it certainly should be to an asbestos producer, that there were dangers involved and they chose to suppress them, I thought" (C22-J5). A third juror from the same case reported that the evidence suggested to him that the companies knew there was a problem and didn't do anything about it: "These guys knew almost at the turn of the century there were problems with this. Basically I came to the conclusion that they did know enough to put warnings out anyway. If they had put the warnings out it probably would have gone a long way toward alleviating them of liability" (C22-J4). Perceived as especially egregious was the company's firing of an employee who attempted to bring the dangers of asbestos to the attention of the company's management: "They fired him after a year, because he found the dangers. . . . I thought, I can't believe it . . . why did they fire him? But see, he knew they were in the wrong and they just didn't want to hear it. They could have licked it back in the 1970s when he found all that danger" (C22-J2).

A juror in a different case "felt they had acted negligently, that the plaintiffs should have been warned by labels or something on the packages that this stuff was hazardous to their health" (C4-J7). This juror felt, though, that the case had "a big block in the middle" where the employer should have been. A central question in this juror's mind was why the plaintiffs' employer had not warned its workers about the potential dangers, illustrating again the complexity of assigning responsibility for worker injuries when employers are usually excluded from litigation because of workers' compensation.

In commenting on how he felt about the specific companies involved in asbestos litigation, one of the jurors observed that at the beginning of the trial, his attitude toward the companies "was neutral, it was okay, it was good," but by the end of the trial it was negative. "The company had been in business for a number of years, however I just think they had piss-poor management. Their management decisions were terrible. . . . They did very little to protect themselves from any future lawsuits. I mean, even if you don't care if people are getting injured, at least, as a good business, somebody in management should at least try to safeguard the corporation, even if you don't care, and they had not done that. . . . It was almost as if they were like an ostrich, just putting their head in the sand. 'We hear you but we don't hear you, there's a problem with our stuff . . . ' Maybe they felt putting a warning of some kind on it might be an admission of guilt, and my impression is they just chose to ignore it because it complicated things" (C22-J7). Similarly, in another case: "I don't think they were responsible companies. I don't think the companies handled it the right way . . . knowing that they had that product and knowing it was dangerous and for years they did not put a warning on" (C26-J6).

The stance that jurors took toward the defendant companies in asbestos trials was not uniformly negative. Some jurors, particularly those in the two cases where the theme of plaintiff responsibility predominated and awards were relatively low, continued to see the companies in a relatively positive light. Consider this juror: "I have a positive reaction because nothing was known about asbestos. . . . They didn't have empirical evidence to prove that it affected people that much until 1946. There were studies made before and reports from Great Britain and so forth earlier than that, but nothing of substance" (C4-J3). This juror described one of the companies as "a first-class corporation" and regarded another positively because it admitted fault and attempted to settle with the plaintiffs. On the same jury was a person who felt sympathetic to a central manufacturer because it had to bear the brunt of the asbestos litigation, and in this juror's view some of the plaintiffs were "trying to get money where I don't think they deserved it" (C4-J4). From the same jury came another observation about the corporate defendants: "I felt like the company wanted to do the right thing. . . . [The attorney for the company] always said these people have been damaged, they deserve an award. I didn't feel like he was trying to cheat these people, but I felt like he was trying to protect his company from [people trying to make it rich]. . . . I think they were negligent, because I thought they had a moral obligation, but I didn't think they did it on purpose" (C4-J8). In the eyes of another juror: "I feel very sorry that they've, I think they've put a very important business out of business because of what's happened. . . . Because of liability, they just put the asbestos people out of business. . . . I don't know if they were as negligent as the courts make them out to be" (C4-J9).

One juror from a case that decided on a relatively low award felt "favorable toward the companies for a lot of the information that I heard" (C26-J1). The juror acknowledged that studies on the impact of asbestos had been done, but pointed out that the study samples were with different types of workers who had more extensive exposure to asbestos. "Back in that period of time, I don't really feel that they knew all the harm that was being caused, and so in turn I didn't really feel I could blame them" (C26-J1). One of the juror's colleagues felt similarly: "I personally don't think at the time that they were manufacturing or selling this product, I didn't think that they were aware that it caused any harm for the knowledge that they had at that time" (C26-J3).

In contrast to many other cases, then, a substantial amount of documentary and deposition testimony demonstrated effectively to some jurors a negative pattern of behavior by corporate management over the years. Jurors responded by forming negative images of the companies, images that featured a profit-motivated lack of concern over injuries and unwillingness to confront problems associated with asbestos. Although many of the relevant parties in the asbestos litigation were quite literally ghosts, having died or retired many years ago, the plaintiffs' attorneys figuratively resurrected them for the lawsuit. The missing parties had more presence in the asbestos litigation than did the corporate defendants in many other cases in the study.

Two Small-Business Disputes

Two other cases that produced a notable number of negative remarks by jurors about the business defendant both involved small companies. One involved a landscaping company, sued for damages over the allegedly negligent application of sod on a home owner's lawn. The business owner testified at length in court about the multiple failures that had occurred, requiring him to install sod or grass seed on several different occasions. Many jurors in this case expressed negative views of the owner and considered his business practices substandard. One juror said that he had not presented himself well in court: "He came off as not well spoken, not terribly intelligent, didn't present himself well, certainly didn't present an image of someone who cared for customers" (C8-J3). As another of the jurors commented: "[The owner] was an obstinate pain in the gluteus maximus, he kept insisting on coming back there to try and correct his wrongdoings and he flat-out refused to say no, he would not let it rest, no matter how much they told him, 'Stay away from our house, we don't want you anywhere near here, don't set foot on our property,' he still came back and did it" (C8-J1).

Jurors reported that they shook their heads in amazement as the owner described on the witness stand why he continued to work on the lawn even though the plaintiffs were telling him to cease. He wanted to make amends and to make his customers satisfied. Of course, he also hoped to stay out of court: "He admitted that he didn't want to go to court, and it was basically in order to get out of going to court he had to redo the lawn, he had to make them happy, and that was the only way he was gonna get out of going to court" (C8-J1).

Yet, as one of the jurors observed: "There were things about him that made him seem like a down-to-earth person. . . . I don't think he appeared to be an intentionally bad person or a person who really tried to rake everybody over the coals and had a bad business because of that. I didn't get that impression. But I got the impression from the things that he said [on the witness stand] that he wasn't really maybe remembering everything the exact way it happened. . . . I think he probably wasn't on top of things the way he should have been as a businessman. Maybe what's happened is there's so much to do there that he needs a business manager to run things a little bit better. . . . But I have the feeling he's relying on people who maybe are not as experienced as they should be and don't know as much about what they're supposed to be doing and yet he's not looking into that" (C8-J6). Another juror, agreeing that the owner was "a good businessman generally," maintained that he got himself into this situation because "he was just too busy, he had too much work. And then when it came down to him being sued he went and did this so he wouldn't be sued" (C8-J2). One of the most positive jurors stated: "I thought he appeared to be a very nice gentleman, he was a businessman, you know. He was there to protect his interest and his business. Unfortunately I think it's just one of those cases where something happened. Unfortunately he procrastinated in taking care of it as he should have. I believe if he had followed up or had called that it would have had a great effect on the trial altogether. I thought it was his problem that he waited until he had a letter from the courts before he [decided to] go and do something" (C8-J4).

Thus, jurors expressed a range of negative views about the owner of the company. They tended to talk exclusively about the individual owner rather than the company itself, illustrating the tendency of jurors to use individual-level examples and analogies when describing corporate entities (see Chapter 4).

The most negative evaluation of a business defendant in the entire group of cases came in a trial in which a worker was injured in an apparently substandard building. A man whom jurors variously described as a "slum landlord" and a "shyster" owned the defendant company. Jurors said that the defendant "did not come across as professional, trustworthy, honest" (C10-J4), and that the jury quickly reached the decision that the defendant was "lying through his teeth" and should lose the case. In one juror's words: "He was into a lot of different things, real-estate-wise, business ventures, and that this was just one thing. It seems like he was trying to use every piece of the law, or bend the law every which way to get what he wanted out of it, you know, to his advantage. . . . It just felt like he should have lived up to the responsibilities" (C10-J8).

Asked about her views of real estate companies that have holdings in different areas of a city, one juror stated: "It's a shame, I feel, the slums down there. That they hold onto this property and they take so much from the poor, I'm really against all of them, that's how I feel" (C10-J1). This juror concluded that the individual "had made up this company. I felt that he was protecting himself, and that's why he had that company name" (C10-J2).

She also said that her general views of companies that own real estate, like the one in the lawsuit, were negative: "I think they let those buildings go down, and they just try to take all they can out of them moneywise. I don't think they renovate enough, they charge terribly high rents, 'cause I have a few friends who have buildings, and I know the rents on those buildings, and usually there is no water in them, no light or water, or the heat is off. You know, there's a lot of problems with these buildings. To me, those landlords just do not care" (C10-J2). Similarly, another juror observed: "The stairs that were taken out because they were damaged [years earlier] were still sitting there. You gotta excuse me, I just don't have too much love for somebody that has a house and just lets it sit and completely deteriorate" (C20-J5).

Thus, unlike most other cases in our study, jurors from the substandard building case often voiced negative comments about the owner and his business enterprises. As in the landscaping case, the business was easily identified with the owner, and the owner was present in the courtroom, so the jurors had an individual party on whom to focus their negative attention. Their overall negative perceptions of the defendant were undoubtedly linked to their judgments that he had negligently caused the worker's injury. However, whether the overall perceptions led to the specific finding of negligence or vice versa could not be determined after the fact.

The fact that some of the most negative evaluations of business litigants came in cases with small business is interesting. Some evidence suggests that people tend to have greater concerns about large businesses than small ones. But national data on convictions of businesses for wrongdoing demonstrate that problems of corporate misbehavior may be more frequent in small, as opposed to large, businesses. Data collected by the U.S. Sentencing Commission, for example, shows that more than 90% of the corporations convicted in federal courts of criminal charges are small businesses.[19] Larger businesses may be in a better position to create and staff compliance programs. Of course, it's also quite possible that larger businesses are committing just as many crimes but avoid indictment through negotiating with regulators or obtaining global settlements.

In sum, as the previous quotations illustrate, jurors occasionally had concerns about the motives of business corporations. Yet when jurors found that a corporation was liable in a civil case, they usually did not conclude that the business had maliciously intended to harm the injured workers or consumers. Nor, with the exceptions noted above, did they express particularly harsh condemnations of the individual business defendant or of the business community in general.

Results of the Project's Attitude Surveys

In attempting to discern whether prejudices or other sentiments toward business affect jury decision making, juror interviews have the obvious advantage of reporting such sentiments directly. Yet jurors may be reluctant to voice strong objections to business parties, or to acknowledge the role of anti-business prejudice in their decision making. Furthermore, people are not particularly good at definitively describing the influences on their own thought processes.

Therefore, I took several other approaches to assessing the role that attitudes toward business played in legal decision making. One method was to ask a number of questions pertaining to business in all three of the studies. The public opinion survey of 450 state residents was designed to provide a representative picture of the local public's views about business. The 269 civil jurors who sat in cases with business and corporate litigants were less representative of the community as a whole, but they were of obvious interest because they had made concrete verdicts about business negligence. The 216 mock jurors provided a useful complement to these other two data sets. As volunteers for a jury study, they represented a unique slice of community opinion.

The research used two standard questions about participants' attitudes toward business, taken from the General Social Survey, a preeminent national survey that has been conducted yearly since 1972. Using these questions allowed me to determine to what extent the participants in my studies were similar to the national public.[20] I was able to make some precise comparisons of the attitudes of participants in my studies with national attitudes toward business by plotting the responses of the participants in my studies against the results of the yearly poll.[21]

This information was important for several reasons. A crucial issue in this research project, in which data were collected from a limited area, is the extent to which the people from this area are comparable to people in other jurisdictions. A community's business climate and local corporate behavior could easily affect citizens' judgments about business in general. Were the people I studied unusually pro- or anti-business? Another purpose of the comparison with national polls is more substantive. The aim is to discover how the nation's citizens view business enterprises and the role of civil litigation in controlling corporate wrongdoing. To that end, the general questions about the business community are fleshed out with additional questions about views of business liability in specific circumstances.

Confidence in Business and Other Institutions

Respondents in my three studies possessed attitudes toward business that were generally in keeping with the national public opinion polls. They showed considerable support for the basis of capitalism, the existence of competition. When asked whether they agreed that "competition in the marketplace keeps costs down for everyone," 61% of the state poll respondents, 63% of the jurors, and 67% of the mock jurors said that they agreed. This local faith in capitalism is consistent with the findings of national polls. National surveys show that the public strongly endorses the free-enterprise system, seeing it as a necessary precondition for free and democratic government.[22] Americans express support for other cultural values underlying a capitalist economy, such as the Protestant work ethic and personal ambition.[23] Business is seen as making valuable contributions to the general welfare.[24] Seven out of ten respondents in one national poll agreed with the statement that "in general, what is good for business is good for most Americans."[25]

Compared to other societal institutions, business engenders a fair degree of confidence among the American public. In national surveys, people are more likely to express a great deal of confidence in the people running major companies than they are to express confidence in the executive branch of government, Congress, organized religion, and the press. In contrast, respondents have less confidence in major companies than they do in medicine, the scientific community, the Supreme Court, and the military.[26] Because the juror interview study included ten medical malpractice cases, it is relevant to note that the institution that engenders the greatest confidence among the American public is the medical community, which ranks above even the Supreme Court and the military.[27] Confidence in economic institutions often follows the business cycle, with lower confidence during recessions and higher confidence in boom times.[28] But even when public confidence in business is low, citizens continue to endorse the basic values of the private-enterprise system.[29]

In this project, to assess general support for and confidence in business, the respondents in all three studies were asked to indicate how confident they were in a number of institutions and professions, including big companies, small businesses, the courts, insurance companies, and lawyers. The extent to which people regard both large and small businesses with confidence is potentially significant, because such overall views might color judgments in specific instances of business wrongdoing. Because insurance companies are major players in civil litigation, lawyers try the cases, and the courts are the sites of civil trials, it was also of interest to examine confidence in them.

In all of the studies (including the national survey and all three study samples), respondents predominantly reported having a moderate degree of confidence ("only some" confidence) in the people running major companies (Figure 6-1). In the national poll, a quarter of the respondents expressed "a great deal" of confidence, about 60% of respondents reported "only some" confidence, and only about 10% said that they had "hardly any" confidence in the people running major companies.[30] The juror sample and the state public opinion sample were generally comparable to the national survey data. As in the national poll, about a quarter reported a great deal of

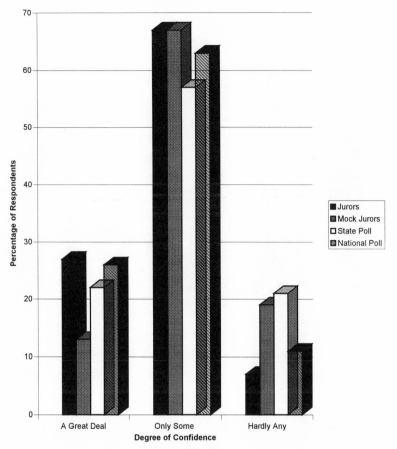

Figure 6-1

Confidence in major companies.

confidence in big business, whereas close to 60% reported some confidence. The state poll respondents were somewhat less confident about big business than the national poll participants. The mock jurors were the least confident about big business; only 13% said they had a great deal of confidence in the people running major companies. In sum, the study participants overlapped to a significant degree with national poll respondents on their degree of confidence in the people running major companies. Jurors showed somewhat more confidence in big business than participants in the other study samples but paralleled the national poll respondents. There is no clear-cut evidence of strong and consistent divergence between the attitudes of

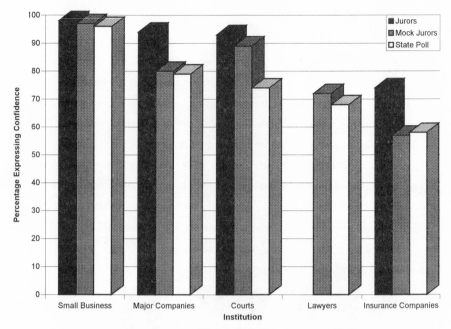

Figure 6-2

Confidence in business and the courts.

the local study participants and the attitudes of the respondents in the national poll. In particular, there is no evidence that the local participants, especially the jurors, are more pro-business than their national counterparts.

It is informative to compare the degree of confidence that people express in major companies to their expressed confidence in other institutions, including small businesses, the courts, lawyers, and insurance companies. Figure 6-2 shows the percentage of participants in each of my three studies who said they had either a great deal of confidence or only some confidence in these specific institutions. Respondents rated small businesses with the highest degree of overall confidence. Ninety-eight percent of the jurors, 97% of the mock jurors, and 96% of the state opinion poll respondents said they had at least some confidence in the people running small businesses. Although jurors were nearly as confident overall about both large and small companies, the other two groups were decidedly more positive about small businesses than about large companies. When one looks at just those who said they had "a great deal" of confidence in small business, the state poll respondents were the most enthusiastic of all. More than half the state poll participants said they had "a great deal" of confidence in small business, compared to 27% of the jurors and 30% of the mock jurors.

Lawyers and insurance companies inspired generally lower levels of confidence. No question about confidence in lawyers was asked of the jurors, but lawyers elicited little confidence among the poll respondents and the mock jurors. The percentages of state poll respondents and mock jurors expressing "hardly any" confidence in lawyers were 32% and 28%, respectively.[31] Respondents in all three studies reported the lowest degree of confidence in insurance companies. The percentages of respondents expressing "hardly any" confidence in insurance companies were 42%, 26%, and 43% for the state poll, jurors, and mock jurors, respectively.

Interestingly, jurors were much more positive about the courts than the other groups, especially the poll respondents. Jurors were twice as likely as the general public to say that they had a good deal of confidence in the people running the courts. It is worthwhile to speculate why the jurors were more confident in the courts. It is possible that people who have little or no confidence in the courts opt out of jury duty, or are eliminated through peremptory challenges or challenges for cause. A more likely possibility is that jurors have spent time in the courts and have seen their operation firsthand. They can answer in the concrete, whereas many respondents to opinion polls are forced to rely on abstractions and stereotypes. Then, too, studies have shown that people's participation as jurors leads them to hold more positive views about jury service and the courts.[32] Finally, it must be remembered that we interviewed civil jurors. They may have focused on civil litigation in answering this question, whereas other participants in the studies may have focused on the criminal justice system. In national surveys, many respondents report the view that the criminal courts are not doing a good job controlling crime.[33]

A similar phenomenon may explain why jurors were less willing than poll respondents to express "a great deal" of confidence in small business. Many of our jurors heard cases in which plaintiffs sued local or regional companies, and listened to evidence about alleged negligence in these businesses. The mock jurors debated a case of a plaintiff injured in a store. In contrast, the poll respondents had the luxury of imagining a more abstract and romanticized notion of the small entrepreneur. The different ways that large and small businesses were evaluated in the state poll is comparable to the results of national surveys. At least when they are asked about their confidence in the abstract, citizens routinely report much more confidence in small businesses than in large corporations.[34]

Business Power

The public appears to prefer the small business to the large. Studies have suggested that many citizens are concerned about the concentrations of power that characterize large business corporations. For example, in a national survey cosponsored by the *National Law Journal* and DecisionQuest, published in 1998, nearly 80% of respondents agreed that "executives of big companies often try to cover up the harm they do."[35] Another way of examining general views about business is to ask whether the respondent believes that business has too much power or too little power in society. Those who indicate that business has too much power are reflecting a negative evaluation, whereas belief that business has the right amount of power indicates contentment with the status quo. A perception of too little power suggests a favorable stance toward business.

When the three groups in my study were asked this question, we found that well over half the respondents (56% of the jurors, 67% of the mock jurors, and 65% of the state poll respondents) believed that business and industry had too much power (Figure 6-3). Jurors were the most likely of the three groups to respond that business and industry had about the right amount of power—nearly twice the rate of the public sample.

The results of a national poll (also shown in Figure 6-3) show that just under half of the respondents (46%) felt that business and industry had too much power. About half the national poll respondents asserted that business had about the right amount of power, a percentage similar to the juror sample but higher than the other two study samples. A comparison of the national poll data with the study samples suggests that in my samples people were more concerned about the amount of power that business and industry possess.

If we consider both the confidence and power questions as overall favorability indices, it is notable that although jurors rated small businesses much less positively than the state poll sample on the confidence question, they were more positive about business on the power question. Ideas about business power may relate more to fears about large companies than to small businesses, and the jurors expressed slightly more confidence in large companies than poll respondents did.

A separate question about big companies confirmed that large business enterprises worry the respondents, particularly those from the state poll. Participants were asked whether they agreed with the following statement: "As they grow bigger, companies usually get cold and impersonal in their relations with people." Fully 79% of

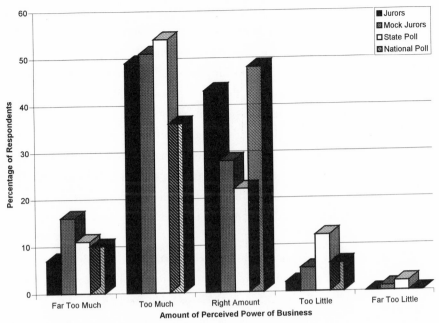

Figure 6-3

Opinions about the power of business.

the state poll respondents agreed, compared to 52% of the jurors and 64% of the mock jurors. Jurors were the most likely to disagree, with 26%, compared to 14% and 15% disagreement for the state poll and the mock jurors, respectively.

The interviews included comments by several jurors about the problems encountered in big businesses. The impersonality of the large corporation was occasionally remarked upon. Can a soulless corporation really care about its individual members? We asked one juror who decided a case involving a Fortune 500 company about her opinion of the company. She responded: "I guess I look at it as a big corporation, I don't really have any firsthand knowledge. My father-in-law used to work for an auto company, but I don't have any family members that work like in a factory or anything. I don't know, I guess I had a fairly good—I mean I know the work is hard and working on an assembly line and that kind of thing is very difficult work. I guess as all corporations, I feel a lot of times things get really impersonal. I guess it's the kind of image that you get of a big corporation. Do they really care about the individual people that are working?" (C14-J1)

During one of the asbestos jury deliberations, two automobile workers talked about their own experiences within a corporate environment. One of them recalled a statement that the other auto worker had made: "You people in here have probably never worked for the type of production company that these companies were. We have. We know what goes on. If it's anything that cuts the bottom line, boy, forget it. It's out. . . . All big corporations, look, the bottom line is profit. If it's not profitable, or anything that cuts into the profit, forget it, we don't do it" (C22-J1).

In the landscaping case (which involved a small rather than a large company), one juror expounded: "I'm kind of aggravated at these big companies today, taking people for their money and, you know, not giving them what they're supposed to have and all. And then when you call them, like [the plaintiff] did with [the company], he never returned her call. Like he didn't want nothing to do with her once he had her money" (C8-J5).

Labor's power and influence have declined substantially over the past several decades,[36] and there is comparatively little contemporary public discussion of conflict between workers and managers in businesses. Traditionally, those who adopted a pro-labor stance have tended to be anti-business. In addition, some lawsuits against businesses involve worker injuries. Under the assumption that there might be a connection between treatment of businesses in litigation and attitudes about labor, we asked the study respondents whether they thought that labor had too much power, about the right amount, or too little power. About half of the respondents from all three samples and the national poll concluded that labor still had too much power. However, the state poll respondents were more likely than the other groups to say that labor had too little power.[37]

In sum, the respondents expressed both confidence in and concerns about business, especially big business, that were similar to the views of people in other jurisdictions, although our respondents were noticeably more worried about the extent of power held by business and industry. Considering these findings, it would be hard to argue that the groups included in my study were strikingly more pro-business than participants in national surveys. The general overlap in responses is an important finding, because it indicates that the people in the current studies are not dramatically different from people in other places, at least with respect to their confidence in business. If such attitudes affect decision making about business behavior either directly or indirectly, then my study can illuminate public reactions to business wrongdoing in other jurisdictions, too. The fact that the study participants don't appear to be unusually pro-business compared to a national sample also helps to address a potential criticism of the juror interviews. As described earlier, strong expressions of hostility toward business litigants were a rarity among the jurors we interviewed. If jurors' general attitudes toward business were markedly more positive than those found in national polls, that might have been an important limitation to the findings of the study.

Opinions about Business Regulation and Litigation

The fear of concentrated business power that was found among respondents in the studies could potentially translate into assumptions that businesses are likely to engage in wrongdoing. Although many Americans are supportive of the aims of business, many citizens believe that business wrongdoing occurs frequently. They express strong desires to punish white-collar criminals.[38] Significant minorities of respondents in one poll thought that businesses, in order to turn a profit, would put workers' health and safety at risk, endanger public health, and harm the environment.[39] Perhaps because of these concerns, there is substantial public support for governmental regulation of business enterprises.[40]

In addition to assessing general views of business, it is highly relevant to try to discover how jurors and the public feel about efforts to control business practices through regulation and litigation. What are their notions about the appropriateness of the legal system to control the business community? More specific questions allowed me to explore people's views of governmental regulation of business as well as civil litigation against business corporations

One set of questions pertained to frequent subjects of business litigation, product and worker safety (Table 6-1). Substantial majorities of all three samples endorsed the value of safe products and a safe workplace. For example, 67% of the jurors, 68% of the mock jurors, and 73% of the state poll participants agreed that "ensuring the safety of products sold to the public is so important that regulations and standards cannot be too high." Majorities of all groups disagreed that requiring products to be 100% safe is just too expensive. Large majorities also believed that companies should be required to tell the public about "any possibility, however small, that its products might be unsafe." Respondents were more optimistic about worker safety: between 40% and 50% of the respondents in the three samples believed that big business is adequately concerned about the safety of its workers.[41]

Turning to questions on the impact of litigation (Table 6-2), one can see evidence that although many respondents believed in regulating business, they were worried

Table 6-1. Opinions about Product and Worker Safety

Item	SA	A	N	D	SD
Ensuring the safety of products sold to the public is so important that regulations and standards cannot be too high.					
Jurors	17	50	11	21	1
Mock Jurors	16	52	10	20	2
State Poll	11	62	9	17	1
Requiring that products be 100% safe is just too expensive.					
Jurors	4	23	15	45	13
Mock Jurors	7	21	9	47	16
State Poll	2	28	8	58	5
A company should be required to tell the public about any possibility, however small, that its products might be unsafe.					
Jurors	34	53	7	7	—
Mock Jurors	35	51	7	7	1
State Poll	26	67	1	6	—
Big business in this country is adequately concerned with the safety of its workers.					
Jurors	7	43	22	24	4
Mock Jurors	4	40	19	33	3
State Poll	1	41	11	42	6

Note: All numbers indicate the percentages of 269 jurors, 216 mock jurors, and 450 state poll respondents giving each response. Responses are: Strongly Agree (SA), Agree (A), Neither agree nor disagree (N), Disagree (D), and Strongly Disagree (SD).

about the negative effects of regulation and litigation on the vitality of business corporations. The state poll respondents were overwhelmingly in agreement that the threat of lawsuits makes it difficult to develop new products, and that the courts have meddled so much in the workplace that it is hard for a business to remain competitive. Most of those polled also believed that the government has gone too far in regulating business.

Compared to the poll participants, the jurors and the mock jurors were more positive about the role of regulation and litigation. More jurors disagreed than agreed, for instance, that courts have meddled so much that it has hurt competition. They also expressed more neutral views about whether the government has gone too far in its regulation of business. Nearly half the mock jurors disagreed that government regulation has gone too far, compared to a third of the jurors and a quarter of the poll subjects. The state poll respondents did not differ from other study participants in their general support for business, so it is likely that their responses to these questions relate more to their views of lawsuits than their views of business.

Mock jurors and state poll participants were also asked their opinions about situations in which they would or would not hold companies legally liable for product injuries. One major issue arises frequently in product liability cases. A company makes what it considers a safe product or machine, relying on current safety information and standards. However, safety standards improve over time. Should a company still be responsible for any damages resulting from the use of older products and equipment? This issue is relevant to asbestos and other product liability cases, where corporate defendants argue that the discovery of product injury occurred a substantial time after the product was introduced in the market.

Study participants thought it was appropriate to hold companies responsible for product defects even if the company relied on the best scientific information at the time (see Table 6-2). Fifty-six percent of the state poll respondents, 54% of the jurors, and 52% of the mock jurors would hold companies liable under these conditions. One interesting result came from the juror interview study. Those jurors who served on asbestos cases were more likely than other tort jurors to say that companies should *not* be responsible under these circumstances.[42] The most likely reason is that defense attorneys in the asbestos trials were partly effective in shifting jurors' views about this issue, which is central to the liability of asbestos companies. For example, some pro-defense jurors conceded that the companies had probably known about the dangers of asbestos but still questioned whether it was appropriate to punish them.

Table 6-2. Opinions about Business Regulation and Litigation

Item	SA	A	N	D	SD
The threat of lawsuits is so prevalent today that it interferes with the development of new and useful products.					
Jurors	8	46	26	20	2
Mock Jurors	13	38	19	28	2
State Poll	8	63	10	20	—
The courts have meddled so much in the workplace that many businesses are not able to remain competitive.					
Jurors	3	26	34	35	3
Mock Jurors	4	22	30	40	5
State Poll	6	55	11	26	1
The government has gone too far in regulating business and interfering with the free-enterprise system.					
Jurors	4	27	36	30	3
Mock Jurors	6	19	27	44	4
State Poll	9	55	11	24	2
Companies should not be responsible for defects in their products if they used the best scientific and safety-related information available at the time.					
Jurors	2	26	18	42	12
Mock Jurors	3	28	16	41	11
State Poll	1	35	8	51	5

	Yes	DK	No
If someone is injured by a machine or product that was made twenty years ago to the best safety standards of that time, do you think the manufacturer should be liable for damages if safety standards have improved since then?			
Mock Jurors	41	28	31
State Poll	41	11	48
National Survey (N=2,008)	40	3	57
If a smoker gets lung cancer from smoking, do you think that the cigarette companies should be liable for damages?			
Mock Jurors	13	14	72
State Poll	12	3	85

Note: All numbers indicate the percentages of 269 jurors, 216 mock jurors, and 450 state poll respondents giving each response. Responses are: Strongly Agree (SA), Agree (A), Neither agree nor disagree (N), Disagree (D), Strongly Disagree (SD), and Don't Know (DK).

The most pro-defendant juror in Case 22 acknowledged: "Their whole case was built upon that the company was aware of the hazards of asbestos and they chose not to take any steps either to correct or inform. . . . To some degree, I think the companies knew of it, but at the same token what was their limit? What was their requirement within the law? What we were asked to do is judge 1990 standards against 1950, 1960, and 1940 standards. The standards now, you can't go back and sue someone for, the standards were different then. And that's what I was having a hard time with. Because within the compounds and the framework of the United States law and government they were working within that framework, so how could I punish them now by 1990s standards? That's wrong, you shouldn't do that" (C22-J8). Another juror from the same case concurred: "I think they should have looked into it and done something about it before. But then this is the early 1990s, and we're talking about the early nineteen hundreds and into the 1930s and 1940s and 1950s. And we all know things now in the early 1990s that we didn't know in 1940, 1950. Even the companies, if they ever even knew all the possibilities and harm. . . . If they were going to get after the asbestos company, they should have gotten after the union and after the cigarette companies, because I think they all had a hand in it" (C22-J3). Thus, though the argument that asbestos manufacturers were only following the safety standards of the day was not ultimately successful in the three asbestos cases in this study (all three cases ultimately resulted in verdicts for the plaintiffs), it resonated well with a minority of pro-defense jurors.

When asked more specifically whether a manufacturer should be held liable for injuries from a machine or product made twenty years ago "to the best safety standards of that time," a plurality of the mock jurors were still willing to find the manufacturer responsible, but state poll respondents were now more likely to disagree that it was appropriate to hold the manufacturer liable. The state poll responses were similar to those obtained in a national survey conducted for Aetna Insurance Company in the 1980s.[43]

When we take both of the questions about product liability together, it seems apparent that there is some significant disagreement among the public about the fairness and appropriateness of holding companies liable under these circumstances. There is little disagreement, though, about whether to hold cigarette companies liable for smokers' lung cancer. Just 13% of the mock jurors and 12% of the state poll respondents would hold cigarette companies legally liable for smokers' lung cancer, a finding that is consistent with predominantly favorable outcomes for tobacco companies in smokers' lawsuits nationwide. These data were collected in the early 1990s, before industry documents about the health effects of tobacco were made public and before the 1999 successes in smokers' lawsuits.

In sum, although study participants expected high safety standards of business, they also expressed considerable concern about the impact of litigation on the health of business enterprises, and reported mixed reactions about the conditions under which they would hold companies liable for products and equipment.

Do General Attitudes Relate to Case Judgments?

The preceding information presents a nuanced portrait of citizens' attitudes and perceptions about business and its legal liabilities. I now turn to the question whether attitudes toward business significantly influence decision making in business cases. To look at this key question systematically across the three studies, I developed a scale, the Business Attitudes scale, to be used in statistical analysis. The Business Attitudes scale included items about confidence in business, business power, safety practices, and liability issues.[44]

Although the questions measured broad support for business entities, the scale was not a unidimensional one. Factor analysis of the scale revealed three distinct factors that were essentially the same across the three studies. The first, Business Support, appeared to tap broad confidence and support for business, especially big business. The second, Business Safety, tapped the dimension of product safety; and a third, Business Regulation, loaded most strongly and consistently on two items having to do with the regulation of the business community: the item about whether competition was effective in keeping costs down, and the item about whether businesses should be liable for products if safety standards had changed.[45]

I then tried to determine to what extent the specific judgments of business wrong-doing that the participants in the three studies made were related to their scores on the Business Attitudes scale.

The Juror Sample. As with the analysis of Litigation Crisis attitudes and case judgments, the juror sample posed the biggest challenge to the effort to determine the relationship of business attitudes and case judgments. Again I used the jury as the unit of analysis. To obtain a summary score of each jury's attitudes toward business, I calculated mean Business Attitudes scale scores for each of the juries separately, by summing the individual jurors' responses on each jury and dividing by the total number of jurors we had interviewed on each jury. I then correlated these mean judgments with the final jury awards in each of the cases, counting the defense verdicts as zero awards. The correlation between the mean Business Attitudes scale response and the jury award was −.20. Looking just at the eighteen non-medical-malpractice tort juries, which pitted individuals against business defendants, the correlation was −.29. Both correlations are in the direction one would expect if positive attitudes toward business were associated with greater leniency toward business defendants, but neither is statistically significant. As the members of the jury collectively supported business more, they showed a slight and nonsignificant tendency to decide on a lower award.[46]

State Poll Participants. In the state poll, respondents held the business defendant to the highest level of responsibility, the nonprofit to an intermediate level, and the individual to the lowest level of responsibility (see Chapter 4). If pro- or anti-business attitudes contribute to this distinctive treatment of business litigants, then we should expect to see strong relationships between the Business Attitudes scale and judgments of the negligence of the business defendant. One would expect little or no relationship between the Business Attitudes scale and case judgments when the

Table 6-3. The Relationship between Attitudes toward Business and Judgments in Business Cases

	Correlations with Business Attitudes Scale	
	State Poll	Mock Jury Study
Total Sample		
Negligence	−.17*	−.32*
Award	−.09	−.22*
Individual Defendant Condition		
Negligence	−.24*	−.31*
Award	−.13	−.30*
Business Defendant Condition		
Negligence	−.08	−.40*
Award	−.13	−.25*
Nonprofit Defendant Condition		
Negligence	−.18*	—
Award	−.02	—

*$p < .05$ (statistically significant)

defendant is not a commercial business, as in the scenarios with individual and nonprofit defendants.

The first column of Table 6-3 displays the correlations between business attitudes and case scenario judgments in the state poll study.[47] The hypothesis that business attitudes drive judgments of corporate responsibility would be supported if attitudes toward business were significantly correlated with scenario judgments in the business defendant condition. In addition, the correlations between such attitudes and scenario judgments should be stronger in the business defendant condition than in the other two conditions. However, just the reverse occurs. The relationships between the Business Attitudes scale and case judgments are not statistically significant in the business defendant condition, but judgments of negligence in the other two conditions and the full sample of participants are significantly related to attitudes toward business.

Another pattern is that all the correlations, even the statistically significant ones, are small, accounting for a very modest proportion of the variation in case judgments. This means that knowing about a respondent's attitudes toward business is not of much assistance in predicting the respondent's reaction to the scenario. One interesting fact is that the influence of business attitudes seemed to be more prominent in the worker injury case. Examining the relationships between the Business Attitudes scale and case judgments in each of the two scenarios, I discovered that the worker injury scenario was judged differently by those who had positive versus negative business attitudes, while in the slip-and-fall scenario, business attitudes played virtually no role.[48]

When I looked more closely at the relationship, it turned out that when people were asked to judge the liability of the business corporation for the worker injury, their attitudes toward business had no impact. Contrary to my expectations, it was in the individual and nonprofit defendant conditions that positive attitudes toward business helped the defendant. In other words, people who were on the whole positive toward business were less likely to find Mr. Jones or the Jones Civic Association negligent for the workers' injuries.[49] It is possible that because the individual and nonprofit defendants' situations were perceived as more ambiguous, attitudes had more of a chance to influence; or these situations may be seen as stronger violations of the ethic of personal responsibility, stretching the boundaries of organizational responsibility too far.

The Mock Jury Experiment. In the mock jury study, every mock juror filled out an individual verdict form before participating in the mock jury deliberation. Therefore, I was able to examine the relationship between their individual predeliberation views and their business attitudes.[50] These data are presented in the second column of Table 6-3.

Business attitudes were more successful in predicting the mock jurors' case judgments. The Business Attitudes scale was significantly related to both negligence judgments and awards in both the individual and business defendant conditions. In the business defendant scenario, knowing an individual mock juror's score on the Business Attitudes scale allowed us to account for about 16% of the variation in that person's negligence judgments. Similar to the state poll, the significant relationships between business attitudes and case judgments were not unique to the business defendant condition, as originally expected. Surprisingly, the Business Attitudes scale was just as likely to be a significant correlate of judgments in the individual defendant condition as in the business defendant condition.

In sum, attitudes about business play a small role in helping to shape judgments of negligence. The statistical relationships between business attitudes and case judgments are not large, but they do tend to point in the same direction across the three studies: those who are most favorable toward business are a bit more likely to take a generous view of civil defendants. To get some perspective on the relative importance of attitudes toward business, I compared their impact with the effect of Litigation Crisis attitudes, shown in Chapter 3 to be related to case judgments. Litigation Crisis attitudes had a more consistent effect. They were more regularly related to outcomes across the three studies than Business Attitudes. For the juror interview sample, a regression analysis used all thirty-six cases and the average Litigation Crisis and Business Attitudes scale scores as predictor variables. Litigation Crisis views were a significant predictor of jury awards, but Business Attitudes were not.[51]

For the mock jury study, both Business Attitudes and Litigation Crisis scores were significant predictors and had about the same ability to forecast negligence judgments.[52] For the state poll participants, across all conditions, both Business Attitudes and Litigation Crisis beliefs were similarly and significantly related to judgments of a defendant's negligence in the scenarios they evaluated.[53]

Another way of examining the relative impact of Business Attitudes and Litigation Crisis views on case outcomes is to look at how jurors in the three different asbestos trials (who viewed the issues differently and arrived at divergent awards) differed in their views of business or litigation. Were the jurors who expressed the greatest condemnation of the asbestos companies those who initially had the least favorable attitudes toward business in general? Attitudes toward business (as measured by the Business Attitudes scale) were not significantly different across the three cases,[54] even though jurors from the high-award case expressed more condemnation of the asbestos companies in the interviews. They did differ significantly, however, in their beliefs about a litigation crisis.[55] Jurors from the cases with low awards were more likely than jurors from the higher-award case to see most lawsuits as illegitimate and frivolous, as measured by the Litigation Crisis scale.

Unexpectedly, in the scenario study and the mock jury experiment, attitudes toward business had a small effect on case judgments across all the conditions, not just the conditions involving a traditional business defendant. Thus, high scores on the Business Attitudes scale were associated with a general tendency to find for the defendant rather than a targeted tendency to find for business defendants. Why? One reason may be linked to the fact that even the individual and nonprofit case scenarios involved some activity that could be broadly construed as a business activity. For instance, in the mock jury study, jurors in the individual condition read a scenario that involved a garage sale at a private home. This was not a traditional business activity, but the home owner could expect to make some money. The individual scenario in the worker injury case involved a home owner hiring people to do yard work, in which the home owner adopted (albeit in a limited and temporary way) the role and responsibilities of a business owner toward his or her employees.

What Shapes Attitudes toward Business?

Another reason that business attitudes may relate to judgments across all conditions and not just in lawsuits against business defendants lies in the fact that the business attitudes measured here, although summarized with a single scale value, are not unidimensional. Furthermore, they do not exist in a vacuum. They are related to an entire host of beliefs, attitudes, and life experiences. Perhaps it is these other attitudes that are really at work in shaping the individual's judgments of civil litigation. For this reason, it is relevant to report what personal characteristics and other attitudes appear to be associated with attitudes toward business.

In regression analyses, three factors were significant predictors of scores on the Business Attitudes scale in all three study samples: educational attainment, self-described political orientation, and gender. People with higher levels of education tended to be more positive about business than people with lower levels of education; conservatives were more favorable than liberals were; and men were more supportive of business than women were.[56] A few other factors were significant predictors in one study or another, but these three appeared to be the most consistent variables associated with favorable attitudes toward business.[57] National studies have also found higher education and political conservatism to be associated with more positive views of business.[58]

On the whole, the material presented in this chapter tends to disconfirm the worst fears of the business community that jurors are strongly anti-business. Jurors' general attitudes about business are generally positive. The ways they discussed their cases reflected more neutral than negative appraisals of business and corporate defendants. It would be unwarranted to conclude, however, that anti-business prejudice never courses through the veins of civil jurors. Three cases in particular, including one asbestos case and two small business cases, appeared to generate substantial negative sentiment among the jurors hearing the case. And although negative views were not expressed consistently in the other cases, there was a smattering of negative commentary about business parties.

The empirical data suggest that a combination of attitudes toward business—including general support for business, attitudes about safety practices, and beliefs about the need for business regulation—can have a small effect on judgments in business cases. Attitudes toward business matter a little bit, then. They matter in cases where the facts are ambiguous, and they matter in some types of cases (not always those involving business defendants) and not others.

A mock jury study published in 1998 shows that in a product liability case purposefully constructed with ambiguous evidence, attitudes toward business can help to shape case judgments. The relationships were modest but consistent with the direction expected from the results presented in this chapter. In that study, mock jurors who were more favorable to business in general and who were more concerned about product safety were also more likely to find the defendant liable.[59] Yet the authors emphasize that by combining all the attitudinal and background variables (including these business-related attitudes), they were able to improve their prediction of juror liability judgments by only a small amount. One of the strongest predictors was a single item that, I would argue, captured the mock jurors' views of litigation crisis: "When plaintiffs sue in a lawsuit and receive money damages, would you say that in general they receive too much or too little?"[60] As in my project, such views about the legitimacy of civil litigation were linked to case-specific judgments.

The discovery of some statistically significant relationships between general attitudes toward business and case decisions is in line with the findings of Chapter 5 that participants' views about the appropriate standard for corporate behavior were associated with their decisions in particular cases. Not surprisingly, scores on the Business Attitudes scale were related to judgments about corporate standards. Nevertheless, it is important to note the difference between higher expectations of business and anti-business prejudice. Even if an individual has a good deal of confidence in business and believes that business is a worthwhile endeavor, he or she might still feel that the profit-making nature of the business enterprise, or the potential reach and impact of its business activities, require it to follow special rules and standards of behavior that do not apply to individuals. For example, recall the corporate manager who served as a juror in the paint-store case. He insisted that the store bear a larger share of the responsibility than the mother because it was in a better position to know the dangers in the place of business. His Business Attitudes scale score was several points higher than that of the average juror, yet he still favored a broad interpretation of the store's responsibility.

It is always possible that jurors might have underreported their biases in order to appear fair. In addition, our group of cases did not involve highly notorious large corporations. For example, public opinion polling has demonstrated that a significant proportion of the public holds negative opinions about multinational oil companies, and if cases involving them had been included in the juror interview study, it is quite possible that jurors' reactions to the liability issues would have reflected their generally negative views. There could also be certain types of cases or issues that rouse public passions against business but that were not tapped in this project. For example, given strong public insistence on environmental safety, corporate defendants in trials charging environmental pollution could well encounter a jury pool predisposed against them. Finally, answers to very specific questions tapping attitudes toward the key issues in particular cases might well have shown some relationships with negligence judgments. Those kinds of questions, though, do not speak to the charge of general anti-business prejudice.

These limitations notwithstanding, the data presented here do provide some reassurance that anti-business prejudice is not as rampant as many corporate executives and their attorneys assume. Attitudes toward business do play some role, but probably not the major one that would have been expected by the business leaders quoted at the beginning of the chapter.

7

THE
ROBIN HOOD JURY

Perhaps no belief about the civil jury in business cases is as widespread as the assumption that it approaches its task as a modern-day Robin Hood, bent on transferring wealth from the rich defendant to the poor plaintiff. Lawyers, business leaders, and policy makers all consider it a truism that juries take the finances of business corporations into account both when deciding liability and when determining how much to award in damages. Jurors are said to penalize corporations for their financial resources, using them as deep pockets from which to compensate undeserving plaintiffs. Writer Peter Huber claims that juries, along with some judges, are "committed to running a generous sort of charity. If the new tort system cannot find a careless defendant after an accident, it will often settle for a merely wealthy one."[1] After a civil jury rendered a multi-billion-dollar punitive damage award against a Louisiana railroad for a chemical fire, corporate defense advocate Victor Schwartz complained: "This case shows that our system has turned into the world's richest roulette wheel."[2] A public service missive from the Mobil Corporation claims: "Jury awards for punitive damages grab headlines as they've spiraled into the millions, not to mention billions of dollars. . . . Plaintiffs' attorneys trolling the waters in the hope of landing a big one, have cast their nets in an ever widening circle that promises to choke business and clog the courts. . . . Defendants with seemingly deep pockets (big companies, professionals, etc.) are paralyzed by the threat of huge jury awards and/or the likelihood of paying damages grossly out of proportion to their share of the blame."[3]

The deep-pockets hypothesis appears to be bolstered by some of the findings of systematic analyses of jury verdicts and awards in corporate cases. In several studies, jury awards to plaintiffs who sued corporations were higher, on the whole, than awards to plaintiffs who sued other individuals.

Researchers at the Rand Corporation conducted one of the first studies documenting this phenomenon. They analyzed jury verdicts in Cook County (Chicago),

Illinois, over two decades from 1959 to 1979, preceding the contemporary period that has given rise to perceptions of litigation crisis.[4] The proportion of business defendants in civil jury trials remained stable over that time period, accounting for about a quarter of all the defendants who faced the civil jury. When the awards for plaintiffs who sued corporations were compared to awards for those who sued individuals, some remarkable differences emerged. The median award against an individual defendant was $5,800, whereas the median award against a corporate defendant was $24,500. Similarly, the average awards were $18,500 and $120,800 for individual and corporate defendants, respectively.[5] Some of the difference in corporate versus individual defendant awards was attributable to the type of case and the severity of the plaintiff's injury. For example, on average, automobile accidents netted lower awards than workplace injuries. However, when the researchers introduced some general controls for case type and injury severity, they found that corporate defendants still paid more than individual defendants did.[6]

Examining juries nationwide in the 1990s, the Civil Trial Court Network Project also showed striking differences in the awards against individual versus business defendants.[7] In one analysis, they compared tort cases in which individuals sued other individuals with tort cases in which individuals sued businesses. The overall win rate was about the same, but the awards were different. The median award for lawsuits against individuals was $22,400, whereas the median award for lawsuits against businesses was more than three times greater, at $69,300. The percentage of awards higher than $1 million also differed, with just 3% of individual tort defendants but 8% of business tort defendants facing judgments over the million-dollar mark.

It is tempting to conclude that these substantial differences between awards in cases with individual defendants and those in cases with corporate defendants show that jurors operate with a deep-pockets mentality, penalizing businesses for their greater financial resources. Before leaping to that conclusion, however, consider that the research in this book has already documented divergent ways that jurors judge individual and corporate liability. Those differences appear to arise not primarily from jurors' hostility toward business but rather from their distinctive standards for business defendants. A considerable number of jurors, and a majority of the public, believe that it is appropriate to hold business corporations to higher levels of responsibility.

Many scholars have pointed to the danger of relying on aggregate statistics like average jury awards to make claims about the psychology of jury decision making.[8]

We must take into account the likelihood that the cases against individuals and businesses differed in a number of other ways, including the extent and type of injuries, the number and type of claims, legal rules, defenses, and settlement practices.[9] Arguably, the most important factor is likely to be the process of settling cases. Different settlement practices by individuals and businesses could account for much of the observed differences in awards. If business defendants routinely settled most small-stakes cases but individual defendants did not, that would leave a range of low- to high-stakes cases for individual defendants but predominantly high-stakes cases for business defendants. Under these circumstances, contrasting individual and corporate cases would be like comparing apples and oranges.[10] Different award judgments would be reasonable in light of the expected value of the cases. Therefore, it is premature at this point to use the award differences to conclude that juries operate with deep pockets.

Legal theory and practice offer conflicting advice about how the resources of a civil defendant are to be considered in litigation. On the one hand, jury instructions about compensatory damages clearly indicate that jurors are not to consider the defendant's financial wealth in arriving at award amounts. On the other hand, some influential tort theorists and certain legal rules appear, implicitly or explicitly, to endorse the notion of distributing the costs of injuries to those who can afford it. Yale Law School professor George Priest describes how early tort theorists promoted cost internalization, that is, charging the costs of injuries to the activities generating them. For instance, under cost internalization, the cost of a worker's injuries in manufacturing a product would be borne by the manufacturer and not the worker. Tort scholars who favored this practice perceived twin benefits. It created incentives for manufacturers to modify the production process to reduce injuries or to seek out safer production alternatives. It also shifted the injury cost from the typically less advantaged worker to the business corporation. Thus, some early tort theorists envisioned the tort system as something of a social compensation scheme, spreading losses across the population and to those who could better afford it rather than leaving the financial burden on the shoulders of the injured.[11]

Tort theories allowing joint and several liability, and proposals for a strict liability rule in the case of defective products, are linked to the idea that defendants are typically in a better position than the injured plaintiffs to handle the expenses associated with the injury. As California Supreme Court Justice Roger Traynor observed in a case supporting strict liability: "Those who suffer injury from defective products are unprepared to meet its consequences. The cost of an injury and the loss of time or health may be an overwhelming misfortune to the person injured, and a needless one, for the risk of injury can be insured by the manufacturer and distributed among the public as a cost of doing business."[12]

Peter Huber observed with considerable cynicism the role of financial wealth in the expansion of liabilities in tort law: "The logic was always the same: People don't kill people; guns, cars, appliances, and airplanes do, or, more precisely, the sellers or manufacturers of those sometimes-lethal objects do the killing. And if not the product itself, then one of its constituent parts, perhaps. Sooner or later, somewhere or other in this kind of chain, there is bound to be a solvent defendant able to foot the bill and likely to be improved by the chastening experience of a lawsuit."[13]

Whether or not jurors consider a defendant's finances in assessing compensatory damages, jurors are specifically instructed in punitive damages cases to take the wealth of the defendant into account to ensure that the punitive damage award will function as an effective deterrent. Dorsey Ellis's review of judicial opinions and academic articles on punitive damages concluded that judges and scholars regularly justified punitive damages not only on the grounds of punishment but also on the basis of deterrence.[14] The effective deterrence of financially strong corporations may require amounts that go beyond the actual damages suffered by the plaintiff, hence the perceived need to inform the jury of the defendant's financial wealth. Whether the possibility of unlimited punitive damages promotes either specific or general deterrence remains the subject of heated debate.[15]

When we think about the jury's task in damage awards from a psychological perspective, it seems possible that jurors could take an equitable approach, rendering awards that vary depending upon relative resources, rather than a strictly equal approach, with awards that are uninfluenced by resources. Psychologists have discovered that people frequently allocate rewards for the completion of tasks equitably, in line with individuals' contributions or resources. In other instances people distribute the same reward to all participants regardless of their contributions or characteristics.[16] Both equality and equity are widely shared social norms. The prevalence of the norm of equity suggests that jurors may consider relative resources as they decide on jury awards.

Speaking of equity, when critics and scholars discuss deep pockets they frequently focus on the situation of a wealthy defendant. But the empty pockets of a defendant could be more salient. If resources do affect jury awards, it could be because jurors *discount* the award against an individual defendant rather than *inflate* the award against a business defendant. Chin and Peterson's research produced evidence of not only higher awards against corporate and government defendants compared to individual defendants, but also lower awards against black defendants compared to white defendants in similar trials. Chin and Peterson observe that the low awards against black defendants "may represent a further aspect of the 'deep pocket' effect, where jurors' perception of defendants' resources influences the size of awards against defendants. If juries perceive blacks as having fewer resources, they might shift less of the burden of damages to black defendants."[17]

In one sense, deep pockets and empty pockets are two sides of the same coin. Yet an emphasis on empty pockets, that is, defendants who are unable to pay to make the plaintiff whole, might alert us to cases in which an equity rule best accounts for jury awards. It is possible that the awards of plaintiffs who sue business corporations might actually be closer to pure levels of compensation. The presumably ample resources or insurance of a business corporation may free jurors to consider only the needs of the plaintiff to be made whole. In contrast, when two individuals are parties to a lawsuit (or when a plaintiff sues a small business), jurors may balance the equities and gauge an award's potentially deleterious consequences on the defendant.

There are, then, some reasons to think that jurors might take the defendant's resources into account in arriving at damage awards. Nevertheless, the results of my research provide mixed evidence concerning the deep-pockets effect.

Background on Jury Awards

When a civil jury determines that the defendant is negligent, it arrives at a monetary award. Most awards consist of what are called compensatory damages, the amount needed to make the plaintiff whole. Compensatory damages for a person suffering a personal injury that interfered with the ability to hold a job, for example, might include lost wages, foregone future raises and promotions, and past and future medical expenses. Compensatory damages may also include payment for the plaintiff's pain and suffering, a component that has engendered controversy and legal reform.[18] In a small number of cases, usually those in which a defendant is alleged to have acted in an intentionally harmful way, the jury is also asked to consider awarding punitive damages. The legally sanctioned purposes of punitive damages include both punishment and deterrence.

Discovering how jurors use information about the financial resources of business defendants is complicated by the limited amount of empirical knowledge about how jurors consider *any* factors in arriving at damage awards. Even though there has been a fair amount of controversy on the topic, scholars have only recently begun systematic study of how jurors decide on awards. Writing a review of the modest research literature in 1989, Professor Edith Greene observed that "very little is known about the ways in which jurors attempt to compensate a plaintiff for injuries that result from the defendant's actions."[19] A decade later, more information about jury awards is available, but the process remains a largely mysterious one.

The Chicago Jury Project first studied the civil jury in the 1950s. Employing a questionnaire sent to judges presiding in civil jury trials, the researchers inquired about the jury's verdict and award, and also what the judge would have decided if the same case had been a bench trial. The judges reported that they would have reached the same verdict as the civil jury 78% of the time, a high rate of agreement. In contrast, judges often disagreed with the specific amounts of jury awards. Jurors awarded more than judges would have in 52% of the cases in which they agreed on liability, and awarded less in 37% of such cases. On the average, jury awards were higher than the judge's preferences about 20% of the time overall.[20] Harry Kalven, Jr., speculated about the causes of the divergent awards (such as the jury's taking the attorney's fee into account), but because he and his colleague Hans Zeisel undertook only preliminary analysis of the civil jury data, they did not produce a systematic picture of the factors that led to higher or lower awards.[21]

In the 1980s and 1990s there have been several large-scale archival studies of jury awards, including the aforementioned projects that found differences in awards for individual and corporate defendants. These and other studies indicate that jury awards are quite variable. On the positive side, there is evidence of what Professor Michael Saks and his colleagues label vertical equity, in that awards are roughly proportional to the seriousness of injury.[22] However, Saks and his colleagues also point to the existence of horizontal inequity, referring to plaintiffs whose injuries appear to be generally comparable but whose awards differ. Furthermore, and paradoxically, plaintiffs who have suffered the most severe injuries, and thus who appear in most desperate need of compensatory damages, tend to be undercompensated compared to less severely injured parties.[23] Those who have suffered small losses tend to be overcompensated relative to those with larger losses. Scholars offer various explanations for the under- and overcompensation patterns. Peter Bell and Jeffrey O'Connell, for example, suggest that people with minor versus major injuries possess different bargaining strengths; those who are seriously injured likely have critical medical and nursing-care needs that make the roulette of trial undesirable.[24] Thus, although some factors, such as seriousness of injury, are strong predictors of jury awards, other unknown variables may also influence the actual amounts. The question we turn to now is whether a corporate defendant's financial strength is one of the variables that affects the jury's award.

A Direct Test of the Deep-Pockets Hypothesis

In real life, the fact that a defendant is a business corporation and the fact that it has substantial financial resources cannot be separated. Therefore, we don't know to what extent the higher jury awards against business defendants are driven by their judgments of business liability, the typically greater financial resources of the corporation, or some entirely separate aspect of the case. It's hard to tease out the causal role of financial wealth in the real world of jury decision making. I shall relate jurors' assessments of how they were affected by the defendant's finances, but relying on juror accounts alone has limits, too. It is difficult to estimate the impact of a specific factor on decision making. Simply because jurors mention a defendant's finances in their deliberations, for instance, is not unequivocal evidence that finances influenced the award. It could be incidental to the decision, an argument advanced to support a position based on other evidence.

In the research laboratory, it is possible to improve on real life, at least for the purpose of testing whether information about finances does affect the jury. In the scenario experiment conducted as part of the state poll, participants read a scenario about either a slip-and-fall accident or a worker injury, with a defendant described as an individual, a nonprofit organization, or a for-profit business corporation.

To test the deep-pockets hypothesis, I varied information about the financial resources of the three types of defendants. In one set of conditions, respondents learned nothing about the defendant's finances; in a second set of conditions, respondents learned that the defendant had low financial resources; and in a third set of conditions, respondents learned that the defendant had high financial resources. There were nine versions in all, with the financial resources of each type of defendant presented in these three different ways.

If the deep-pockets explanation is true, then there should be significant differences in awards (and, perhaps, even in negligence judgments) for the three conditions varying financial information. When no information is presented, if respondents hold different assumptions about the financial worthiness of individuals, nonprofit groups, and business corporations, then their awards should track their assumptions. So, if people assume that businesses are richer than individuals and they follow a deep-pockets approach, then the awards against business corporations will be higher than the awards against individuals. But when actual financial information about the defendant's status is presented, defendants with low assets should have to pay less than defendants with high assets. Therefore, if jurors draw on a deep-pockets ideology, awards should be smaller in the low-assets condition and larger in the high-assets condition, regardless of whether the defendant is an individual, a nonprofit organization, or a business corporation.

In my scenario experiment, however, no significant differences in negligence or awards due to financial resources emerged. The average award recommendations were virtually identical regardless of whether people were given no information, information that the defendant had low assets, or information that the defendant had high assets.[25] Similarly, average negligence judgments were virtually identical.[26] To examine the possibility that the deep-pockets effect occurs only with business corporations, I also analyzed the impact of finances on negligence and award judgments in the business cases alone. The pattern was the same: the financial information had no effect on either negligence or award decisions.

As expected, the information about finances affected the perceived likelihood that the defendant could pay the award.[27] In the high-assets condition, participants were more likely to say that the defendant would be able to pay the award, compared to participants in the other two conditions.[28] This is important, because it indicates that people heard and understood the financial information, even though it didn't influence their judgments about an appropriate award.

From a scientific point of view, it is essential to be cautious in interpreting a finding of "no difference."[29] Even if an effect is substantial, it might not be detected in one research project. In any single study, there can be a multitude of other reasons why no differences are observed. In studying factors that affect jury awards, there is the additional problem that jury awards are highly variable and it may be hard to discern the impact of a particular factor.

Fortunately, several other studies have now examined the deep-pockets hypothesis. The findings of these other projects are consistent with mine. In Robert MacCoun's study, citizens from a California jury pool assessed six different personal injury cases in which the defendant was described as a poor individual, a rich individual, or a corporation. People did not differentiate between wealthy and poor defendants in their liability or award judgments.[30]

Neil Vidmar's extensive project on medical malpractice juries undertook two variations on a test of the deep-pockets explanation of jury awards in medical malpractice cases. In the first study, a group of 147 jurors was presented with the case of a woman who had broken a leg and suffered complications. The broken leg was the result (in one set of conditions) of medical negligence or (in another set of conditions) of an automobile accident. Furthermore, the negligence was attributed to either one person, two people, or a hospital or corporation. The jurors were told that negligence and the amount of compensatory damages were undisputed, and that their sole task was to decide on a figure for pain and suffering. Vidmar reasoned that if a deep-pockets approach accounted for medical malpractice jury awards, then the awards should be higher for medical malpractice than for the auto accident; furthermore, it should be lowest in the case of the single defendant and highest for the hospital and corporate defendants, with their greater resources. In a result consistent with my research, however, Vidmar found that awards did not increase with the presumed financial resources of the defendant.[31] A second, similar study by Vidmar also found no significant differences in awards for pain and suffering in auto negligence versus medical malpractice cases. In the second study, the participants were asked directly whether the defendant's ability to pay was considered in arriving at an award. Fully 70% of the participants said no. Of those who said they did consider the defendant's ability to pay, more than half said they would have decreased the award if they thought the defendant could not pay or there was no insurance to cover the award.[32]

Vidmar points out that his null results should be interpreted with some caution, because the awards were highly variable, making it more difficult to detect a deep-pockets effect. In addition, he varied the type of cases and defendants rather than their net worth. Nevertheless, Vidmar's basic results are consistent with mine and MacCoun's and add to some increasing doubts about the veracity of the deep-pockets theory of jury awards.

A recent mock jury experiment of a complex product liability dispute varied net worth, as my project did, and found no support for the deep-pockets effect.[33] In this project, the net worth of a company was made known to mock jurors before they deliberated on compensatory damage awards. One set of juries learned that the company was valued at $11 million, whereas the other set heard that the company's value was much higher, at $611 million. Yet those who heard about the higher net worth did not reach higher compensatory damage awards.[34] The collected experiments suggest that when other factors are held constant and financial resources are varied, financial resources have no discernible impact on the size of awards given by mock jurors.

The experiments are optimal for disentangling some of the potential influences on jury awards. An experimental design allows us to make claims about the causal role (or lack thereof) of financial information. Nevertheless, the nature of laboratory research could conceivably limit the impact of financial information. In the fuller context of a trial, with greater background knowledge about both the defendant and the plaintiff, the desire to compensate the plaintiff fully or to consider the financial equities of a judgment against the defendant may be more pressing. Another factor not explicitly varied in the experiments was the likelihood of insurance, a topic frequently brought up in juror interviews and in mock jury discussions. Let's turn to the richer but messier world of the juror interviews for a complementary perspective.

Looking for Evidence of Deep Pockets in the Juror Interviews

In the juror interviews, we provided multiple opportunities for jurors to discuss the effects of the financial wealth of the parties on their decision making. In every interview, whether the jury had decided in favor of the plaintiff or not, we probed what evidence was presented about the finances of each party in the lawsuit, and whether jurors had learned about any insurance coverage of the plaintiff or the defendant. We asked what impact their knowledge about financial resources or insurance had on them as they considered the case. With the members of juries who reached a monetary award, we asked specifically whether certain issues were discussed or considered by the jury in arriving at its award, including the facts that the defendant could afford a large amount, that the defendant was a corporation, or that the plaintiff or defendant had insurance.

The first point to be made is that there is a striking asymmetry in the evidence presented about plaintiffs and the evidence presented about defendants. Jurors generally learned a fair amount about the finances of the plaintiff and very little about those of the business defendant. The plaintiff's occupation, salary, and medical and other living expenses were often included in the trial as legally relevant evidence pertaining to compensatory damages. Expert economic testimony for plaintiffs suing for lost wages typically included salary histories and projections of future salary increases. Assessments about the plaintiff's finances were presented, directly through evidence and also indirectly through inferences. For example, in a case involving a knee injury, jurors concluded that the plaintiff was in financial straits: "At some point in the trial [the plaintiff's] finances were talked about in detail. It was mentioned that she was in need of money not because she was so deeply in debt, that wasn't talked about, but because she was separated from her husband for eight or nine years, she was having to support herself" (C2-J1).

In contrast to the voluminous information about the plaintiff's financial situation, jurors reported that they usually learned little, if anything, about the financial resources of the business defendants. The ghostly status of the corporate entity carried through to the financial domain. Very little economic information about business defendants was submitted as evidence at trial, leaving jurors to speculate about the financial health of the company on the basis of its size and the type of business. Even so, the relative financial resources of the parties were probably obvious. Jurors routinely assumed that individual plaintiffs were less well off than the doctors or businesses they sued. In the cases in which business plaintiffs sued business defendants, there were substantial differences in the size of the companies and hence their relative financial resources.

Whatever their views of the comparative financial strengths of the plaintiff and the defendant, only a minority of jurors acknowledged that these financial disparities influenced how they thought about the case or arrived at an award. In reflecting on the factors that their jury considered in arriving at an award, most jurors I interviewed said that finances were not a significant factor. The law specifically instructs jurors to consider the defendant's financial strength in cases with a punitive damages phase. Therefore, I shall present data for cases with and without punitive damages separately.

Most directly linked to the deep-pockets hypothesis are jurors' reports of whether they had considered that the defendant could afford a large amount. The majority (77%) of the jurors in cases without punitive damages said that their juries neither discussed nor considered whether the defendant could afford a large amount during the award phase of the deliberation. Eighteen percent said that they had considered it, whereas another 5% had discussed it but had not used it in decision making.

The fact that the defendant was a corporation was also considered by only a minority of jurors during the award discussion. For jurors who decided cases without punitive damages, the majority, again 77%, stated that their jury had not discussed or

considered the fact that the defendant was a corporation during the award deliberations. Sixteen percent said that their jury considered the fact that the defendant was a
corporation during the award phase of the deliberation, and another 7% stated that
their jury had discussed the fact that the defendant was a corporation but did not use
the information in arriving at their award. The finding that a minority of jurors took the
defendant's corporate identity into account in the award phase is consistent with the
pattern (described in Chapter 4) that only a minority of jurors reported being influenced by corporate identity in their decision making.

As expected, the jurors' reports about the extent to which they considered the
defendant's ability to pay were quite different in the punitive damages cases. Twenty-
eight jurors from cases with punitive damages award discussions reported on the
factors they considered in arriving at an award. Among these jurors, seventeen (61%)
said that they had considered whether the defendant could afford to pay a large
amount, and another nine (32%) said that their jury had discussed but had not used
the defendant's ability to pay. Just two jurors (or 7%) from punitive damages cases
said that they had not discussed or considered the defendant's ability to pay.

Comments from jurors across a range of cases flesh out the reasoning behind the
majority view that financial differences between the parties were largely irrelevant.
They reportedly focused on whether or not negligence was proven, on plaintiff need,
and on fairness issues.

Jurors who awarded a substantial sum in a dental malpractice case made characteristic remarks. Asked whether they assumed that the doctors had more money than
the plaintiffs, jurors routinely replied yes, "of course I assumed that" (C16-J4). Yet
follow-up questions about the impact of this financial disparity resulted in denials:
"As a layperson I would assume that the oral surgeon would make more money, and
close behind him would be the orthodontist or they might even be equal. I don't know
what they make. And [the plaintiff] would be last. . . . But that had nothing to do with
the decision" (C16-J1).

In a medical malpractice case, a juror expressed the equality perspective suc-
cinctly: "Just because you can afford more than I can afford doesn't mean that you
should pay more than I do. It's not fair" (C23-J2). In a contract case involving a
relatively small company, jurors also reported that the financial situation of the
parties did not affect them: "No, we really didn't take that into consideration about
what they could afford or not afford. . . . If anything, we didn't think either one of them

could afford to pay anything, I guess, not really. . . . We didn't care whether they could pay it or not" (C30-J1). This juror went on to say that if the company had been larger, it is possible that the award might have been larger. Other jurors from the same case confirmed that insurance was not mentioned in any way in their discussions.

In a tort case involving a company truck that hit and injured the plaintiff, jurors learned a fair amount about the plaintiff, who was asking for lost wages. "The company we learned nothing, of the plaintiffs, we learned everything" (C18-J7). The plaintiffs were not well off. Yet, characteristically, jurors stated that the poor financial state of the plaintiffs, and the difference in presumed financial resources between the defendant company and the plaintiff's family, "didn't influence me" (C18-J1).

In the knee injury case, although the jury learned of the plaintiff's poor financial situation, jurors stated that the financial status of the plaintiff was not considered: "No, basically, we just zeroed in on the injury, how much we felt the injury was worth," commented one juror (C2-J2). "No, I didn't consider that at all," said another (C2-J3). A third juror, however, observed that the evidence of poverty could act as a two-edged sword. She favored an award and said that the relative resources of the plaintiff and the defendant did not personally affect her. But other jurors appeared to downgrade the plaintiff's request because she appeared needy:

Interviewer: What did you learn about the financial resources of the parties, beginning with the plaintiff?

Juror: It was brought up that she was made to look like she needed money.

Interviewer: Okay, and how did that affect the way you thought about the case?

Juror: It didn't affect me as much as it affected some of the other jurors. I think you're entitled to a fair settlement whether you're rich or whether you're poor. I don't think that should have anything to do with it. And I firmly believed she was hurt and I firmly believed she suffered hurt from her injury, and that should have been the basis of how much we decided to give her. Not the fact that she needed money or that this is a big corporation, they could have given her money or anything like that.

Interviewer: But the other jurors viewed it as she needed money and is doing this to try and get money?

Juror: Yes, yes. . . . The older men on the jury, there were at least three of them, felt that she was doing it for money. That she should be awarded some settlement, but the injury wasn't great enough to award her that much. (C2-J5)

In an asbestos case, one of the most plaintiff-blaming jurors saw the plaintiffs as relatively comfortable. I asked her:

Interviewer: Did you think that because you saw the plaintiffs as pretty well off it was less necessary to give them an award from the companies? Or, did you feel like the companies have plenty of money, so they could afford to help out these plaintiffs?

Juror: No, I didn't feel as though the companies should have to help them out. They went to work. They got their salary. I think they were told they could get a big lump sum, because I felt as though [the plaintiff's attorney] has made a fortune off asbestosis cases.

Interviewer: If the plaintiffs had been really poor, would that have changed your thinking at all?

Juror: No, I don't think so. I really don't. (C4-J1)

In an auto accident case a juror specifically argued against the deep-pockets approach, emphasizing the fairness of treating parties equally: "I just think that just because [corporations] have the more money, and the more financial background, and stability, I don't think that is any more reason to make them pay out any more money than a person paying out of their own pocket. You know, especially if the injury in both cases is the same" (C35-J4).

One of the auto accident cases involved a man hit by a fuel truck. The plaintiff and his wife, both African American, were seen as "living pretty close to the edge" (C31-J2). Their poor financial picture led one juror to state: "The worst thing was, and this has nothing to do with it except it was my opinion, I felt the plaintiff and his wife probably could use the money. More money than we gave them. Just for living, you know. But, and that made me feel bad that we didn't award more, but that was not the point of the whole thing, you know. So we couldn't do that. And that way I felt bad for [the plaintiff]" (C31-J2). Another juror from the fuel truck case also denied that the financial status of the parties was taken into account in arriving at an award: "No. We took mostly into account what the economist had said. How much it would take for them to have that type of care" (C31-J3).

Asked about the impact of the doctor's financial resources in a medical malpractice case, one juror reported: "All twelve of us, I think we did what was right, not just because this guy had a lot of money. . . . I kind of felt that [the plaintiff] should have got something, but you couldn't have gave him something without making this guy guilty of malpractice, and that wasn't right" (C33-J1).

In another medical malpractice case, one juror said that the doctor's income was bound to be higher than the plaintiff's was, but she did not consider it. She noted, however: "I think there was a certain amount of jealousy too, a little. Some of the jurors did not want [the plaintiff, the mother of a young man who had died] to get any sort of a sizable award. . . . She had received an award from the hospital and the anesthesiologist. They settled out of court and they settled before it really went to jury trial. And I think that one of the jurors felt that she had already received enough" (C19-J1). A similar sentiment was voiced in an asbestos case:

Juror: I think they were compensated by [their employer] through workman's comp.
Interviewer: Did that make a difference to you that they'd already been compensated before the trial even started?
Juror: Not really. I mean you do think in the back of your mind like, "oh, [your company's] paid you." They were suing like fifteen different companies; we only saw these five. They settled with all the other ones, and we were wondering like, did they get enough money from it? But then you also have to wonder, look what this stuff has done to their body. (C26-J7)

In sum, those who reported that they did not consider the defendant's financial resources justified their approach on fairness grounds, or maintained that their focus was on the negligence of the parties or specific amounts needed for compensation rather than on how much a defendant could afford. Several comments reflected concern that plaintiffs might be unjustly overcompensated, relative to their injuries, through multiple lawsuits and settlements. These perceptions are more consistent with attitudes concerning a litigation explosion than with Robin Hood tendencies.

Jurors' Concerns about Excessive Awards

In discussing whether they were affected by the financial disparities between plaintiff and defendant, a number of jurors saw fit to discuss their perceptions of the litigation explosion and the existence of many excessive awards. In line with jurors' concerns about the legitimacy of plaintiff claims (see Chapter 2), jurors occasionally talked about the *plaintiff's* (rather than the juror's) perception of the corporation as a deep pocket: "I think that she feels [as] if it's an organization [that] ought to pay for this, there's more responsibilities, more money behind this organization than is an individual, and this is why she's pressing for these extra dollars down the line. . . . She seemed to be exaggerating, and taking advantage of the fact that it's an organization that's gonna be paying these things, instead of an individual, so let's hit the organization. Let's get the biggest amount of monies" (C6-J5).

In a case involving a woman hit by a fire truck, one juror reported that she entered the jury room believing that the plaintiff deserved an award, but only the minimum necessary award. The plaintiff's expert economist, in this juror's view, had come up with a figure that was too large. "In my past history, I have felt that whiplash cases had astronomical awards. Ridiculous. Absolutely couldn't see how they were justified. And I thought, 'We'll have no such nonsense in this case. I won't stand for that.' But I realized that we were all pretty much of the same mind, that no one was going for the large award" (C6-J4). Other effects of high awards were also noted: "I'm very concerned about our health today, what you're paying for health. And this is what's going to happen also for our car insurance. People are able now to go into court and sue for a million dollars. Well, eventually you and I are going to pay for those kinds of things. That's my feeling on this. Are we going to just knock all the corporations out, or are we going to make them give one person a million dollars for something? I think they should be justly awarded, but I didn't think they deserved that kind of money" (C22-J3).

Jurors frequently brought up their concerns about the impact of jury awards on business costs and insurance rates (see Chapter 3). Illustrating that theme, one juror reported that he had to convince some of the older people on the jury that whether or not an insurance company paid the award should not affect the size of the award: "It was like they were basing it on well, the insurance companies are going to pay it anyway. And we're saying wait a minute. . . . If this was coming out of your pocket, what would you do? And we kept saying if it is coming out of your pocket, it's coming out of our pocket because this is what drives up insurance and all these people get these exorbitant amounts of money" (C35-J6). Another juror reported that in the jury room, the idea that insurance would cover any award "got met with a resounding wave of, 'well it's coming out of our pockets because you know it's just like oil insurance and everything.' So once that was brought up, their minds were kind of like changed" (C31-J7).

In a job discrimination case against a state college, jurors commiserated with the plaintiff, who had been fired after teaching for many years. Nevertheless, several jurors I interviewed noted that when the defendant was a state institution, the tax-payers became the deep pockets. "I said, you know, folks, let's not forget that if a judgment is made for the plaintiff, it will in all probability be paid for by an insurance company. Who has insured the college against legal action. And that will ultimately be translated into the higher premium rates for the college, which you and I as taxpayers of this state in addition to the kids who are attending classes there are gonna have to pay for. So don't think that money comes out of the blue to make these settlements. The only place they're gonna come from is from the taxpayers who subsidize the college and I think very wisely choose to do so, and the students who attend classes there" (C34-J1). Another juror on the case sounded a similar theme: "I was thinking that if we did end up going with the plaintiff, I personally felt that the money would be coming out of my pocket, you know with taxes going toward the college, that the tax money that I'm paying for the college to be in school would be going into her pocket where I really didn't think it should. Because, you know, she never helped herself, so why should we give her money for not being able to help herself?" (C34-J9)

Likewise: "When you're supported by the taxpayers, that's you and me, I don't think that makes you a deep pocket. . . . I don't think that she should win just because there's a deep pocket. And . . . taxpayers shouldn't be considered deep pockets" (C34-J5). This juror, however, proceeded to deny that the public nature of the institution affected the outcome, which went against the plaintiff: "I really didn't let that influence me. It was just a matter of whether I thought she was wronged or not." Thus a number of comments relating to finances and awards were consistent with the views of a litigation crisis held by the vast majority of jurors.

In most cases, jurors expressed disdain for the large awards that other juries had given and that were publicized in the media. But occasionally the existence of other high awards cut the other way. One juror in the sports injury trial reported that a colleague who favored a higher award exclaimed: "Elizabeth Taylor got fourteen million for breaking her toe. This guy's a paraplegic, how much is he going to get for pain and suffering? Not a nickel? You're not going to give him a dime. And Elizabeth Taylor in California in a big court case in all the papers walked out of the courtroom with fourteen million dollars" (reported by C1-J2). Although this sort of comment was infrequent, it is intriguing that one juror used a well-publicized high damage award to support his argument for increasing the award in the case he was deciding.

Data collected by researchers Edith Greene, Jane Goodman, and Elizabeth Loftus suggest that the perceived prevalence of high damage awards may influence jurors' judgments about appropriate awards in just this way.[35] Greene and her colleagues conducted a mock juror study in which participants rendered a decision about damages and answered other questions. As part of the study, mock jurors estimated the percentage of plaintiffs who received jury damage awards higher than one million dollars. The jurors tended, on average, to overestimate the percentage of these high damage awards, consistent with the perception of litigation crisis. The relevant result for the current discussion is that those participants with the highest estimates of million-dollar damage awards tended to award the most to the plaintiff in the case before them. This seems to contradict my general finding that those who are most concerned about a litigation crisis tend to favor lower awards. Greene and her colleagues found that mock jurors who believed that damage awards were excessive were more likely to favor lower awards, too, on average. But they speculate that the perception of frequent million-dollar awards works against this overall tendency, by increasing the going rate, or the benchmark against which the juror's own case is evaluated.

A Deep-Pockets Perspective

Few jurors stated explicitly during the interview that they took finances into account in their decision making. Jurors sometimes talked about how their colleagues advanced the view that a business or insurance company could afford an award, only to be shot down by others on the jury. Nevertheless, a few jurors did advance a deep-pockets approach, including jurors in punitive damages cases.

A number of jurors admitted considering the defendant's ability to pay in deliberating about the award because they wanted to assure themselves that their award would not destroy or seriously harm the defendant. In one asbestos case, for instance, the juror reported that his jury considered the financial resources of the asbestos manufacturers in light of the award the jury reached:

Interviewer: This idea that large corporations can afford more, was that something that was discussed during deliberation?

Juror: Yeah, they kept coming up and saying they were bigger companies, and we thought that they could handle it more so than a smaller company. A smaller company, a big award would wipe them out. . . . I didn't want to wipe them out, and I know a lot of other people didn't want to wipe them out. . . . I think we finally had come to the conclusion of how much we were gonna pay, which was pitiful. We figured what we had decided what we were gonna pay wasn't gonna wipe these corporations out. When the bottom line came down to it, they could've probably paid it out in a lump sum. (C4-J8)

A juror in another asbestos trial expressed some concern about the impact of awards on the health of the companies: "We assumed that [the companies] were very well off, but also by the same token you've got to remember that [a company that went bankrupt] was a leading company at one time. And when I hear now that they have nothing but a fund, they just turned over their assets and it was put into a fund for this, that's kind of scary, when you stop and think about it. Will they be able to pay these people? . . . I'd rather see them get [a modest award] than be awarded a big amount and not get it" (C22-J3).

One juror in the fuel truck case disagreed with the low award her jury reached, explicitly advocating a deep-pockets strategy. She believed that the plaintiff had been "mistreated" by the jury, that he "should have gotten more than what he got." Furthermore: "That company should have paid because they're, I mean they have money that they could have paid. I mean they make money every time you turn around. They make money and make money" (C31-J1).

There were apparently instances in which jurors who favored a higher award attempted to convince others by referring to the defendant's ability to pay. In the landlord case, the first juror we interviewed said that she personally had not been affected but that others on the jury mentioned it: "I didn't myself but some people said he has the money, there were little remarks that he can afford it" (C10-J1). Another juror agreed, "We definitely discussed [whether the defendant could afford a large amount]. We didn't think that anything we dished out was really going to hurt [the defendant]" (C10-J4). Another juror on the case agreed: "That came into play several times. Basically saying that, 'don't worry, he can afford'" (C10-J5). In a workplace accident case against a large company, one juror recalled "somebody saying that whatever we awarded was a drop in the bucket. We didn't really have any feeling that this was something that was going to break them. . . . We didn't sit there and worry about, 'Oh my, where is this person going to get the money to pay all this?'" (C14-J6). Thus, one theme of those who said they considered the defendant's ability to pay was sensitivity to the impact of the award on the defendant, reflecting the desire to compensate the plaintiff without drastically harming the defendant.

Punitive damages cases showed the most frequent consideration of the defendant's financial resources. In these cases, jurors appeared to follow the court's instruction that punitive damages should be large enough to hurt the defendant company. In the lemon law case, which resulted in punitive damages, seven out of the eight jurors we interviewed acknowledged taking the defendant's ability to pay into account. One juror noted that the judge's instructions required it: "If you were gonna punish the corporation, it had to be something that would hurt them more than if they sued you or me, that was the idea that I got" (C25-J1). Another juror agreed: "If somebody hit me up for ten dollars, it's gonna hurt me. But these corporations, you give them a five-thousand-dollar fine, that's nothing to them. . . . For it to filter down not only from top management but to the people who work on the cars . . . then you gotta hit them in their pocketbook" (C25-J3).

In a contract case that involved punitive damages, one juror stated that he had considered the defendant's financial resources during the award process: "Because [the defendant's] a very big corporation, for the large amount of money involved, I don't think that it would have hurt the corporation very much" (C11-J2). This juror believed that the punitive damages award was insufficient and that the plaintiff company should have been awarded more "for all the trouble and the heartache they went through . . . it was unfair." His colleague agreed: "[The defendant] could afford a large amount, yes we talked about that, they could afford a large amount" (C11-J5). Another juror agreed that the financial differences between the corporations had affected them "maybe in the deliberation room when we were all sitting around and you have to figure out how much should [the plaintiff company] get for compensation or whatever, and we're like well [the defendant's] a big company, they could stand to lose. . . . You sat around and you were talking about how much compensation should they get, and we were like well if we only award them a little bit, it's not like punishment for [the defendant] because it's like nothing to them if you award them a little bit. But if you award them a little bit more, then they'll feel it, you know, like they'll know that they did wrong." Illustrating again the jurors' tendency to compare corporations to individuals, this juror went on to say, "I guess it's like with the kid. If you tap its hand, then it's not going to bother him but if you smack him hard then they're going to feel it" (C11-J4).

In a breach-of-contract case over an international shipment that resulted in punitive damages, the judge reportedly told the jurors after the trial that he agreed with their verdict but "thought we went a little too steep on the award." This jury suspected that even though they held the defendant company liable, the plaintiff was unlikely to recover. As one juror reported, the jury gave both compensatory and punitive damages "even though we all agreed on the same point that he wasn't going to get a dime of it because [the defendant company] didn't even exist anymore and [the business owner was working as an employee of another company]. So we knew that he probably wouldn't have gotten a dime of it, but it was just the principle that he should have gotten that" (C13-J6).

To sum up, most comments about deep pockets appear to be the result of jurors reassuring one another that the award will not seriously damage the defendant, which implies that jurors do occasionally consider equity issues in the award process. Jurors' remarks reflect concern about emptying a corporate defendant's pockets, ruining a business through high awards. Others comments indicate that jurors in punitive damage cases consider the deterrent impact of an award.

The Role of Insurance

The notion of deep pockets can encompass not just the economic reserves and holdings of a company but also its ability to use insurance to handle injuries caused by negligence. It will be recalled from Chapter 6 that citizens expressed very little confidence in the insurance industry. In fact, of all the institutions mentioned in my survey, insurance companies elicited the least confidence. This raises the question of how insurance was considered as juries deliberated about awards. Were jury awards higher because business defendants had insurance to cover plaintiffs' injuries?

Information about the defendant's insurance coverage is typically withheld from the jury on the grounds that it might lead them to increase their awards without regard to liability or plaintiff need. For instance, Federal Rule of Evidence 411 states: "Evidence that a person was or was not insured against liability is not admissible upon the issue whether the person acted negligently or otherwise wrongfully." The rule is routinely justified on the grounds that insurance is of questionable probative value and is often prejudicial.[36] The commentary to Rule 411 specifically notes the possibility that "if the jurors hear about insurance coverage, or the lack of it, they may decide the case on the basis of the deepest pocket, rather than on the facts."[37]

In one early study of the impact of insurance on juries, conducted in the 1950s, people on jury duty in St. Louis and Chicago participated in a mock jury experiment. They listened to a tape-recorded trial of an auto accident and were asked to assess damages. One group of jurors learned that the defendant did not have insurance to cover the award. A second group was told that he did have insurance. A third group was informed that the defendant had insurance but was admonished by the judge to disregard it.

The results were interesting. The juries who were informed that the defendant had no insurance to cover the accident awarded an average of $33,000. The juries who were told that he had insurance (but received no admonition from the judge) gave a slightly higher average award of $37,000. The big surprise, though, was the average award of the group admonished by the judge: $46,000! The judicial instruction to disregard the insurance information apparently boomeranged, drawing jurors' attention to the insurance information and causing a much higher award.[38] Although an analysis of the tape-recorded jury deliberations showed that jurors who were admonished to disregard insurance did not discuss it with one another, it nevertheless influenced their awards. This project underscored the potential significance of insurance information, at least for its time.

It is an open question whether similar results would be obtained today, with the ubiquity of auto insurance and the prevalence of homeowner's and business liability insurance. Most jurors assume that corporate defendants have insurance to cover the costs of plaintiff injuries. In today's lawsuits, whether jurors are explicitly informed about insurance may have little bearing on their decision processes.

In the interview study, a significant number of jurors reported discussing some aspect of insurance (either the plaintiff's or the defendant's) during deliberation. Consideration of insurance was more frequent than consideration of corporate identity or the defendant's ability to afford a large amount. In their deliberations about awards, 23% of the jurors reported considering the issue of the defendant's insurance, and another 14% said their jury had discussed the issue of insurance but had not used it in reaching an award amount. Thus, more than a third of the jurors (37%) reported at least discussing the issue of the defendant's insurance. A smaller number (23%) said they had either considered or discussed whether the plaintiff's insurance had covered some of the medical and other expenses associated with the injury. Jurors who reported discussing or considering the defendant's insurance were also more likely to discuss the plaintiff's insurance. Combining the reports of the two types of discussion, a total of 44% of the jurors I interviewed said that their juries had at least discussed either the defendant's or the plaintiff's insurance in the process of arriving at an award.

In personal injury cases, jurors on occasion questioned whether the plaintiffs' injuries and medical expenses were fully covered by medical insurance or worker's compensation. Hospital and doctor bills often contain notations about insurance information. Such bills were frequently introduced as evidence pertaining to compensatory damages and were sent to the jury room. Therefore, jurors were sometimes able to confirm that the plaintiff's medical bills were at least partially covered by medical insurance. For example: "He was covered under his mother. . . . I did see that on the chart when he was admitted [to the hospital]" (C19-J1). Jurors used the identity of the plaintiff's employer to estimate the likelihood of medical insurance: "He was working for [a large company] and we said he's gotta have hospitalization, I mean it's a very large organization" (C20-J7).

But the lack of explicit information in other cases could be frustrating. Asked whether the plaintiff was fully insured for past medical bills, one juror responded: "That's a question I would have liked to have asked. . . . I mean his insurance could have covered it 100%, and we wouldn't have known that. I thought that was important that they should have presented it" (C33-J5). Another juror reported that information about prior payments would have affected the jury's award: "We would have liked to have known how much the fire company had already paid, since they admitted guilt. We felt that they had to pay something. We didn't know how much this woman had already collected. That shouldn't have affected us, but we wanted to know" (C6-J4). This juror explained:

Juror: All we really knew was that the insurance had run out, that they were now on their own. But we didn't know what kind of insurance they might have had. All we knew was that the two years of the medical treatment that she had had that had been paid for. We didn't know how it had been paid for. I guess we assumed that since the fire company had admitted guilt that they had done it.
Interviewer: How do you think it would have influenced your award if you knew that she had continuing medical coverage?
Juror: Oh, they might, that bunch might have given her even less. (C6-J4)

One worker injury case was unusual because the injured workers were assumed *not* to be covered by worker's compensation insurance: "I assumed that they didn't [have worker's compensation] from the testimony that they were being paid by Mr. —— [a subcontractor] in cash. And it was brought out that they, that nothing was being withheld from their payment and their wages. I assumed that they were just getting paid for the job and were not covered by insurance" (C27-J3).

If jurors did learn about insurance that the plaintiff carried, they sometimes wondered why the plaintiff sued: "The only thing that was part of the records was that he had some type of insurance and the plaintiffs were asking money damages covering the medical bills and the funeral expenses, which had already been paid. So a lot of the jurors thought, why are they asking for that, since it's obviously already been paid for" (C19-J2).

Some jurors had personal experiences that gave them insight into how insurance companies might respond to a jury award that included medical expenses: "I guess his [medical expenses] were being picked up. But we [compensated him] because we all kind of believed from our personal experiences that once the award was made that probably the HMO or any Blue Cross or Blue Shield carrier would probably go back there and try to recover the costs. . . . I had a personal experience myself in an automobile accident years ago. . . . The insurance company of the person who hit me, when they finally settled the claim, Blue Cross and Blue Shield, I don't know how they knew it but they did, they sent me a bill for the emergency room services and I had to cash a check and then send money back to them. . . . Some other people had had some similar experiences" (C27-J2).

As for the defendants, in keeping with standard practice, jurors were usually not explicitly informed about whether they had insurance coverage:

Interviewer: What about the possibility that the defendants or the company carried insurance? Did you think about that at all?

Juror: We thought about it, but that was never pointed out and it was never presented, never. Nobody asked. And we didn't know if we could ask.

Interviewer: Did the fact that so many people have insurance influence the size of your award at all?

Juror: No. It was done entirely different. (C35-J2)

Although they were usually not informed about the insurance status of the business defendant, jurors regularly assumed that the business defendant was covered for accidental injuries. Often business insurance was so taken for granted that jurors reported never giving it a thought: "I really didn't think about it at all, you know, how they could pay" (C28-J4). "I was not really concerned with that because I assumed as a organization of that size with those potential liabilities that they would have the type of insurance to protect themselves" (C28-J6). In a medical malpractice case: "Obviously there was insurance companies somewhere back there. I mean we all knew that. The money wasn't going to come out of his pockets for that" (C19-J7).

One juror from the fire truck case reported: "I guess we were all kind of using our knowledge of how a volunteer fire company would have to be set up businesswise. It would have to have its own insurance, for liabilities, and their drivers and everything, so we never really thought too much about them, because just to be in that kind of position you know you're going to be sued. . . . Anything you do anymore, it's like cops, you have to have some kind of insurance. Because you're gonna make a mistake, or even if you don't make a mistake someone's gonna sue you just because things didn't end up the way they wanted" (C6-J7). But another juror in the fire truck case suggested that any driver would be covered by insurance: "I don't think it would make much difference whether it's a fire company or an individual, because they're insured, you're insured pretty good either way, you should be. Maybe more so with the fire company, but . . . if I had a truck and I was involved in this here, I don't think it would make much difference. . . . You know, if you win, you're gonna get the money" (C6-J8).

A minority of jurors apparently felt that the presence of the defendant's insurance made reaching an award easier, because the money wasn't coming directly from the bank account of the defendant. This perspective, however, was strongly contested by their fellow jurors, who countered that the case should be decided on the merits rather than on who was able to afford it, and that relying on insurance increased business costs and insurance rates. One juror observed:

> The fact was mentioned that there was insurance. It was one thing that came up in the jury room. Are they suing because they feel that an insurance company has deep pockets? It didn't really matter who was going to pay; they probably should get what they are entitled to. They shouldn't get any more than that simply because it was an insurance company, someone that you couldn't see. . . . The majority of the [jurors] expressed contempt for people who tried to get large awards simply because an insurance company is involved rather than the bearings of the case. But of course insurance money ends up coming out of all of our pockets. . . . I just got the impression that the plaintiffs felt that there was a corporation involved, there was an insurance company involved, and they should see what they could get. (C35-J3)

A juror from the same case stated that although insurance and financial resources of the parties didn't influence her thinking, "there was a lot of talking about it. Like when we were trying to put a dollar amount on how much money we were going to award him, it was like who is going to be paying the money, the insurance company, or does it come out of his [driver's] pocket, or is the company going to pay for it? And the foreman said it doesn't matter who's paying for it, we have to come up with an amount. We can't base our figure on who is paying it, we have to base it on what the case is worth" (C35-J4).

In contrast, another juror felt that it was easier to make the award because the defendant was a corporation with insurance:

Interviewer: You said that you assumed that the defendants had insurance. How did that affect the way you thought about the case?

Juror:	It helped us make this decision that was better only moneywise because I knew it wasn't coming out of the driver's.
Interviewer:	And if it had been coming out of his pocket? How would that have been different?
Juror:	I don't know, I might've fought harder when I was on the jury to see if we could ask the judge questions or bring in more evidence. (C6-J7)

In the paint-store case, which ended in a defense verdict, none of the jurors we interviewed admitted that they took insurance into account. But one juror told us: "I didn't think about [whether the corporation had insurance], but that was raised in the jury room. And that was one of the things that some people thought, one of the reasons why people thought at the beginning that we ought to award something, because it was of no effect to the company at all because they had insurance for these kinds of things" (C20-J9). In the blood-bank case, a juror commented on insurance and jury awards: "I'm not one that's gonna say, 'Aw, listen, you know, let the insurance pay it.' I'm really pretty much against that. I, you know, just you think, it's a big corporation, you know, let's soak the rich kind of thing. I don't go very well with that. I don't have that attitude. I don't know whether anybody else did, to tell you the truth" (C28-J8). Reflecting on the forty-five thousand dollars that her jury awarded, this juror observed: "Well, that's not gonna break the blood bank. . . . Somewhere along the line, I think, they probably have some kind of insurance coverage. But again, I feel strongly that just because you have insurance coverage, you shouldn't get soaked by it" (C28-J8).

In one auto accident trial, in which jurors decided only the liability issue, one juror recounted a discussion on the jury about who would pay the award: "They said, how is this guy gonna pay for this? Who's gonna pay for this? Is his insurance? Well, we don't know. Nobody told us. . . . You know that they had liability insurance and certainly the jury award was . . . within the range of any liability insurance. . . . There was some discussion about what is fair here, but the comment was made several times, 'Hey, high awards, all that does is make our automobile insurance go up.' So, now it's interesting. You get into the jury room and there is personal interest involved whether you want it to be or not" (C29-J1).

A juror who participated in a case that decided for the defendant reported an experience in another jurisdiction: "[Whether the college had insurance] never came out. And maybe it's just as well, because I did sit on a civil case in New York State where the rationale, we had a hung jury finally, was that sure, the plaintiff made the mistake, but the insurance company, they got lots of money, let them pay. . . . Very,

very disappointing experience. . . . I think that's a terrible idea. I feel very strongly about that. I mean, there's right and there's wrong. And the fact that they're insured doesn't make any difference" (C34-J6).

A juror from a dental malpractice case commented on the role of insurance in the jury's thinking: "We did figure that she probably had insurance to pay part of it, but then we decided that doesn't make any difference. That shouldn't come into it. . . . We knew that [the dentists] would all have insurance, all doctors have insurance. The only thing that we were concerned with is doctors like him are what make the insurance rates go up higher, and that's why our fees go higher, and it's a shame that he's practicing. If there was some way that we could get people like him out or to pay his own insurance or something, you know he might be more responsible if he had to pay a little bit more. But it's not fair to all the good doctors to have to pay a high rate of insurance because of a few like him. It's not fair that we have to pay the difference because of a few like him" (C36-J3).

The consequences of a jury award on a doctor's insurance premiums were considered by one medical malpractice juror: "I don't know how this insurance works, but if let's say there are several cases of malpractice, are their premiums raised? You know, the same as if you've had an automobile accident and it's your fault, your premiums are raised. So maybe someone would think to themselves oh yes, sue, he has insurance, and they think it is not going to hurt the doctor at all, but I think that it must so the doctor is as careful as he can be. . . . I don't look at it as the fact that they have insurance, that insurance will cover it. I don't look at things that way, personally" (C19-J1). In another medical malpractice case, a juror admitted to being influenced by the fact that the doctors were probably insured against the claims:

Juror: I'm not sure it influenced me very much, but I know that it had some effect on me. I would bet that it did. I don't know how much.
Interviewer: How do you think it would influence someone?
Juror: I think that it would tend to give them a bigger judgment, knowing full well that it wasn't coming out of the doctor's pocket. At least directly. Maybe indirectly, like an increase in medical insurance. (C23-J3)

This juror's colleagues, however, all spoke against this idea: "I felt that whether they had insurance or didn't have insurance wasn't a reason to decide the case for which way. It's insurance, that's what insurance people are for, they're there to insure these guys. But did he or did he not commit malpractice? That was what the question was.

Not whether he was insured or not and should we give him two billion dollars or whatever" (C23-J1). This juror admitted that the fact of insurance "did enter into [the other jurors'] heads that they could award a large amount because the doctors surely had insurance. . . . That doesn't sit well with me. Just because you have insurance doesn't mean you should get slapped with, I mean when you do get to have claims to insurance, usually they raise your rates. Well, I don't think that's quite fair" (C23-J1). Similarly: "Personally, sure I thought about [the doctors' insurance]. But then you also think about malpractice suits insurance. I mean that's why our premiums go up is because they can't stay in business" (C23-J2). The other two jurors we interviewed from this case also said that they were not affected by the role of insurance.

In an auto accident case, jurors discussed the potential role of insurance:

Interviewer: Did you think about whether or not [the defendants] carried insurance to cover accidents like this one?

Juror: I thought about it. The question was never raised.

Interviewer: Do you think it would have made a difference in your thinking if you'd known either one way or another?

Juror: Boy, I would like to say I'm pure enough [laughing] to say no to you, but I don't know. Because I have to admit to you when I was sitting there listening to the case, I had all kinds of questions in my mind about well, who's paid for this so far? But that was not part of the case, it was not raised even to be objected to by either of the attorneys, so that was a piece of information that we didn't have. Would I be influenced by that? Depends on how big the numbers get, probably. . . . I'm influenced certainly by these astronomical awards for some things that you read about in the newspaper. So to the extent that I found myself involved in some set of astronomical numbers, had I known who had paid for what, I'd be hard put that I wouldn't be influenced by that. That's all I'm saying. This case didn't reach those kinds of numbers. (C31-J4)

This quotation suggests that even if the deep-pockets effect is hard to pin down in small-stakes cases, it might be easier to locate in the "astronomical numbers" cases. Let's take a look at how jurors in those cases describe their use of the defendant's financial resources.

High-Award Cases

The high-award cases are a natural place to look for evidence of a deep-pockets approach. The Rand study found that differences between awards to plaintiffs who sued individuals and awards to those who sued businesses were more pronounced in the severe-injury cases.[39] It is also consistently found that plaintiffs who suffer the most severe injuries are the most undercompensated. Even if deep pockets don't drive jury awards in most cases, perhaps they do in the extreme-injury cases. Because jurors seem to consider the impact of their award on both parties, the ample resources of a corporate defendant might reduce jurors' concerns about detrimental impact on the defendant while allowing them to compensate a severely injured plaintiff fully. Therefore, it is valuable to take a close look at how jurors in these cases talked about the financial resources of the defendant companies.

In my study, jurors' reports of considering whether the defendant could afford a large amount, or of considering the defendant's or plaintiff's insurance, did not differ significantly between high-award cases (those in which the verdict was $1 million or greater) and lower-award cases. The "no difference" finding has to be considered tentative, however, in that just thirty-six jurors were included in the high-award cases. Even so, the juror interviews are consistent with the view that the defendant's finances were not the major reason for the high damage awards. Jurors occasionally spoke of the defendant's resources, and there were even a few instances that reflected apparent deep-pockets rationales, but these occurred just as infrequently in the high-award cases as in the remainder of the trials.

In the highest medical malpractice award, in which the plaintiff lost part of his lung, the jury awarded a compensatory damage award that reportedly exceeded the plaintiff's settlement request. Was the jury's generosity linked to its members' views of the doctor's financial wealth? Jurors' interviews provided little, if any, evidence that the jury had taken the doctor's insurance explicitly into account in the award process. Whether the defendant could afford a large amount "was not a consideration at all" (C12-J2). "We assumed that he probably [had insurance]. Quite frankly, that was not even a consideration of mine. One way or another I didn't really care if he had insurance or not" (C12-J2). Similar sentiments were expressed by most of this juror's colleagues. One of the jurors reported that during deliberations she acted to try to keep the award to a reasonable amount: "It was the first time I've ever served on jury duty, and in the past when I'd read about these million-dollar awards, I thought, that's just insane. And I said so to my fellow jurors. . . . I was one of the outspoken people working on keeping it down. Just because in principle, you know, horrendous huge awards are, sometimes they're out of hand" (C12-J3).

In the sports injury trial, a multi-million-dollar-award case, several jurors made comments about the plaintiff's insurance for the catastrophic injury and about the financial resources of the company. The jurors were so interested in the extent to which the plaintiff's medical bills had been covered that they asked the judge for the information:

Juror: We sent notes to the judge. . . . We did ask if he had insurance, if he had school insurance, or does the board of education have insurance to cover this sort of thing. And, have you been paid in monies by any other insurance company, and would he be getting any other insurance from insurance companies. . . .

Interviewer: What did the judge tell you about the insurance?

Juror: It could not be revealed. . . . We were a little disappointed. We thought it would be helpful to know this. And, I guess we were going to [decrease our award, taking into account] any amounts that he had previously been paid, or would be getting. (C1-J1)

Asked whether the likelihood of the company's insurance affected her thinking, this juror said, "I guess it has to, in some form, certainly, you know they have insurance, I guess you feel that that's what their insurance is for, and they can probably afford" (C1-J1). She described the general feeling of the jurors that "since we made the decision that the company was guilty, let's make him comfortable to age fifty-eight, but let's not go overboard." Another juror in the sports injury trial observed, about the likelihood of the plaintiff's insurance: "With what I know about insurance, that usually catastrophic injuries are covered, to a certain extent, and then after that, the well goes dry, and you're sort of on your own" (C1-J2). Although this juror assumed that the defendant company had insurance, he said it did not affect his thinking. The jury concluded that the company could afford the multi-million-dollar award without loss of jobs (C1-J2). Another juror stated that he did not consider whether the company could afford a large amount, but assumed that it could (C1-J3). One juror, who described himself as "instrumental in bringing the dollar amounts down" (C1-J5), also said the jury did not consider whether the company could afford the award, and that they assumed it had insurance for that purpose.

Two of the jurors were holdouts who initially favored a defense verdict. They eventually agreed to vote in favor of liability. Interestingly, these two holdout jurors provided perhaps the clearest evidence for the deep-pockets hypothesis in my entire study. Both the holdouts said the company's financial resources had influenced them: "I guess [the difference in financial resources] swayed me, in a way. Because of the fact that they had money. I mean, that they wouldn't be substantially, they wouldn't be financially crippled if they had lost the case," stated the first juror (C1-J5). The other juror used similar reasoning:

Interviewer: What do you think was the most critical thing that took you away from being for the company to being for [the plaintiff]?

Juror: Probably what seemed fair to me, in my mind what is fair. For a person to have to live in such constant torture every day, and not grant that person a little bit of softness in this life that we're passing through, to me seemed to be brutally cruel, to refuse this to this person. As compared to a big company that's indifferent and has a tremendous amount of money. And it has prepared itself to meet cases like this, so that's why I shifted to his side. (C1-J4)

The fact that the pro-defense jurors engaged in explicit consideration of the defendant's deep pockets was contrary to my expectations. I anticipated that pro-plaintiff jurors would be stronger advocates for the deep-pockets approach, but that did not turn out to be true among the jurors I interviewed from the sports injury trial.

In an auto accident case that resulted in a multi-million-dollar award, several comments suggested that jurors might have been affected by the defendant's ability to pay for the plaintiff's extraordinary medical bills and lifetime nursing care. This case involved a company driver who ran a red light while reading the paper, hitting and catastrophically injuring the plaintiff, who was riding a motorcycle. Liability was not a significantly disputed issue in the case, leaving jurors to focus on an appropriate award. One juror remarked that it may have made "just a little bit of a difference": "Well, you always feel like, well, it's a company, it can spare the money, you would always kind of have that in the back of your mind but I really didn't focus on it, that was just a thought" (C21-J6). Similarly: "We weren't angry or hostile with [the defendant], but we figured I think they maybe could afford this better than this poor man" (C21-J7). One juror stated that the existence of a corporation in the case made "a difference in the monetary value of the case. Because [the corporation] had more money than the average person that would hit someone else. So they were more responsible, not that they were more responsible, but they had more money in back of them" (C21-J3). When asked whether she considered that when the jury was trying to think about an award, however, the juror contradicted herself, saying: "No, no. That didn't come into effect in his damages at all. . . . When we actually sat down and figured out the money that we were going to award the gentleman, we didn't take into consideration [the corporation]. . . . It's not the fact that they had more money, it's just the fact of what [the plaintiff] needed during his lifetime after the accident" (C21-J3). In the same case, another juror, asked whether the defendant would be able to pay the award, remarked: "I think they're gonna have a little problem with this. Their insurance company's not gonna just write you a check because somebody said so. I don't know, it'll probably affect their rates" (C21-J2).

In sum, analyzing the interviews in the high-award cases revealed some occasional deep-pockets reasoning on the part of individual jurors. Yet it was no more frequent than in cases that produced lower awards. Most jurors in high-award cases, as in other trials, focused on the issue of negligence and on the specific needs of the plaintiff in arriving at award decisions.

Mock Jurors' Comments about Financial Resources during Jury Deliberations

Another approach to examining the role of financial resources is to observe whether mock jurors spoke about resources and insurance during their videotaped jury deliberations. This also allows us to assess whether financial resources and insurance are considered differently in cases with individual defendants and those with corporate defendants. In analyzing the videotaped deliberations of the mock jurors, research assistants observed regular discussions about the plaintiff's and the defendant's insurance in both experimental conditions. All twelve juries that decided the case against the individual defendant mentioned insurance, as did nine of the twelve juries that decided the case against the corporate defendant.[40]

In the mock juries that decided the case with the individual defendant, Mr. Wilson, comments about the possible impact of insurance included both plaintiff and defendant insurance. For instance, mock jurors in one group reviewed the plaintiff's medical bills and speculated about her income and financial resources to cover the bills. They inferred that she was relatively well-to-do because she had a private room at the hospital. In another jury with an individual defendant, one member speculated about the plaintiff's finances: "We don't know anything about this woman, for all we know she could own a big hotel, we don't know if she's a single mother" (Group 32, J3). In another individual defendant case with a defense verdict, one juror observed: "It's unfortunate, but let's pray that she's got insurance" (Group 25, J1). In discussing an award in another individual defendant case, one juror asked whether they should assume that the insurance company would pay 80% of the expenses; another expressed the view that the insurance company was likely to be reimbursed from any jury award that covered medical expenses. In one individual defendant case in which the mock jury reached a defense verdict, several jurors asserted that the likelihood that the plaintiff had medical coverage was a major reason for not awarding her monetary damages.

This group, like many others in the individual defendant condition, also expressed concern about whether the defendant had insurance to cover such an award. Another individual condition jury was very concerned about the impact of its $500,000 award on Mr. Wilson: "This could really wipe someone out. . . . He's probably gonna lose his insurance coverage" (Group 22, J4). And the broader impact was noted: "These awards, we all end up paying" (Group 22, J1). In another individual defendant case, a juror observed that homeowners' insurance was designed to cover accidents occurring in the home. Yet after the jury arrived at an award of $600,000, one juror predicted about the defendant: "His premiums are gonna go up" (Group 15, J6). In another individual defendant case, mock jurors also queried whether the defendant had homeowners' insurance and whether insurance covered the costs of the accident. One juror warned that they could not assume that the defendant was covered by insurance. Jurors in another individual defendant case, who doubted that any homeowner carried a million-dollar policy, expressed a similar concern. Yet another mock jury with an individual defendant discussed Mr. Wilson's insurance company and its right to appeal their verdict and $700,000 award. Thus, in the individual condition mock juries, there was explicit consideration of the plaintiff's medical insurance and the likely impact of an award on the defendant.

In contrast, there did not appear to be as much concern in the corporate defendant mock juries about the potentially negative impact of a jury award on the defendant. There was, however, the same interest in the plaintiff's insurance. For instance, in a case with a defense verdict, jurors wanted to know about insurance payments to determine what to award the plaintiff: "If her injuries were covered by insurance, then how would that happen . . . that the furniture company's insurance would reimburse her insurance company?" (Group 18, J1). Another juror replied: "If she wins the case the furniture company will pay, if she loses the case Blue Cross and Blue Shield will obviously have to pay for part of it" (Group 18, J4). One mock juror sympathized that the plaintiff was "probably sitting at home with a pile of medical bills," speculating that she might be dropped by the insurance company as a result of her medical expenses (Group 28, J1). In another mock jury, one juror observed: "They didn't say whether she had medical insurance" (Group 17, J4). However, a fellow mock juror replied that whether she had insurance was irrelevant to the case: "Blue Cross, Blue Shield, insurance has nothing to do with it" (Group 17, J1). Mock jurors appeared to want information about insurance so that they could assess the money needed by the plaintiff.

In another mock jury deciding the corporate defendant case, one juror observed: "We have to put some negligence on the store or she'll be covered zero" (Group 30, J6), suggesting that the percentage of plaintiff fault was at least partly driven by concerns that the plaintiff receive some financial compensation. In the same jury, jurors questioned whether the store could afford to pay the medical bills. One colleague gave a deep-pockets response: "They both have insurance. . . . Nobody's paying for it" (Group 30, J2). In another corporate case, a juror wondered, "I don't know what kind of medical plan she had" and later justified their jury award: "They [defendants] probably have insurance, they can afford it" (Group 20-J4).

Members of one mock jury deciding the corporate case reflected a range of perspectives about insurance. As with the jurors we interviewed from actual cases, an awareness of skyrocketing insurance premiums as a result of large jury awards was a frequent theme in this group and others:

J4:   Does the insurance company decide based on what we say?

J5:   We don't want to make her wealthy, but we don't want to see her groveling with nothing to eat. Their insurance is gonna cover that, right?

J2:   You have to understand that every time the store pays one of these claims, you're paying for it because the prices go up. (Group 18)

In another corporate defendant mock jury that arrived at a $2 million award, there were a number of comments about the impact of awards on insurance: "This is part of the reason the insurance companies get outrageous, because the money has to come from somewhere" (Group 14, J3). In another case: "Insurance has just gone out of the ceiling, there's no end to it" (Group 29, J2). Similarly, in another corporate condition mock jury that decided on a $1.05 million award: "Their insurance rate is going up, and you're going to pay for it the next time you go in to buy" (Group 27, J3).

Thus the comments by the mock jurors reinforce the general pattern found in the interviews. A minority of jurors reflected a deep-pockets perspective, and there was a good deal of interest in the insurance situation of both defendant and plaintiff. Yet mock jurors also expressed concern about the impact of high awards on business and society. Mock jurors in the individual defendant condition appeared to be more concerned than mock jurors in the corporate condition about the effect of their award on the defendant's financial picture.

Concluding Comments about the Deep-Pockets Explanation

The deep-pockets explanation for differential treatment of the corporation found only a modest degree of support in the research conducted as part of my project. The Robin Hood jury appears to be nearly as mythical as the character on which it is based. The clearest evidence against the deep-pockets hypothesis comes from the experimental study that tested the deep-pockets approach. Contrary to predictions of the deep-pockets theory, the provision of financial information in the scenario experiment had absolutely no effect on negligence judgments or recommended awards. Study participants did pay attention to the financial information, so the lack of effect cannot be attributed to a failure to notice the financial worth of the defendant. The null results are supported by the findings of several other studies that also failed to find a deep-pockets effect when financial information was varied.

Most jurors I interviewed confirmed this finding, reporting that they did not take financial disparities into account. But can we trust what jurors say about the role of finances in their decision making? We know that jurors, like the rest of us, aren't always able to accurately determine the impact of various factors on their decision making. With finances there is the additional issue that admitting that a defendant's resources played a part in the award goes against the norm of equality and might be considered to be socially undesirable. However, jurors often appeared to speak with candor and in ways that portrayed them in a less-than-favorable light. They acknowledged taking into account attorneys' fees, although many knew that this was forbidden by the court. Fully 80% of the jurors admitted that during award deliberations, their jury had discussed or considered the fact that attorneys' fees must be paid.[41] More important, the jurors' claims that finances played little or no role in award decisions are supported by the experimental studies that varied financial wealth of defendants and found no impact.

Critical commentary about the deep-pockets effect focuses attention on the supposed inflation of awards against wealthy business defendants. But my research hints that the *empty* pockets of a defendant (business or individual) are more significant. In the mock jury study, mock jurors considering a lawsuit against the individual defendant sometimes expressed concern that the defendant might be unable to pay. In many cases in my interview study, the twin assumptions that the business would be able to pay and that businesses were insured were virtually automatic. Jurors reported that they didn't even think about it. Most jurors appeared to assume that the financial resources or insurance to compensate for business-related injury would be adequate, leaving them to concentrate on the needs of the plaintiff. Yet jurors sometimes attempted to gauge the impact that an award would have on the business defendant. The undercompensation of the most severely injured plaintiffs, a well-known phenomenon of the tort system, could be at least partly attributable to jurors' failure to compensate fully because they are concerned about the negative consequences to the defendant.[42] Although I didn't find clear evidence of a deep-pockets orientation in my studies, whether jurors inflate or discount under other circumstances is a question worthy of additional study.

The focus of jurors and mock jurors on the insurance of both parties in the lawsuit suggests that any full consideration of deep or empty pockets must take the fact of insurance into account. Insurance seems to be an important factor to jurors, since close to half of the jurors reported discussing either the plaintiff's or the defendant's insurance during the deliberation over the award. It was also a frequent topic in the mock jury deliberations, as participants attempted to judge how much money the plaintiff needed to be compensated and to assess the actual financial impact on the individual or company defendant. In both the juror interview study and the mock jury project, precise evidence about the extent of insurance was minimal or nil, and jurors had to rely on their own suppositions.

Although jurors appear savvy about general trends in insurance (including the extent of business and automobile insurance, and the impact of an accident or injury on insurance rates), other possibilities might not be considered. For example, what about the uninsured defendant or plaintiff? The extremely large deductibles that many corporations carry? Businesses or agencies that self-insure? Another point about the existence of insurance is that it does not appear to be a one-sided consideration. If jurors are influenced by insurance, then they seem to care about both the plaintiff's coverage for medical expenses and the business defendant's coverage for consumer or worker injury. It would be useful to replicate the Chicago Jury Project's insurance study today to determine how explicitly varying insurance information (for both plaintiff and defendant) affects contemporary jurors. It is possible that the high likelihood of insurance today has helped to level the playing field between individuals and business corporations and between businesses of different sizes. Although it is still possible that a consideration of financial wealth affects jury decision making in corporate cases, the claim that it is a major factor appears to be unwarranted, based on the evidence I gathered in this project.

8

MYTHS AND REALITIES OF THE
CIVIL JURY IN BUSINESS CASES

Recall some of the arguments for why the civil jury should not decide cases with business parties:

- "Juries face accidents up close, viewing them in the lurid setting of an individual tragedy already completed. . . . The only human reaction to the individual tragedy viewed close up, is unbounded generosity, which any large corporation or insurer can surely afford to underwrite."[1]
- "The presence of juries increases the lottery aspects of the tort system. Skillful plaintiffs' attorneys may select only the most appealing clients, and focus their efforts primarily on mobilizing the sympathy of the jury. . . . The resultant verdict may have little to do with the merits of the case, and everything to do with theater."[2]
- "Jury awards for punitive damages grab headlines as they've spiraled into the millions, not to mention billions of dollars. . . . Plaintiffs' attorneys trolling the waters in the hope of landing a big one, have cast their nets in an ever widening circle that promises to choke business and clog the courts. . . . Defendants with seemingly deep pockets (big companies, professionals, etc.) are paralyzed by the threat of huge jury awards and/or the likelihood of paying damages grossly out of proportion to their share of the blame."[3]
- "Is it any surprise that many commercial contracts these days have a clause where each party waives its right to a jury trial? Doesn't that tell you something? That they are not willing to trust twelve peers off the street with the complexity of their business transaction."[4]

Claims like these are leveled against the civil jury every day, in newspapers, board meetings, and coffee shops. Critics accuse the lay jurors of bringing their sympathies for the plaintiff and their biases against business into the courtroom, reaching into the deep pockets of corporations to reward plaintiffs even when the negligence of the corporations has not been proven. The failings of the civil jury in business cases are seen as a drain on American business competitiveness.

In spite of these serious charges against an important legal institution, until now there has been little empirical study of how juries operate in lawsuits with business litigants. It is time to take stock. Which of these charges against the civil jury in business cases have been supported, and which have been refuted, by the empirical findings of my research project? Let us address the three main charges against the civil jury in business cases: that it is pro-plaintiff, that it is anti-business, and that it is motivated by deep pockets.

The Myth of the Pro-Plaintiff Jury

The first claim, that juries are pro-plaintiff, cannot be supported. The studies that have contrasted judicial views and civil jury verdicts find substantial overlap between judge and jury, and when their decisions diverge, juries are no more likely to favor the plaintiff in civil litigation, including litigation with business defendants. My research and that of others also contradict the popular perception that jurors are uniformly sympathetic to plaintiffs who bring claims against businesses. A more accurate characterization is that jurors are often suspicious and ambivalent toward people who bring lawsuits against business corporations. Jurors and the public are deeply committed to an ethic of individual responsibility, and they worry that tort litigation could be fraying the social fabric that depends on a personally responsible citizenry. Even in my sample of cases, which had a higher-than-average win rate, a substantial number of jurors described hostility toward the plaintiffs in their civil lawsuits. Jurors reported examining plaintiffs' claims with a critical eye, probing for ways in which plaintiffs were responsible for their own injuries and assessing the degree to which they could be overstating their injuries. Part of the jury's task, as they saw it, was to be vigilant about spotting frivolous lawsuits.

These attitudes are consistent with the general tendency among members of the public to question the general validity of lawsuits and to believe that the amount of litigation is out of control. The jurors' concerns about the legitimacy of plaintiff claims and their beliefs in a litigation explosion were linked to judgments that favor defendants, including business defendants, in civil lawsuits.

Although I conducted my research in only one jurisdiction, the critical stance toward the civil plaintiff is not merely a local phenomenon. The mistrustful attitudes about civil litigation that I uncovered are virtually identical to those found in national surveys and in polls in other jurisdictions. Across the country, Americans express deep concern about spiraling litigation and unjustified lawsuits. Media reporting and advertising campaigns by business and insurance are certainly part of the reason why Americans are convinced that there is a substantial amount of frivolous litigation. Yet jurors and other citizens respond to the news reports and advertisements because they resonate with their own concerns that expansive rules of civil liability might undermine our societal commitment to individual personal responsibility.

Although the phenomenon isn't just a local one, my conclusion that juries are not particularly pro-plaintiff may not apply in every area. Some lawyers identify certain states, such as Texas, as highly pro-plaintiff. Research projects on civil jury awards show a good deal of variability across jurisdictions, suggesting that local practices and legal cultures could be important influences on the behavior of civil juries.[5] In all three of my studies, I found that attitudes about a litigation crisis were significantly associated with judgments in civil cases. That relationship leads me to predict that in jurisdictions with local cultures that are more supportive of civil litigation, jurors would tend to take a more plaintiff-oriented approach to civil lawsuits against business. A business might conceivably win a close case in one jurisdiction but lose in another. Nevertheless, the nationally shared suspicions about civil litigation indicate that these pro-plaintiff jurisdictions, if they exist, are in the distinct minority.

The Myth of the Anti-Business Jury

The second claim, that civil jurors are hostile to business, also does not find much support in a close empirical analysis. The jurors I interviewed did not display the widespread hostility to business litigants that is commonly asserted. Instead, jurors and the public supported business as a general rule, and worried about how excessive litigation might detrimentally affect the strength of the business community. Jurors expressed concern about the effect of an award on the business defendant, wondering whether it might lead to a loss of jobs or otherwise harm the company. Most business litigants in the cases that were part of this study were described in a neutral or positive light. In a minority of cases, jurors levied some harsh comments against particular business defendants, but to the extent that I could determine through interviews, their criticism seemed to be linked largely to trial evidence of business wrongdoing rather than to jurors' preexisting anti-business hostility. In fact, general attitudes toward business were only modestly related, at best, to judgments of business wrongdoing.

My study allowed me to move beyond a focus on whether jurors were hostile toward business to examine how their consideration of a business corporation compared to their treatment of an individual person. There was substantial overlap, whether we rely on jurors' own assessments or on experimental comparisons. Jurors appeared to adopt an individual template, regarding the business corporation as a "person" for the purposes of determining liability. As they decided whether a corporation should be held liable, they reasoned whether a similarly situated individual would be responsible. Indeed, many jurors stated that the presence of a corporation made little or no difference to their decision making. However, jurors did not appear to equate the business corporation with an ordinary, run-of-the-mill person. The analogy that better captures jurors' predominant view is that of a professional individual, such as a doctor or a scientific expert, who possesses a substantial degree of knowledge and resources.

The experiments and interviews showed that under some circumstances the behavior of a corporate litigant is evaluated differently than the actions of an individual litigant. Experiments that varied the identity of the defendant in mock trial simulations showed that business corporations are held to a higher standard of behavior. What might be viewed as accidental and excusable for an individual is seen as negligent for a corporation. Many members of the public, including jurors, endorsed the position that corporations, because of their greater knowledge, resources, and potential impact, should be held to a higher standard of responsibility than individuals. My research suggests that in particular kinds of cases, such as asbestos and product liability trials, a distinctive approach to corporate negligence is even more likely. Here the jurors reflect some of the same motivations that have led lawmakers over the past several decades to create a broad range of special rules of business responsibility. Taken as a whole, the findings indicate that the higher standards that jurors insist upon for business corporations are derived from specific expectations about what is necessary and desirable for business actors, rather than generally negative (or positive) views of the business community. My finding that citizens hold business litigants to higher standards converges with the results of independent studies carried out in California, North Carolina, and even Japan.

Attitudes toward business were not as strongly and reliably related to case judgments as were attitudes about the civil justice system. Nevertheless, there was a good deal of overlap between how participants in my project viewed the business community and how respondents in national surveys perceive business. One exception was that my study participants seemed to be more concerned about the power of big business than are national survey respondents. To the extent that such attitudes about the business community were sometimes related to case outcomes, I predict that in jurisdictions with more positive attitudes toward business, jurors would at times display a tendency to favor the defendant in business trials. However, as my research and that of many other psychologists document, the general attitudes that jurors possess are likely to play only a small role in their verdicts.

It is worth emphasizing again that my jury trial sample contained predominantly tort trials in which individual litigants sued business defendants, and I focused on personal injury tort cases in my line of experiments. In jurisdictions with different case mixes, or in types of trials that are not reflected here, juries could take different approaches that I was not able to observe.

Given that business-business litigation has increased over time, it would be instructive to examine in greater detail how jurors respond to such cases. Do jurors still attempt to fashion an individual template for the evaluation of corporate behavior when both parties are corporations and the issue is a business dispute that bears little relation to ordinary individual experience? Do they try to construct a David-and-Goliath scenario, pitting a larger and stronger corporation against a smaller one?

Another issue to be explored is whether the plaintiff-blaming phenomenon that is so evident in my work with tort cases also dominates contract cases. Some scholars have hypothesized that people do not derogate the individual who brings a contract claim with the same degree of fervor that they reserve for the tort plaintiff.[6] I looked at too few contract cases to make systematic comparisons, but the possibility is intriguing. If jurors do not come to a contract case with the same distrust of plaintiff claims, what other jury dynamics come into play? Similarly, do jurors hold to the same high expectations for business litigants when the behavior is a failure to comply with a contract instead of the infliction of personal injury?

The Myth of the Robin Hood Jury

The findings reported in this book also cast doubt on the jury's identity as a modern-day Robin Hood. Most jurors stated that the business defendant's financial status had little impact on their decision making; some stated that it would be unfair to consider the defendant's finances. They were more concerned, they said, with assessing the defendant's negligence and the plaintiff's needs. By themselves, those reports might be subject to question, because they could be affected by the jurors' inability to discern the impact of finances on their own decision making, or to their desires to present themselves in a socially desirable light. Nonetheless, supporting the jurors' claims are the results of experimental tests of the independent effect of deep pockets on case judgments and awards. An experiment that I conducted, and subsequent research by other investigators, varied the financial resources of a defendant, but it made no difference in negligence or award judgments. Research projects in California, North Carolina, and Illinois have all looked for the predicted relationship between an increase in a defendant's financial wealth and awards to plaintiffs who sue them.[7] But all the projects thus far have failed to find the predicted deep-pockets effect. These research findings from the juror interviews and the experiments are contrary to expectations. However, the convergence across methods and studies increases my belief that a defendant's financial resources are not a major factor leading to high jury awards.

Why? One possibility is that the equity norms that would support higher awards against wealthier defendants are balanced in the jury room by equality norms that value equal treatment. Another is that what has appeared to be jurors' deep-pockets approach toward business defendants is better explained by their beliefs that for-profit businesses should cover the full costs of injuries associated with making their products. This approach overlaps with the cost internalization arguments of some tort theorists. A third possibility is that the ubiquity of insurance makes the actual net worth of a business defendant essentially irrelevant.

The potential impact of insurance, and the way assumptions about insurance could interact with jurors' concerns about the equities between the parties, deserve further study. The interviews and experiment revealed that jurors and mock jurors show keen interest in the insurance held by both plaintiffs and defendants. Jurors, deprived of information about insurance coverage (save what they deduced from the trial evidence and their life experiences), routinely speculated about insurance as they attempted to assess the bottom-line cost of a plaintiff's injuries. They sometimes requested details about insurance, only to be rebuffed by the judge, who informed them that the law forbids divulging that information.

In a country where it is now routinely expected that businesses are insured, does it make sense to withhold the details of insurance information from the jury, as current law requires? The experimental findings that mock jurors do not vary their awards after learning of a defendant's net worth suggest that informing jurors of insurance might have little or no impact. Net worth may not be critically important so long as a business defendant is presumed to hold liability insurance. How insurance information affects juries, and how it interacts with the norms of equity and equality, should be examined empirically.

Should We Continue to Rely on Civil Juries
for the Resolution of Business Disputes?

In the policy debate over the role of the civil jury, many of those who wish to limit the civil jury have rested their arguments at least partially on untested beliefs about how juries function in lawsuits with business and corporate parties. My project was designed primarily to address critiques of the civil jury relating to its partiality, bias, and differential treatment of business corporations. Critical commentary about the jury's continuing role in deciding cases with business litigants includes both the assertions of bias that my research explored and also claims of fact-finding incompetence that other investigators have studied more directly. Before drawing conclusions about the policy implications of my own research, it is worthwhile to review this important body of work. After all, even if the claims of jury bias are more myth than reality, as I maintain, if jurors are unable to comprehend the sometimes complex legal and evidentiary issues of business disputes, that is cause for concern.

Research projects by a number of scholars have investigated the fact-finding competence of the civil jury. That research reaches largely positive conclusions about the jury's fact-finding abilities, although areas of vulnerability can be identified.

First, projects comparing judicial and jury case judgments find substantial overlap. Judges presiding over jury trials have been asked to give their views about the adequacy of the jury's verdict or even to provide hypothetical verdicts themselves. The projects show that judges agree with the vast majority of civil jury verdicts. The high agreement rate was first found in the 1950s and has continued in contemporary times, even though civil jury trials today doubtless include more complex evidence. Trial judges surveyed about their views of the civil jury system voice strong support for it, although they are willing to consider reforms that could improve the jury trial.[8] Because judges are legal experts, their support for the soundness of jury verdicts, and the agreement between judges and juries, are reassuring. Both the heterogeneity of the jury's membership and its ability to pool collective memory and correct errors in deliberation undoubtedly promote the competence of the civil jury.

Even if the jury proves to be competent in most cases, some trials with business and corporate parties are likely to present extremely challenging evidence. Consider the Benlate cases presented in Chapter 1. When jurors decide issues of product liability, toxic torts, medical malpractice, or contract disputes, they must evaluate often complex and conflicting expert testimony. Do they fall back on biases and prejudices when confronted with evidence only an expert could love?

Neil Vidmar's extensive study of medical malpractice juries, which included complex cases, reached a largely positive conclusion about the competence of the civil jury. Vidmar combined analyses of court files with interviews with attorneys and examination of the insurers' closed claim files, and undertook experiments comparing the judgments of lay jurors and legal professionals. Contrary to the claims that juries are biased against doctors, Vidmar found that jury verdicts converged with medical experts' judgments of negligence in specific cases, that damage awards were roughly proportional to the seriousness of the injuries, and that, if anything, juries appeared to be slightly more supportive of doctors than of plaintiffs.[9]

Richard Lempert reviewed case studies of jury performance in twelve complex cases, most of which included business and corporate parties. The trials presented major challenges to the jury in that they frequently included evidence that only the experts themselves were likely to understand easily. There was an additional complication in that, probably because of the length of some of these trials, a number of the juries included few or no college-educated jurors. Nevertheless, Lempert concluded: "A close look at a number of cases . . . does not show juries that are befuddled by complexity. Even when juries do not fully understand technical issues, they can usually make enough sense of what is going on to deliberate rationally, and they usually reach defensible decisions. To the extent that juries make identifiable mistakes, their mistakes seem most often attributable not to conditions uniquely associated with complexity, but to the mistakes of judges and lawyers, to such systematic deficiencies of the trial process as battles of experts and the prevalence of hard-to-understand jury instructions, and to the kinds of human error that affect simple trials as well."[10]

The general thrust of the studies is positive about the civil jury's competence. Yet research has identified specific problem areas. Jurors have particular trouble understanding judicial instructions and complex statistical or technical expert testimony.[11] Non-experts tend to have difficulty with statistical evidence and to underestimate its relevance and weight.[12] Jurors themselves identify expert evidence as challenging, although a thorough review of research on jury reactions to expert testimony gave the jury a good report card.[13]

Jury competence may be further compromised by the fact that the presentation of complex evidence takes place within an adversarial setting. As Stephen Saltzburg cogently observes, "Adversarial attorneys in our system do not always have an incentive to make things clear and to promote understanding. There are times when confusion and ambiguity promote the odds of one party's prevailing. . . . Even if one side makes heroic efforts to educate the jurors about all disputed issues, the other side may strain to muddy the water."[14] All of this suggests that we should be vigilant about continuing to study and scrutinize the civil jury's ability to comprehend trial evidence, particularly in complex business litigation. There may well be disputes involving business that are beyond the ability of a lay jury (or even a judge) to decide rationally.

Jury Competence and Jury Reform

The challenges to jury competence described above might lead some to recommend the elimination or at least the further diminution of the civil jury in business cases. An alternative to these drastic options is targeted jury reform. A number of jurisdictions have embarked on reforms of the jury system that are designed to enhance jury competence.[15] For example, the state of Arizona has enacted a comprehensive set of trial reforms with the aim of making jurors more active participants and the trial process more educational. Under these reforms, instructions are given in plain English, jurors can take notes, and they are allowed to ask questions of witnesses. Civil jurors in Arizona may also discuss the evidence among themselves as the case proceeds rather than wait until the final deliberation, when memories may have faded.[16]

The process by which juries arrive at damage awards deserves close scrutiny. In particular, we should explore options for providing jurors with more guidance than the court currently gives. Although I could not confirm a deep-pockets approach in jury damage awards, many jurors I interviewed conveyed their feeling that arriving at a monetary award was the most daunting aspect of jury service. How, they asked, did the court expect the jury to come up with a reasonable amount if it gave the jurors no direction and limited information?

Studies have shown that a percentage of civil jury awards are modified after the trial.[17] Exactly how many of these modifications result from settlements between the parties is not clear, but at least some modifications reflect the judge's assessment that the jury got it wrong on the specific award amount. Of course, the judge has some distinct advantages over the jury in the award decision. He or she can research comparable cases and develop a sense of the going rate for an injury.[18] Juries are deprived of this sort of comparative data.

Developing tools for juries—such as comparative information or schedules that provide suggested ranges of award amounts—could be useful but would be enormously difficult and politically contentious. The federal sentencing guidelines in criminal cases, which were created to reduce sentencing variability, have been controversial and heavily criticized. Promulgating a set of guidelines designed for jury awards in civil cases would doubtless create comparable difficulties and similar furor. Nonetheless, providing some guidance or mechanisms for reducing the variability in jury awards would go a long way toward dealing with the perceptions that the civil jury is a highly unpredictable body. Projects are now under way comparing the impact of various approaches to regulating jury damage awards.[19] I would urge that empirical study of these alternative methods not be limited to their impact on award amounts and variability. The evaluations should also assess the potential effects of these modifications on the broader purposes of the civil jury trial.

Beyond Fact-Finding Competence: Other Functions of the Civil Jury

The discussion of the civil jury's fact-finding competence should not distract us from the reality that the evaluation of the central issues in most trials depends on basic human judgment, not on highly technical issues understood by only a few experts. Was a store negligent for leaving dangerous objects where children could get them? Should a car dealership be sanctioned for failing to address repeated problems with an owner's new car? Here the jury's ability to represent the community and its range of values arguably makes it superior to a single judge. The jury includes representatives of both constituencies—the business person and the consumer.

The strongest argument in favor of the jury's continuing role is that it incorporates into its verdicts in business and corporate cases the public's sense of the responsibility and role of the corporation in contemporary society. The range of views that jurors convey in their interviews indicates vigorous debate and difference of opinion about where individual responsibility ends and corporate responsibility begins. My research reveals that juries and their verdicts reflect societal tension over the appropriate level of business responsibility. Civil juries help to define, and redefine, this line between individual and corporate accountability. Indeed, in some cases in which juries resist expansive rules of business liability, the jury can be the corporation's best friend in the courtroom! Traditional and widely held beliefs about the importance of individual responsibility are challenged by the complexities of the modern social world. The continuing presence of the jury in civil litigation allows that debate to be crystallized in the evaluation of specific cases.

As our collective understanding of the line between individual and corporate responsibility shifts, expanding corporate responsibility in some domains and contracting it in others, the jury's verdicts embody that changing understanding. Noted Yale law professor Peter Schuck, commenting about the tort system and the jury, observed: "Tort liability, more than most areas of law, mirrors the economic, technological, ideological, and moral conditions that prevail in society at any given time. . . . The master ideas that drive tort doctrine—reasonableness, duty of care, and proximate cause—are as loose-jointed, context-sensitive, and openly relativistic as any principles to be found in law. . . . Legal principles, after all, are neither self-sustaining nor self-defining; their true significance only emerges as they are applied to actual disputes. The institution of the jury, as much as legal doctrine, infuses tort law with new life and meaning in the light of new configurations of social facts and values."[20]

Other functions and purposes of the civil jury system must also be considered in thinking about the desirability of retaining the civil jury in cases involving business litigants. The civil jury, for instance, is important not only because of the specific cases that the jury hears but also because of its signaling function for the much larger number of cases that are settled based on assumptions about what a jury would do with the cases if they went to trial.[21] My project found little support for many prevalent assumptions about the civil jury in business cases. The signals broadcast by the civil jury, conveyed by the media, and received by parties with preconceptions, are full of error and noise. To the extent that my own research and that of others correct misimpressions of the civil jury, its ability to operate as a signpost may be improved.

Other effects of the jury pertain to its impact on the jurors themselves. It has been claimed that jury service both educates the public and legitimates the justice system. De Tocqueville, who wrote in 1835 about the American civil jury, remains one of the most eloquent spokespersons for the educational role of the civil jury: "Juries, especially civil juries, instill some of the habits of the judicial mind into every citizen, and just these habits are the very best way of preparing people to be free. It spreads respect for the courts' decisions and for the idea of right throughout all classes. . . . [The jury] should be regarded as a free school which is always open and in which

every juror learns his rights . . . and is given practical lessons in the law. . . . I do not
know whether a jury is useful to the litigants, but I am sure that it is very good for
those who have to decide the case."[22] As is commonly found in post-trial studies of
jurors, the jurors I interviewed were very positive about their jury experience, rating it
an average of seven on a ten-point scale.[23] Jury duty could translate into a greater
appreciation for the legal system, as shown by the reflections of this juror:

> We were a group of people that came together, just a bunch of strangers, and we did
> the job. What I did find is that everybody was uniquely interested, concerned, and
> involved in what they were doing, and I think that everybody assumed their role as a
> juror with a great deal of conviction and responsibility. And that was people from all
> walks of life. I mean there were young men there that like to run around in a pickup
> truck and drink beer, there were people who were married and trying to raise
> families and advance their career. There was the whole spectrum there. And yet I
> think the junior single members had the same dedication as the [responsible senior
> individuals]. I'm very proud of the jury in that respect . . . and I'm also proud of our
> society for the same reason, because I think that that random jury is probably
> representative of most of the juries that serve. In the end, I have a great deal more
> faith in our judicial system from that experience, because I think that it was fair to
> all parties, and I think that this random jury that was entrusted with this decision
> was a good jury. (C13-J4)

My research and this book have concentrated on the jury's role. There are broader
questions about how well the civil justice system serves its key goals of deterring negligent behavior, delivering compensation, and protecting consumers and the workforce. Numerous business leaders have complained that the constant threat of litigation has paralyzed them or dramatically lessened their ability to innovate and hence
compete in the marketplace. The jury is but one part of that system, but because
business leaders often associate it with unpredictability and business hostility, it has
become a lightening rod for criticism and attack.

How well the civil justice system fulfills its broad goals is the subject of extensive
and vigorous debate; fully addressing it would go far beyond the scope of this book.[24]
Nevertheless, it is tempting to speculate how the civil justice system would be affected by removing or reducing the jury's role. I predict that a civil justice system
without a jury would evolve in a way that more reliably served elite and business
interests, although the changes might be small and difficult to detect. Under the
current system, the verdicts of judges and juries overlap to a considerable degree, but
when they diverge, the jury is more likely to incorporate community notions of justice

into its decisions, because judges represent a narrower slice of society than jurors do. It is often assumed that the jury is the prime culprit in the variability of damage awards, but it is possible that jury awards, which constitute group products, could actually be more stable than the damage awards of individual judges.[25]

In addition, the continuing presence of the jury has the potential to offset some of the well-known advantages of repeat players in the legal world, such as business corporations.[26] The jury's presence might reassure some cynics who believe that wealthy parties can purchase favorable legal outcomes from the decision maker. Consider the remarks of Portland attorney Gregory Kafoury: "In our nation, we see the Congress, the presidency, and the state legislatures largely bought and paid for. . . . When a great corporation comes before 12 citizens, it cannot rig the outcome. And if the jury says 'Off with your head!' the company gets hurt. It gets hurt financially, it gets hurt in the press, and it gets hurt in the stock market."[27] A vigorous debate is currently raging over whether the civil jury should remain the decision maker for punitive damages, with some scholars arguing that juries' punitive damage awards are erratic and infected by biases.[28] Lempert argues that removing the punitive damages decision from juries to judges would produce a host of undesirable spin-off effects, such as incentives for the trial bar and companies to lobby for and against judicial candidates.[29] Although financially well-to-do litigants will always have substantial advantages in civil litigation, the continuing presence of the civil jury allows citizens the opportunity to resolve significant cases of individual and business rights and responsibilities.

Whether the hypothesized increased responsiveness of the civil justice system on account of the jury might be outweighed by other potential drawbacks remains an open question, and one that is difficult to study. Even though my research casts doubt on the supposed pro-plaintiff, anti-business tendencies of the civil jury, the fact remains that the presence of the jury in the civil justice system allows members of the public some modest say over the practices of the modern corporation. On balance, is giving jurors that voice positive or negative? Does the presence of the civil jury enhance or lessen the degree of care in business activity? Does it undermine innovation? Whatever the jury's independent contribution, are there more efficient and effective methods of promoting the deterrence and compensation goals of the civil justice system? Having presented an empirically based portrait of the civil jury's approach to business cases, I leave these questions for other citizens and scholars.

NOTES

CHAPTER 1 The Debate over the Jury's Role in Business Cases

1. Weiser, Carl (1993, July 21), Farmer: "Improved" Benlate cost me $4 million, *News Journal*, p. A1.
2. Weiser, Carl (1993, July 29), DuPont exec: Benlate was a "good product," *News Journal*, p. A1.
3. Weiser, Carl (1993, August 10), What the jury didn't hear in Ga., *News Journal*, pp. A1, A4.
4. Weiser, Carl (1993, July 31), DuPont chemist silenced, *News Journal*, p. A1.
5. Weiser, Carl (1993, August 11), Take DuPont to woodshed, lawyer cries, *News Journal*, p. A1.
6. For discussion of the image of the civil jury, see Hans, Valerie P. (1993), Attitudes toward the civil jury: A crisis of confidence? in Robert E. Litan (Ed.), *Verdict: Assessing the civil jury system* (pp. 248–281), Washington, D.C.: Brookings Institution.
7. McMurray, Scott (1993, August 13), DuPont settles lawsuit over fungicide for small fraction of damages sought, *Wall Street Journal*, p. A3.
8. Woolner, Ann (1993, August 16), Jury was leaning toward DuPont: Jurors say plaintiffs didn't have much of a case, *Fulton County Daily Report*, pp. 1, 4–5.
9. McMurray, *supra* note 7.
10. Woolner, *supra* note 8, at 1; Weiser, Carl (1993, August 13), Benlate lawsuit settled: Growers' attorney concedes, *News Journal*, p. A1.
11. Woolner, *supra* note 8, at 4.
12. *Id.*
13. Weiser, *supra* note 10, at 1.
14. Woolner, *supra* note 8, at 4.
15. *Id.* at 5. It is interesting to note that jurors did not behave passively when the judge ruled against DuPont on this matter. Rather, they actively speculated about the absence of testimony and witnesses, and made inferences about the missing information. For an interesting discussion of how jurors often respond in active and unanticipated ways to efforts to "blindfold" them, see Diamond, Shari Seidman, Jonathan D. Casper, & Lynne Ostergren (1989), Blindfolding the jury, *Law and Contemporary Problems, 52,* 247–267.
16. Cornish, Neil (1994, May 12), DuPont wins Fla. lawsuit, *News Journal*, p. A1.
17. Brienza, Julie (1995, April), Benlate DF suits continue to mount; DuPont sanctioned, *Trial, 31,* 96–98.
18. *Id.* at 98.
19. *Id.* at 96–98.
20. Mantius, Peter (1999, January 1), Hawaii court released DuPont's test results, *Atlanta Constitution*, p. 15A.
21. Pedreira, David (1999, January 1), DuPont's $11 million endowment ends Benlate suit in Georgia, *Tampa Tribune*, Florida/Metro section, p. 1; Sissell, Kara (1999, January 13), DuPont settles Georgia Benlate inquiry, *Chemical Week*, p. 10.
22. Matsuura v. E. I. DuPont de Nemours and Co., 166 F.3d 1006 (9th Cir. 1999).

23. Kirschner, Elisabeth (1996, June 17), DuPont loses Benlate birth defect trial, *Chemical and Engineering News, 74,* 7; Bork, Diana Culp (1996, June 26), A Florida judge lets junk science into her courtroom, *Wall Street Journal,* pp. A15, A19.

24. E. I. DuPont de Nemours and Co. v. Castillo, 1999 Fla. App. LEXIS 1447 (Court of Appeal of Florida, 3d district).

25. Hollingsworth, Jan (1998, August 20), Health problems blamed on Benlate, *Tampa Tribune,* p. 1; Rougvie, James (1999, February 20), US court ruling puts Scots families' claims in jeopardy, *Scotsman,* p. 7.

26. Kirschner, Elisabeth (1996, July 29), DuPont faces recent Benlate losses on health and plant damage claims, *Chemical and Engineering News, 74,* 20–23. The billion-dollar figure appeared in a number of news reports; see Ruling ok's new lawsuits against DuPont (1999, February 3), *Los Angeles Times,* p. C3; Pedreira, *supra* note 21.

27. Van Duch, Darryl (1997, October 13), Bad PR spurs cave-ins, *National Law Journal,* pp. A1, A6–A7. The quotation is from p. A7.

28. My summary is necessarily brief and paints with a broad brush. Several classic citations include more detailed analysis: Friedman, Lawrence M. (1985), *A history of American law,* 2d ed., New York: Simon and Schuster; Horwitz, Morton J. (1977), *The transformation of American law, 1780–1860,* Cambridge: Harvard University Press; and Hurst, James Willard (1956), *Law and the conditions of freedom in the nineteenth-century United States,* Madison: University of Wisconsin Press. For challenges to the economically based instrumentalist views of Hurst and Horwitz, see Karsten, Peter (1997), *Heart versus head: Judge-made law in nineteenth-century America,* Chapel Hill: University of North Carolina Press; and Schwartz, Gary (1981), Tort law and the economy in nineteenth-century America: A reinterpretation. *Yale Law Journal, 90,* 1717–1775.

29. Friedman, *supra* note 28, at 185–187.

30. *Id.* at 470. See Lamson v. American Axe & Tool Co., 177 Mass. 144, 58 N.E. 585 (1900).

31. In the nineteenth century, the existence of contributory negligence was a complete defense. Today, most jurisdictions have replaced contributory negligence with a standard of comparative negligence. See Epstein, R., C. Gregory, & H. Kalven (1984), *Cases and materials on torts,* 4th ed., Boston: Little, Brown. Historically, the jury showed ambivalence toward the contributory negligence doctrine, an ambivalence that some cite as playing a causal role in the shift toward comparative negligence. See Kalven, Harry Jr., & Hans Zeisel (1966), *The American jury,* Boston: Little, Brown; and the discussion on the jury's response to contributory negligence (pp. 43–47) in Landsman, Stephan (1993), The history and objectives of the civil jury system, pp. 22–60 in Litan, *supra* note 6.

32. Farwell v. Boston & Worcester Railroad Corporation, 45 Mass. (4 Metc.) 49 (1842).

33. Discussions of the jury's decline may be found in Horwitz, *supra* note 28, especially chapter 3; and Note: The changing role of the jury in the nineteenth century (1964), *Yale Law Journal, 74,* 170–192. See also Hans, Valerie P., & N. Vidmar (1986). *Judging the jury.* New York: Plenum, pp. 38–40.

34. Karsten, *supra* note 28.

35. Friedman, *supra* note 28, at 468.

36. *Id.* at 482.

37. McEvoy, Arthur F. (1995), The Triangle Shirtwaist Factory fire of 1911: Social change, indus-

trial accidents, and the evolution of common-sense causality. *Law & Social Inquiry, 20,* 621–651.

38. *Id.* at 637.

39. *Id.* at 637–638.

40. Priest, George L. (1991), The modern expansion of tort liability: Its sources, its effects, and its reform, *Journal of Economic Perspectives, 5,* 31–50. As Priest observes, before the 1960s "a ladder was a ladder, and a fall was a deviation from normal consumer use," and "no one thought to sue ladder manufacturers for injuries suffered from falls off ladders" (p. 38). By the 1990s, lawsuits alleging product defects against ladder manufacturers and others were common. See also Priest, George L. (1985), The invention of enterprise liability: A critical history of the intellectual foundations of modern tort law, *Journal of Legal Studies, 14,* 461–527.

41. E.g., Greenman v. Yuba Power Prod. Inc., 59 Cal.2d 57, 377 P.2d 897, 27 Cal. Rptr. 697 (1963); *Restatement (Second) of Torts,* section 402A (1964).

42. E.g., Sindell v. Abbott Laboratories, 26 Cal.3d 57, 607 P.2d 924 (1980), *cert. denied,* 449 U.S. 912 (1980).

43. Brickey, Kathleen F. (1984), *Corporate criminal liability: A treatise on the criminal liability of corporations, their officers and agents,* Wilmette, Ill.: Callaghan.

44. Dunworth, Terence, & Joel Rogers (1996), Corporations in court: Big business litigation in U.S. federal courts, 1971–1991, *Law & Social Inquiry, 21,* 497–592.

45. Professor Marc Galanter of the University of Wisconsin's School of Law analyzed trends in federal court statistics over time, from 1960 to 1986, and discovered dramatic increases in court filings for various types of commercial litigation, including contract litigation, intellectual property disputes, and bankruptcy cases. Galanter, Marc (1988), The life and times of the big six; or, the federal courts since the good old days, *Wisconsin Law Review, 1988,* 921–954. See also Galanter, Marc, & Joel Rogers (1991, April), *A transformation of American business disputing? Some preliminary observations,* working paper DPRP 10–3, Institute for Legal Studies, University of Wisconsin, Madison.

46. Business cases clog courts (1995, August 5), *National Law Journal,* p. A1 and section C. The complexity of the cases may be one reason why the cases do not proceed more swiftly through the courts. Another possibility is that large corporations have the financial resources to litigate vigorously, which prolongs litigation and makes cases more difficult to resolve.

47. Friedman, Lawrence (1985), *Total justice,* New York: Russell Sage Foundation.

48. For example, comparisons of manufacturers from the 1960s to the 1990s have revealed that manufacturers today are more likely to rely on new forms of contracts to regulate their dealings with other companies, such as contractors and suppliers, than they were in the 1960s, when companies depended more on general norms and customs of business than on the law. Compare the classic study of the minimal use of formal contracts by manufacturers in Macauley, Stewart (1963), Non-contractual relations in business: A preliminary study, *American Sociological Review, 28,* 55–67; with Esser, John P. (1996), Institutionalizing industry: The changing forms of contract, *Law & Social Inquiry, 21,* 593–629, showing the rise of "relational" contracting.

49. Galanter & Rogers, *supra* note 45. See also Kenworthy, Lane, Stewart Macauley, & Joel Rogers (1996), "The more things change . . . ": Business litigation and governance in the American automobile industry, *Law & Social Inquiry, 21,* 631–678.

50. Peterson, Mark (1987), *Civil juries in the 1980s: Trends in jury trials in California and Cook County Illinois*, Santa Monica, Calif.: Rand Corporation.

51. *Id.* at 11.

52. Ostrom, Brian, David Rottman, & Roger Hanson (1992), What are tort awards really like? The untold story from the state courts, *Law and Policy, 14*, 77–106.

53. Data were collected for all civil jury trials in forty-five jurisdictions during the 1992 fiscal year. A figure of 53% for business defendants in all civil jury trials in the Civil Trial Court Network Project was obtained through online analysis using the database Web site (http://teddy.law.cornell.edu:8090/questata.htm). See also Ostrom, Brian J., David B. Rottman, & John A. Goerdt (1996), A step above anecdote: A profile of the civil jury in the 1990s, *Judicature, 79*, 233–241. Based on the same data set, Ostrom et al. report that 47% of all tort jury trials listed a corporation as a defendant, 5% included an insurance company as a defendant, and another 11% specified a hospital or medical company as a defendant.

54. In online analysis, business plaintiffs accounted for 11% of all plaintiffs in all civil jury trials. In contrast, individuals accounted for 87% of the plaintiffs. In tort trials, the predominance of individuals was even more pronounced; they accounted for 95% of all plaintiffs.

55. See, for example, Dunworth and Rogers, *supra* note 44, at 555, figure 19, showing that more than 90% of cases involving large corporations end early in the litigation, primarily through dismissal or a default judgment. A low rate of civil cases resolved by jury trials was also found in a study of New Haven Superior Court cases in the years 1919–1932, where 4% of cases filed were resolved by jury trial. Cited at p. 49 in Landsman, *supra* note 31.

56. Ostrom et al., *supra* note 53, at 234.

57. Dunworth & Rogers, *supra* note 44, at 555, figure 19. For a discussion of the decline in civil trials, including jury trials, see Alschuler, Albert W. (1990), The vanishing civil jury, *University of Chicago Legal Forum, 1990*, 1–24.

58. Ostrom et al., *supra* note 53, at 234.

59. Galanter, Marc (1993), The regulatory function of the civil jury, pp. 61–102 in Litan, *supra* note 6.

60. See Lempert, Richard (1981), Civil juries and complex cases: Let's not rush to judgment, *Michigan Law Review, 80*, 68–132. The discussion of the political role of the civil jury may be found on pp. 80–84; and in Landsman, *supra* note 31, at 52–53. For a thoughtful analysis and critique of the idea that the civil jury plays a significant political role, see Priest, George L. (1993), Justifying the civil jury, pp. 103–136 in Litan, *supra* note 6.

61. Adler, Stephen J. (1994). *The jury: Trial and error in the American courtroom*, New York: Times Books. The quotation is from p. 146.

62. Nader, Ralph, & Wesley J. Smith (1996), *No contest: Corporate lawyers and the perversion of justice in America*, New York: Random House. The quotation is from p. 258.

63. *Id.* at xxvi.

64. E. I. DuPont de Nemours and Co. v. Castillo, see p. 3, note 1, of downloaded LEXIS opinion: "We agree that this was error. We find that this evidence was vague and indefinite. Whatever relevance it may have had was greatly outweighed by its potential to unfairly prejudice the jury." The note continues with citations to a later scientific study that failed to confirm the clustering.

65. See Adler, *supra* note 61, at 146, for discussion of this point.

66. Angell, Marcia (1996), *Science on trial: The clash of medical evidence and the law in the breast implant case,* New York: Norton. The quotation is from page 74.

67. Vamos, Mark N. (Ed.), The verdict from the corner office (*Business Week*/Harris Executive Poll) (1992, April 13), *Business Week,* p. 66. See also the accompanying article, Galen, Michele, with Alice Cuneo & David Greising (1992, April 13), Guilty! Too many lawyers and too much litigation: Here's a better way, *Business Week,* pp. 60–65.

68. This appears to be especially true at the start of product liability litigation, when the evidence about product effects is still developing.

69. Diamond, Shari Seidman (1993), Order in the court: Consistency in criminal court decisions, in C. James Scheirer & Barbara L. Hammonds (Eds.), *Psychology and the Law,* vol. 2 of *The Master Lecture Series* (pp. 123–146), Washington, D.C.: American Psychological Association; Hensley, Thomas R., & Scott P. Johnson, Unanimity on the Rehnquist Court, *Akron Law Review, 31,* 387–408 (showing that 60% of U.S. Supreme Court opinions from 1953 to 1990 were not unanimous).

70. Vamos, *supra* note 67.

71. See Huber, Peter, & Robert E. Litan (1991), *The liability maze: The impact of liability law on safety and innovation,* Washington, D.C.: Brookings Institution; Litan, Robert E. (1991), The liability explosion and American trade performance: Myths and realities, in Peter H. Schuck (Ed.), *Tort law and the public interest: Competition, innovation, and consumer welfare* (pp. 127–150), New York: Norton.

72. Garber, Steven (1993), *Product liability and the economics of pharmaceuticals and medical devices,* Santa Monica, Calif.: Rand Corporation. See also Eads, George, & Peter Reuter (1985), *Designing safer products: Corporate responses to product liability law and regulation,* Santa Monica, Calif.: Rand Corporation.

73. Sanders, Joseph (1992), The Bendectin litigation: A case study in the life cycle of mass torts, *Hastings Law Journal, 43,* 301–418.

74. See Tort Policy Working Group, United States Department of Justice (1986), *Report of the Tort Policy Working Group on the causes, extent, and policy implications of the current crisis in insurance availability and affordability;* Council on Competitiveness (1991), *A report from the President's Council on Competitiveness: Agenda for civil justice reform in America;* Hensler, Deborah (1992, February–March), Taking aim at the American legal system: The Council on Competitiveness's agenda for legal reform, *Judicature, 75,* 244–250.

75. Daniels, Stephen (1989), The question of civil jury competence and the politics of civil justice reform, *Law and Contemporary Problems, 52,* 269–321.

76. Gillespie, Ed, & Bob Schellhas (Eds.) (1994), *Contract with America,* New York: Times Books, p. 147. See also the Republicans' follow-up book, Moore, Stephen (Ed.) (1995), *Restoring the dream,* New York: Times Books, which points to excessive litigation as a "major impediment to creating a prosperous and growing economy" (p. 157).

77. Sanders, Joseph, & Craig Joyce (1990), "Off to the races": The 1980s tort crisis and the law reform process, *Houston Law Review, 27,* 207–295; Schmitt, Richard B. (1995, June 15), While Congress debates, states limit civil lawsuits, *Wall Street Journal,* pp. B1, B8.

78. Chesebro, Kenneth J. (1993), Galileo's retort: Peter Huber's junk scholarship, *American University Law Review, 42,* 1637–1726. See especially the discussion on pp. 1714–15, note 344, on the nature of tort-reform organizations and the industry and insurance organizations that

support them financially. Other analyses of the role of business in tort reform may be found in Schmitt, Richard B. (1994, March 10), Powerful companies unite to push for legal reform, *Wall Street Journal*, p. B1; Schmitt, Richard B. (1995, February 13), GOP drive to curb liability suits emboldens the business lobbyists, *Wall Street Journal*, p. B2; Hofmann, Mark A. (1994, April 4), Big names try to keep low profile, *Business Insurance*, p. 3.

79. Henderson, James A., Jr., & Eisenberg, Theodore (1990), The quiet revolution in products liability: An empirical study of legal change, *UCLA Law Review, 37*, 479–553; Eisenberg, Theodore, & James A. Henderson, Jr. (1992), Inside the quiet revolution in products liability, *UCLA Law Review, 39*, 731–810.

80. See the analysis in Hans, Valerie P., & Andrea Appel (1999), The jury on trial, in Walter F. Abbott & John Batt (Eds.), *Handbook of jury research*, Philadelphia: American Law Institute.

81. 116 S. Ct. 1384 (1996).

82. *Id.* at 1395.

83. BMW of North America, Inc. v. Gore, 116 S. Ct. 1589 (1996).

84. *Id.* at 1682, note 34. Justice Breyer's concurrence quoted the language of Pacific Mutual Life Insurance Co. v. Haslip, 499 U.S. 1, 18 (1991).

85. Daubert v. Merrell Dow Pharmaceuticals, Inc., 509 U.S. 579 (1993).

86. Kumho Tire Company v. Carmichael, 119 S. Ct. 1167 (1999).

87. The call for more empirical study of the civil justice system has been made in Galanter, Marc, Bryant Garth, Deborah Hensler, & Frances Zemans (1994), How to improve civil justice policy, *Judicature, 77*, 185, 229–230; Saks, Michael J. (1992), Do we really know anything about the behavior of the tort litigation system—and why not? *University of Pennsylvania Law Review, 140*, 1147–1292; Schuck, *supra* note 71.

88. Dunworth & Rogers, *supra* note 44, at 499–500.

89. Some of the results from the research project have appeared in scholarly journals. See Hans, V. P., & W. S. Lofquist (1992), Jurors' judgments of business liability in tort cases: Implications for the litigation explosion debate, *Law & Society Review, 26*, 85–115; Hans, V. P., & K. Sweigart (1993), Jurors' views of civil lawyers: Implications for courtroom communication, *Indiana Law Journal, 68*, 1297–1332; Hans, V. P., & W. S. Lofquist (1994), Perceptions of civil justice: The litigation crisis attitudes of civil jurors, *Behavioral Sciences and the Law, 12*, 181–196; Hans, V. P. (1996), The contested role of the civil jury in business litigation, *Judicature, 79*, 242–248; and Hans, V. P. (1998), The illusions and realities of jurors' treatment of corporate defendants, *DePaul Law Review, 48*, 327–353.

90. One pretest case fell outside the one-year boundary. Cases that settled during trial and two cases involving a conflict of interest were excluded.

91. See Ostrom et al., *supra* note 53, at 240.

92. To assess the comparability of the types of cases, I compared my sample with the civil jury trials in the Civil Trial Court Network Project using the online database (see note 53). Using all jury trial disposition methods, all plaintiff types, and business and hospital defendant types, I observed a good deal of similarity. For example, 74% of the CTCN sample included tort cases, compared to 78% tort cases in my sample. Automobile torts represented 20% of the CTCN sample and 22% of my sample; product liability and toxic substances were less frequent (with combined totals of 8% of the CTCN cases and 11% of my sample). Differences included the fact that my sample had fewer cases of premises liability (20% of the CTCN

sample but only 6% of my sample) and more cases of medical malpractice (12% of CTCN cases but 28% of my sample). My sample included 4 cases (11%) of worker injury, but the CTCN coded these as "other torts" rather than counting them separately, so a direct comparison isn't possible (personal communication with Brian Ostrom, March 30, 1999).

93. For example, in their sample of all tort cases, the NCSC study found a median jury award of $52,000 and a mean award of $455,000. See Ostrom et al., *supra* note 53. The mean and median awards in my sample of business and corporate cases are higher. The reasons why cases involving businesses and corporations might produce higher-than-average awards are taken up at length in Chapter 7. In my group of thirty-six trials, there were two multi-million-dollar awards that skewed the average award upward. The first case in which we interviewed jurors was purposefully selected after the conclusion of the trial because it resulted in a multi-million-dollar award. The second was included in the year-long sample of cases and was, at the time, a record-breaking award in the jurisdiction. The inclusion of the first case raised the mean award for the thirty-six cases by approximately one hundred thousand dollars, while the inclusion of the second raised the mean by approximately three hundred thousand dollars.

94. For the limitations of retrospective questions, see Pearson, Robert W., Michael Ross, & Robyn M. Dawes (1992), Personal recall and the limits of retrospective questions in surveys, in Judith M. Tanur (Ed.), *Questions about questions: Inquiries in the cognitive bases of surveys* (pp. 64–65), New York: Russell Sage Foundation; Nisbett, Richard E., & Timothy Wilson (1977), Telling more than we can know: Verbal reports on mental processes, *Psychological Review, 84,* 231–259.

95. The state is not named, in order to decrease the likelihood of identifying the cases from the juror interview study, which was conducted in the same state.

CHAPTER 2 Blaming the Victim in Civil Lawsuits against Business

1. 13 Barb. 2 (N.Y. 1853), p. 15, quoted in Landsman, Stephan (1993), The history and objectives of the civil jury system, in Robert E. Litan (Ed.), *Verdict: Assessing the civil jury system* (pp. 22–60), Washington, D.C.: Brookings Institution. The quotation is from p. 45.

2. Frank, Jerome (1936), *Law and the modern mind,* New York: Tudor Publishing. The quotation is from pp. 177–178.

3. Huber, Peter (1988), *Liability: The legal revolution and its consequences,* New York: Basic Books. The quotation is from p. 185. See also Olson, Walter K. (1991), *The litigation explosion: What happened when America unleashed the lawsuit,* New York: Dutton ("Juries' damage calculations are more influenced by sympathy," p. 335).

4. Zuger, Martin (1983), *Public attitudes toward civil justice,* cited in Saks, Michael J. (1998), Public opinion about the civil jury: Can reality be found in the illusions? *DePaul Law Review, 48,* 221–245; poll data cited are on p. 243.

5. Clermont, Kevin M., & Theodore Eisenberg (1992), Trial by jury or judge: Transcending empiricism, *Cornell Law Review, 77,* 1124–1177.

6. See the discussion of the trial judge's decision, and the subsequent decision by an appeals court to uphold the judge's exclusion, in Green, Michael D. (1996), *Bendectin and birth defects: The challenges of mass toxic substances litigation,* Philadelphia: University of Pennsyl-

vania Press. See pp. 233–235. Case citation is *In re* Richardson-Merrell, Inc., "Bendectin" Products Liability Litigation, 624 F.Supp. 1212, 1224 (S.D. Ohio 1985), *aff'd*, 857 F.2d 290 (6th Cir. 1988), *cert. denied*, 488 U.S. 1006 (1989).

7. Federation of Insurance and Corporate Counsel, *Handling sympathy in jury trials* (n.d.), videocassette.

8. In our jury study, "C" refers to the number we assigned to each case, and "J" refers to the number we assigned to each juror who heard a particular case. Case numbers and juror numbers correspond to the order of interviews, not to numbers assigned by the court. Jurors' comments have been edited slightly for readability, but the jurors' own language was preserved whenever possible, even if it was not grammatically correct.

9. This juror was one of the two holdouts for a verdict for the defendant: "I was on the company side. . . . I didn't want to be emotional" (C1-J4). He ultimately changed his mind and voted for the plaintiff; he was one of the few jurors in the entire project who explicitly stated that the defendant's deep pockets influenced his change of heart (see Chapter 7).

10. This juror went on to say, however, "But I believe that when you're playing any sport, you should be provided the best possible equipment that you can have" (C1-J1). Thus, even though she held the plaintiff to a standard of personal responsibility for playing sports, she also acknowledged the duty of such others as coaches, staff, and manufacturers to provide equipment that reduced the chance of injury.

11. For a fuller discussion of loss of consortium claims, see Hans, Valerie P., & Michelle Hallerdin (1992, March 13), Juror skepticism toward plaintiffs: The example of loss of consortium claims, Paper presented at the biennial midwinter meeting of the American Psychology-Law Society, San Diego.

12. Hans, V. P., & K. Sweigart (1993), Jurors' views of civil lawyers: Implications for courtroom communication, *Indiana Law Journal, 68,* 1297–1332.

13. The correlation between the item about the legitimacy of lawsuits and the mock juror's individual perception of plaintiff responsibility was .19 ($p = .02$); the item also correlated significantly with individual judgments of negligence ($r = -.19, p = .005$) and with individual recommendations of award ($r = -.19, p = .006$).

14. The correlation between opinions about the legitimacy of plaintiff grievances and opinions about the negligence of the defendant was statistically significant ($r = -.10, p = .03$), as was the relationship between opinions about the legitimacy of plaintiff grievances and recommended award ($r = -.11, p = .03$). Curiously, a direct question about the plaintiff's responsibility was not significantly related to the general item about the legitimacy of plaintiffs' claims ($r = .05, ns$).

15. For a general review of the relevant studies, see Hans, Valerie P. (1993), Attitudes toward the civil jury: A crisis of confidence? pp. 248–281 in Litan, *supra* note 1.

16. Taylor, H., M. R. Kagay, & S. Leichenko (1987), *Public attitudes toward the civil justice system and tort law reform,* survey conducted for Aetna Life & Casualty by Louis Harris and Associates, copy available from Louis Harris and Associates, 630 Fifth Avenue, New York, N.Y.

17. To sue or not to sue? Public backs liability reform (1991, August), *Public Pulse*, p. 6.

18. Aronson, Peter, David E. Rovella, & Bob Van Voris (1998, November 2), Jurors: A biased, independent lot, *National Law Journal*, pp. A1, A24, A25. Data cited in the text come from the online database of findings from the poll cosponsored by the National Law Journal and

DecisionQuest. Responses to the question cited in the text were obtained at http://www.nlj.com/1998/decisionquest_survey/q01_06.html.

19. Engel, David (1984), The oven bird's song: Insiders, outsiders, and personal injuries in an American community, *Law & Society Review, 18,* 551–581.

20. *Id.* at 559.

21. Clermont & Eisenberg, *supra* note 5.

22. For an excellent discussion of the problems of making direct inferences about jury behavior from jury verdict statistics, see Vidmar, Neil (1994), Making inferences about jury behavior from jury verdict statistics: Cautions about the Lorelei's lied, *Law and Human Behavior, 18,* 599–617.

23. Kalven, Harry, Jr., & Hans Zeisel (1966), *The American jury,* Boston: Little, Brown.

24. Hans, Valerie P. (1998), Illusions and realities in jurors' treatment of corporate defendants, *DePaul Law Review, 48,* 327–353.

25. Feigenson, Neal, Jaihyun Park, & Peter Salovey (1997), Effect of blameworthiness and outcome severity on attributions of responsibility and damage awards in comparative negligence cases, *Law & Human Behavior, 21,* 597–617.

26. *Id.* at 611.

27. Lerner, Melvin (1990), *Belief in a just world: A fundamental delusion,* New York: Plenum.

28. See also Tennen, Howard, & Glenn Affleck (1990), Blaming others for threatening events, *Psychological Bulletin, 108,* 209–232.

29. Lerner, Melvin, & Dale Miller (1978), Just world research and the attribution process: Looking back and ahead, *Psychological Bulletin, 85,* 1030–1051; and Shaver, Kelly (1985), *The attribution of blame: Causality, responsibility, and blameworthiness,* New York: Springer-Verlag.

30. Bellah, Robert N., Richard Madsen, William M. Sullivan, Ann Swidler, & Steven M. Tipton (1985), *Habits of the heart: Individualism and commitment in American life,* Berkeley: University of California Press. The quotation is from p. 25.

31. Beta weights for a modified Litigation Crisis scale (it was necessary to remove the item about the legitimacy of plaintiff claims for accurate analysis) were .34 for the juror sample, .50 for the mock juror sample, and .32 for the state poll (all p's $<$ .001). The Litigation Crisis scale and its correlates are discussed in greater detail in Chapter 3.

32. Chi square (2 d. f.) = 8.89, p = .01.

33. Chi square (2 d. f.) = 6.68, p = .035.

34. Diamond and her colleagues make a similar point in analyzing results from a large mock jury study using a product-liability fact pattern. In their study, women, minority jurors, and less-educated and lower-income jurors were more likely to find for the plaintiff in that case; yet when all these and other background characteristics were combined, they explained only about 5% of the variation in mock juror responses. Diamond, Shari S., Michael J. Saks, & Stephan Landsman (1998), Juror judgments about liability and damages: Sources of variability and ways to increase consistency, *DePaul Law Review, 48,* 301–325. Data cited are on pp. 306–307.

35. Hans and Ermann found no differential fault in a study of worker injury (Hans, Valerie P., & M. David Ermann [1989], Responses to corporate versus individual wrongdoing, *Law & Human Behavior, 13,* 151–166). Furthermore, in the public opinion scenario study described in

Chapter 4 of this book, the case of worker injury did not produce different judgments of plaintiff responsibility in the scenarios with individual, as opposed to corporate, defendants.

36. MacCoun reported no differences in plaintiff fault in a study that compared scenarios with individual defendants to those with corporate defendants. MacCoun, Robert J. (1996), Differential treatment of corporate defendants by juries: An examination of the "deep-pockets" hypothesis, *Law & Society Review, 30,* 121–161.
37. Hans, Valerie P. (1990), Attitudes toward corporate responsibility: A psycholegal perspective, *Nebraska Law Review, 69,* 158–189. See discussion on pp. 177–178.
38. Id.
39. Van Voris, Bob (1997, July 14), Smoke clears in Mississippi, *National Law Journal,* p. A6. See reports of the settlement between state attorneys general and the tobacco companies in: 46 states agree to $206 billion tobacco settlement, (1998, November 23), *Liability Week,* No. 44, Vol. 13; Frankel, Alison (1999, January–February), After the smoke cleared, *American Lawyer,* p. 48.
40. Friedman, Lawrence (1985), *Total justice,* New York: Russell Sage.
41. Friedman, Lawrence M. (1990), *The republic of choice: Law, authority, and culture,* Cambridge: Harvard University Press.
42. Rabin, Robert L. (1993), Institutional and historical perspectives on tobacco tort liability, in Robert L. Rabin & Stephen D. Sugarman (Eds.), *Smoking policy: Law, politics, and culture* (pp. 110–130), New York: Oxford University Press.
43. Black, Donald (1987), Compensation and the social structure of misfortune, *Law & Society Review, 21,* 563–584; Coleman, James S. (1982), *The asymmetric society,* Syracuse: Syracuse University Press.
44. Schwartz, John (1999, February 11), Jury awards ex-smoker $51.5 million, *Washington Post,* p. A2.
45. McCall, William (1999, March 31), $81 million awarded to family of a smoker, *Boston Globe,* p. A3.

CHAPTER 3 Citizens' Attitudes about Civil Litigation

1. Gerlin, Andrea (1994, September 1), How a jury decided that a coffee spill is worth $2.9 million. *Wall Street Journal,* p. A1.
2. Aks, Judith H., William Haltom, & Michael W. McCann (1997, May 31), Media coverage of personal-injury lawsuits and the production of legal knowledge, Paper presented at the annual meeting of the Law and Society Association, St. Louis; Haltom, William (1998), *Reporting on the courts: How the mass media cover judicial actions,* Chicago: Nelson-Hall Publishers. Discussion of media coverage of the McDonald's coffee-spill case is at 223–229.
3. Huber, Peter (1988), *Liability: The legal revolution and its consequences,* New York: Basic Books; Olson, W. K. (1991), *The litigation explosion: What happened when American unleashed the lawsuit,* New York: Dutton.
4. Cong. Record E548 (1995, March 8). Representative Packard's comments were made in the 104th Congress, during discussions of proposed legislation to limit punitive damage awards by civil juries and to make suing doctors and manufacturers more difficult.
5. See the extensive discussion of the use, and misuse, of litigation horror stories at pp. 37–46

in Daniels, Stephen, & Joanne Martin (1995), *Civil juries and the politics of reform*, Evanston, Ill.: Northwestern University Press.

6. The current Web site reporting these stories is http://www.atra.org. I visited the ATRA Web site (formerly located at aaabiz.com/atra/ath.htm) on February 25, 1997, June 18, 1997, and May 12, 1999. The gambling, rock concert, and milk-a-holic stories were on the Web site on May 12, 1999.

7. The story was presented at http://pages.prodigy.com/cala/new11.htm (January 7, 1997, press release). I visited the site on February 25, 1997, June 18, 1997, and May 12, 1999.

8. The quotation is from ACEC's Web site, section on Legal Affairs (http://www.acec.org/bsaf/legal.htm#reform), describing the value of the annual litigation survey. Indeed, a number of stories from engineers collected during the annual survey also appeared on ATRA's Web site as illustrations of frivolous litigation. There are close ties between the two organizations, with ACEC members serving on ATRA's Board and in other leadership roles.

9. Excellent and detailed analyses may be found in Daniels & Martin, *supra* note 5; Galanter, Marc (1983), Reading the landscape of disputes: What we know and don't know (and think we know) about our allegedly contentious and litigious society, *UCLA Law Review, 31*, 4–71; Galanter, Marc (1986), The day after the litigation explosion, *Maryland Law Review, 46*, 3–39; Hensler, Deborah (1992, February–March), Taking aim at the American legal system: The Council on Competitiveness's agenda for legal reform, *Judicature, 75*, 244–250; Saks, Michael J. (1992), Do we really know anything about the behavior of the tort litigation system—and why not? *University of Pennsylvania Law Review, 140*, 1147–1292; Saks, Michael J. (1998), Public opinion about the civil jury: Can reality be found in the illusions? *DePaul Law Review, 48*, 221–245; and Vidmar, Neil (1995), *Medical malpractice and the American jury: Confronting the myths about jury incompetence, deep pockets, and outrageous damage awards*, Ann Arbor: University of Michigan Press.

10. Saks, "Do we really know anything," *supra* note 9, at 1160, n. 34. References to original sources and footnotes were deleted from the quotation.

11. See Daniels & Martin, *supra* note 5, at 268–269, n. 66.

12. Kritzer, Herbert M. (1980–1981), Studying disputes: Learning from the CLRP experience, *Law & Society Review, 15*, 503–524; Miller, Richard E., & Austin Sarat (1980–1981), Grievances, claims, and disputes: Assessing the adversary culture, *Law & Society Review, 15*, 525–565.

13. See Miller & Sarat, *supra* note 12, at 544, figures 1A and 1B, for the general contours of the disputing pyramid (figure 1A), and the distinctive patterns in tort, discrimination, and post-divorce cases (figure 1B). Although these specific types of cases follow the general pyramid shape, there are some interesting differences among them. For instance, compared to the overall numbers, many more post-divorce cases and many fewer discrimination cases result in court filings. Miller and Sarat found that households making tort claims were more likely than other claimants to be accepted, reflecting "a highly institutionalized and routinized system of remedies provided by insurance companies, and the well-established customary and legal principles governing behavior in this area." Id. at 542.

14. Kritzer, Herbert M., W. A. Bogart, & N. Vidmar (1991). The aftermath of injury: Cultural factors in compensation seeking in Canada and the United States, *Law & Society Review, 25*, 499–543.

15. Miller & Sarat, *supra* note 12, at 551–553, 560.

16. Hensler, Deborah R., M. Susan Marquis, Allan F. Abrahamse, Sandra H. Berry, Patricia A. Ebener, Elizabeth G. Lewis, E. Allan Lind, Robert J. MacCoun, Willard G. Manning, Jeannette A. Rogowski, & Mary E. Vaiana (1991), *Compensation for accidental injuries in the United States*, Santa Monica, Calif.: Rand Corporation.

17. *Patients, doctors, and lawyers: Medical injury, malpractice litigation, and patient compensation in New York: The report of the Harvard Medical Practice Study to the State of New York* (1990).

18. Danzon, Patricia (1985). *Medical malpractice: Theory, evidence and public policy*, Cambridge: Harvard University Press.

19. Saks, "Do we really know anything," *supra* note 9, at 1186–1189.

20. Vidmar, Neil, & Regina A. Schuller (1987), Individual differences and the pursuit of legal rights: A preliminary inquiry, *Law and Human Behavior, 11*, 299–317.

21. Attorneys undertake calculations to determine which cases they should accept and which cases they should settle or take to trial. On the selection of cases for trial, see Priest, George L., & Benjamin Klein (1984), The selection of disputes for litigation, *Journal of Legal Studies, 13*, 1–55; also Gross, Samuel R., & Kent D. Syverud (1991), Getting to no: A study of settlement negotiations and the selection of cases for trial, *Michigan Law Review, 90*, 319–393.

22. Galanter, "Reading the landscape of disputes," *supra* note 9.

23. Galanter, "The day after the litigation explosion," *supra* note 9; Galanter, Marc (1988), The life and times of the big six; or, the federal courts since the good old days, *Wisconsin Law Review, 1988*, 921–954; Galanter, Marc (1994), News from nowhere: The debased debate about civil justice, *Denver University Law Review, 71*, 77–113; Galanter, Marc (1996), Real world torts: An antidote to anecdote, *Maryland Law Review, 55*, 1093–1160; Galanter, Marc (1998), An oil strike from hell: Contemporary legends about the civil justice system, *Arizona Law Review, 40*, 717–752.

24. See Galanter, "Real world torts," *supra* note 23, at 1103–1105 (based on National Center for State Courts data from twenty-two states during 1984–1993).

25. *Id.* at 1105–1109.

26. *Id.* at 1109.

27. See Galanter, "The life and times of the big six," *supra* note 23, at 942–945; Dunworth, Terence, & Joel Rogers (1996), Corporations in court: Big business litigation in U.S. federal courts, 1971–1991, *Law & Social Inquiry, 21*, 497–592.

28. See Fleming, J. J., & L. C. Schwarz (1991, December), Juror opinion survey reveals obstacles for litigators, *Inside Litigation, 5*, 21–24; Greene, E., J. Goodman, & E. F. Loftus (1991), Jurors' attitudes about civil litigation and the size of damage awards, *American University Law Review, 40*, 805–820; Hans, V. P. (1993), Attitudes toward the civil jury: A crisis of confidence? in R. E. Litan (Ed.), *Verdict: Assessing the civil jury system* (pp. 248–281), Washington, D.C.: Brookings Institution; Taylor, H., M. R. Kagay, & S. Leichenko (1987), Public attitudes toward the civil justice system and tort law reform, Survey conducted for Aetna Life and Casualty by Louis Harris and Associates, copy available from Louis Harris and Associates, 630 Fifth Avenue, New York, N.Y.; To sue or not to sue? Public backs liability reform (1991, August), *Public Pulse*, p. 6.

29. Taylor et al., *supra* note 28.

30. Fleming & Schwarz, *supra* note 28.

31. Samborn, Randall (1993, August 9), Anti-lawyer attitude up, *National Law Journal, 15*, pp. A1, A20, A22.

32. *Lawsuit abuse in California: A study of lawsuit abuse performed for the Pacific Research Institute by Charlton Research Company* (n.d.) (distributed by Citizens Against Lawsuit Abuse). This pamphlet describes key results of a telephone survey of six hundred people in the Los Angeles media area, conducted in December 1993.

33. Vamos, Mark N. (Ed.), The verdict from the corner office (*Business Week*/Harris Executive Poll) (1992, April 13), *Business Week*, p. 66. See also the accompanying article, Galen, Michele, with Alice Cuneo & David Greising (1992, April 13), Guilty! Too many lawyers and too much litigation: Here's a better way, *Business Week*, pp. 60–65.

34. Songer, Donald R. (1988), Tort reform in South Carolina: The effect of empirical research on elite perceptions concerning jury verdicts, *South Carolina Law Review, 39*, 585–605.

35. Taylor et al., *supra* note 28.

36. Hans, Valerie P., & Krista Sweigart (1993), Jurors' views of civil lawyers: Implications for courtroom communication, *Indiana Law Journal, 68*, 1297–1332; Samborn, *supra* note 31.

37. The reliability of the scale was acceptable across all three studies, with alpha equal to .65 for jurors, .74 for mock jurors, and .60 for state poll respondents.

38. For details of the statistical analyses, see Hans, Valerie P., & William S. Lofquist (1994), Perceptions of civil justice: The litigation crisis attitudes of civil jurors, *Behavioral Sciences and the Law, 12*, 181–196. When I speak in the text of items being strongly associated with a dimension or a factor, I refer to the loadings of the items in factor analysis, a statistical technique that allows analysts to reduce a set of items to one or more underlying dimensions or factors.

39. To tap respondents' sense of political efficacy, I used a scale developed originally by Campbell, Gurin, and Miller to assess the extent to which people think that such individual efforts as voting and other political actions can create political change (Campbell, A., G. Gurin, & W. E. Miller [1954], *The voter decides*, Evanston, Ill.: Ron Peterson). We predicted that a strong sense of political efficacy should be related to a sense that the legal system was responsive to the citizenry. See the discussion of political efficacy in Hans & Lofquist, *supra* note 38, at 184, 190–191. For evidence about the overall decline in public trust in law and government, see Tyler, Tom R. (1998), Public mistrust of law: A political perspective, *University of Cincinnati Law Review, 66*, 847–875.

40. Sorrentino, R. M., & J. E. Hardy (1974), Religiousness and derogation of an innocent victim, *Journal of Personality, 42*, 372–382.

41. Greenhouse, C. J. (1989), Interpreting American litigiousness, In J. Starr & J. F. Collier (Eds.), *History and power in the study of law: New directions in legal anthropology* (pp. 252–273), Ithaca, N.Y.: Cornell University Press.

42. *Id.* at 266.

43. Taylor et al., *supra* note 28; see also Astolfo, T. A. (1991), *Attitudinal predictors in a negligence case*, masters' thesis, Florida International University, Miami, Fla.

44. Friedman, Lawrence (1985), *Total justice*, New York: Russell Sage.

45. Sarat, Austin (1977), Studying American legal culture: An assessment of survey evidence, *Law & Society Review, 11*, 427–488; Bennack, Frank A., Jr. (1983), The public, the media,

and the judicial system: A national survey on citizen awareness, *State Court Journal, 7,* 4–13; National Center for State Courts, *How the public views the state courts: A 1999 national survey,* Williamburg, Va.: National Center for State Courts.

46. See generally Hans, Valerie P., & Juliet L. Dee (1991), Media coverage of law: Its impact on juries and the public, *American Behavioral Scientist, 35,* 136–149; Graber, Doris (1980), *Crime news and the public,* New York: Praeger; Roberts, Julian V., & Anthony N. Doob (1990), News media influences on public views of sentencing, *Law and Human Behavior, 14,* 451–468; Stalans, Loretta, & Shari S. Diamond (1990), Formation and change in lay evaluations of criminal sentencing: Misperception and discontent, *Law and Human Behavior, 14,* 199–214.

47. Aks et al., *supra* note 2; Haltom, *supra* note 2.

48. Gerlin, *supra* note 1.

49. *Id.*

50. Aks et al., *supra* note 2; Haltom, *supra* note 2.

51. McDonald's coffee award reduced 75 percent by judge (1994, September 15), *Wall Street Journal,* p. A4.

52. McDonald's settles lawsuit over burn from coffee (1994, December 2), *Wall Street Journal,* p. B6.

53. Aks et al., *supra* note 2, at 5; Haltom, *supra* note 2.

54. Aks et al., *supra* note 2, at 15.

55. Bailis, Daniel S., & Robert J. MacCoun (1996), Estimating liability risks with the media as your guide: A content analysis of media coverage of tort litigation, *Law and Human Behavior, 20,* 419–429. They studied *Time, Newsweek, Business Week, Fortune,* and *Forbes* for the years 1980–1990, employing a keyword search designed to identify articles on tort litigation. The computer search located 249 articles on civil litigation, which formed the basis for their content analysis.

56. *Id.* See tables 2 and 3, and pp. 423–426. The mean awards followed a similar pattern.

57. Daniels & Martin, *supra* note 5.

58. Daniels presents and critiques the themes of several advertising campaigns that appeared during the 1980s, sponsored by business and insurance groups. Daniels, S. (1989), The question of jury competence and the politics of civil justice reform: Symbols, rhetoric, and agenda-building, *Law and Contemporary Problems, 52,* 269–310.

59. Loftus, Elizabeth (1979, January), Insurance advertising and jury awards, *American Bar Association Journal, 65,* 68–70.

60. Schmitt, Richard B. (1997, March 3), Can corporate advertising sway juries? *Wall Street Journal,* pp. B1, B3.

61. *Id.* at B1.

62. *Id.* at B1, B3.

63. Kahneman, Daniel, Paul Slovic, & Amos Tversky (1982), *Judgment under uncertainty,* Cambridge: Cambridge University Press. See also the discussion in Greene, Edith (1990), Media effects on jurors, *Law and Human Behavior, 14,* 439–450.

64. Alschuler, Albert W. (1998), Explaining the public wariness of juries, *DePaul Law Review, 48,* 407–417. The argument about juror behavior is on p. 409. Alschuler could be right that general attitudes become less important in the context of a trial, but my data showing the significant effect of litigation crisis attitudes on jury decisions indicate that they do not become irrelevant.

65. Greene et al., *supra* note 28, found lower awards in a mock case among jurors who supported tort reform; see also Astolfo, *supra* note 43 (residents of Dade County, Florida, who more strongly supported tort reform recommended lower awards for a hypothetical plaintiff who sued a corporation than those whose support for tort reform was lower). Diamond and her colleagues found that attitudes toward litigation affected judgments of liability. Diamond, Shari S., Michael J. Saks, & Stephan Landsman (1998), Juror judgments about liability and damages: Sources of variability and ways to increase consistency, *DePaul Law Review, 48,* 301–325. Data cited are from table 1, p. 307.

66. The correlation between the awards and the mean Litigation Crisis scale scores among all thirty-six juries is $-.48$ ($p = .003$).

67. Litigation Crisis scale scores were correlated overall with poll participants' scenario judgments of negligence ($r = -.18, p < .05$) and recommended award ($r = -.24, p < .05$). The same pattern was present in each of the three defendant type conditions, and correlations ranged from $-.13$ (*ns*) to $-.37$ ($p < .05$).

68. The mock jury study included thirty-four groups, ten of which decided a high-liability version of the case and twenty-four of which decided a version where liability issues were more ambiguous. Theoretically, attitudes can have the most impact when the evidence in a case is ambiguous rather than strongly slanted to one side or another. Using all thirty-four cases, the overall relationship between litigation crisis views and negligence was $r = -.26, p = .001$, and with the relationship between litigation crisis views and award the r was $-.23, p = .001$. Using just the moderate-liability cases, the correlations with Litigation Crisis views increased slightly, to $-.29$ for negligence and $-.26$ for award. For both the full sample and the moderate-liability cases, correlations in the two experimental conditions between negligence, awards, and litigation crisis views ranged from $-.22$ to $-.34$, and were all statistically significant.

69. Of course, asking the questions before presenting the scenarios creates the risk of alerting people to litigation crisis issues, which might then have a greater impact on decision making. There is also the possibility that some third unknown factor influenced both tendencies to side with defendants and litigation crisis attitudes, and accounts for the correlation between them.

70. Hayden, Robert M. (1991), The cultural logic of a political crisis: Common sense, hegemony and the American liability insurance famine of 1986, *Studies in Law, Politics, and Society, 11,* 95–117. See also Greenhouse, C. J. (1989), Interpreting American litigiousness, in J. Starr & J. F. Collier (Eds.), *History and power in the study of law: New directions in legal anthropology* (pp. 252–273), Ithaca, N.Y.: Cornell University Press; Engel, David M. (1984), The ovenbird's song: Insiders, outsiders, and personal injury in an American community, *Law & Society Review, 18,* 551–582; Galanter, "Real world torts," *supra* note 23, at 1153–1158.

71. Durkheim, Emile (1984), *The division of labor in modern society* (Translated by W. D. Halls), New York: Free Press.

CHAPTER 4 The Personhood of the Corporation

1. Coffee, John C. (1981), "No soul to damn, no body to kick:" An unscandalized inquiry into the problem of corporate punishment, *Michigan Law Review, 79,* 386–459; Fisse, Brent (1983), Reconstructing corporate criminal law: Deterrence, retribution, fault, and sanctions,

Southern California Law Review, 56, 1141–1246; Stone, Christopher D. (1975), *Where the law ends: The social control of corporate behavior,* New York: Harper and Row.

2. See, for example, Nader, Ralph, & Wesley Smith (1996), *No contest: Corporate lawyers and the perversion of justice in America,* New York: Random House; Samuels, Warren J., & Arthur S. Miller (Eds.) (1987), *Corporations and society: Power and responsibility,* New York: Greenwood Press.

3. Allen, William T. (1996, Nov. 12), Economics and moralism in corporation law, Talk presented to the Legal Studies Program, University of Delaware, Newark. For a discussion of limited liability, see Hovenkamp, Herbert (1991), *Enterprise and American law, 1836–1937,* Cambridge: Harvard University Press, pp. 49–55.

4. My brief account of the historical development of the corporation misses many of the subtleties. For fuller accounts, see Friedman, Lawrence M. (1985), *A history of American law,* 2d ed., New York: Simon and Schuster; Horwitz, Morton J. (1977), *The transformation of American law, 1780–1860,* Cambridge: Harvard University Press; and Hurst, James Willard (1956), *Law and the conditions of freedom in the nineteenth-century United States,* Madison: University of Wisconsin Press.

5. Friedman, *supra* note 4, at 188.

6. *Id.* at 191.

7. See, generally, Hurst, *supra* note 4.

8. *Id.* at 84.

9. Tomlins, Christopher L. (1993), *Law, labor, and ideology in the early American republic,* Cambridge: Cambridge University Press; Tomlins, Christopher L. (1985), *The state and the union: Labor relations, law, and the organized labor movement in America, 1880–1960,* Cambridge: Cambridge University Press.

10. Santa Clara County v. Southern Pacific Railroad, 118 U.S. 394 (1886).

11. *Id.* at 396.

12. Quoting from the brief of one of the lawyers, Horwitz notes that it emphasizes the transitive quality of actions against the corporation: "Whatever be the legal nature of a corporation as an artificial, metaphysical being, separate and distinct from the individual members . . . these metaphysical and technical notions must give way to the reality. The truth cannot be evaded that, for the purpose of protecting rights, the property of all business and trading corporations IS the property of the individual corporators. A State act depriving a business corporation of its property without due process of law, does in fact deprive the individual corporators of their property. In this sense . . . there is no real distinction between artificial persons or corporations, and natural persons." Horwitz, Morton J. (1987), *Santa Clara* revisited: The development of corporate theory, pp. 13–63 in Samuels & Miller, *supra* note 2. The quotation is from p. 17 (emphasis deleted).

13. Samuels, Warren J. (1987), The idea of the corporation as a person: On the normative significance of judicial language, pp. 113–129 in Samuels and Miller, *supra* note 2.

14. See the essays in Samuels and Miller, *supra* note 2, particularly: Samuels, *supra* note 13; Flynn, John J. (1987), The jurisprudence of corporate personhood: The misuse of a legal concept (pp. 131–159); and Benjamin, Martin, & Daniel A. Bronstein (1987), Moral and criminal responsibility and corporate persons (pp. 277–282).

15. Meir Dan-Cohen, citing the classic work of Berle and Means (Berle, Adolf A., Jr., & Gardiner C. Means [1932], *The modern corporation and private property,* New York: Macmillan) and

other work that confirmed their initial insights into the separation of stock ownership and corporate control, as well as work that shows the conflicting perspectives of corporate actors and officers, argues: "When a corporation can no longer be identified with a relatively homogeneous group of shareholders, when its behavior can no longer be portrayed as the inert mechanical execution of an owner's will, and as our attention is drawn to its distinctive organizational properties and processes, the posture of simply equating the corporation via personification or aggregation to a natural person loses whatever surface plausibility it might once have had." Dan-Cohen, Meir (1986), *Rights, persons, and organizations: A legal theory for bureaucratic society,* Berkeley: University of California Press. The quotation is from p. 21. See also Stone, *supra* note 1.

16. Fox, Dennis R. (1996), The law says corporations are persons, but psychology knows better, *Behavioral Sciences and the Law, 14,* 339–359; Tomkins, A. J., B. Victor, & R. Adler (1992), Psycholegal aspects of organizational behavior: Assessing and controlling risk, in D. K. Kagehiro & W. S. Laufer (Eds.), *Handbook of psychology and law* (pp. 523–541), New York: Springer-Verlag.

17. Arthur Miller argues: "Corporations, at least those of giant size, are private governments and should be recognized as such. Their power and influence, both externally in the national political order and internally in the so-called corporate community, make them a true form of governance." Miller, Arthur (1987), Corporations and our two constitutions, pp. 241–262 in Samuels & Miller, *supra* note 2. The quotation is from p. 242.

18. This Modern Federal Jury Instructions version may be found in Sand, L., J. Siffert, S. Reiss, J. Sexton, & J. Thrope (1988), *Modern federal jury instructions, civil,* vol. 3, 72–2, instruction 72–1.

19. Dan-Cohen, *supra* note 15, at 13.

20. Although there are many businesses (particularly small businesses) that are not incorporated, and corporations that are not for-profit businesses, the vast majority of business defendants in my sample were also corporations. I treat businesses and corporations interchangeably in this chapter's discussion, while recognizing that they are not always identical.

21. McConnell, Allen R., Steven J. Sherman, & David L. Hamilton (1994), On-line and memory-based aspects of individual and group target judgments, *Journal of Personality and Social Psychology, 67,* 173–185. These researchers conclude that under typical circumstances, memory for individuals should be better than memory for groups. They suggest that for groups that are perceived as very unified and whose members have strong bonds, memory should improve.

22. Nisbett, Richard E., & Lee Ross (1980), *Human inference: Strategies and shortcomings of social judgment,* Englewood Cliffs, N.J.: Prentice-Hall.

23. Hamilton, V. Lee, & Joseph Sanders (1992), *Everyday justice: Responsibility and the individual in Japan and the United States,* New Haven: Yale University Press. Different dimensions of social relationships are presented on p. 11.

24. Summer v. Tice, 33 Cal. 2d 80 (1948).

25. Fox, *supra* note 16, at 348–349; Tomkins et al., *supra* note 16.

26. Darley, John M., & Bibb Latane (1968), Bystander intervention in emergencies: Diffusion of responsibility, *Journal of Personality and Social Psychology, 8,* 377–383.

27. Hans, V. P. (1990), Attitudes toward corporate responsibility: A psycholegal perspective, *Nebraska Law Review, 69,* 158–189; Kelman, H. C., & V. L. Hamilton (1989), *Crimes of obe-*

dience: Toward a social psychology of authority and obedience, New Haven: Yale University Press.

28. The names of the company and the juror given here are fictitious. The juror used her own name and that of her employer in her interview.

29. M. David Ermann, a colleague of mine at the University of Delaware, is a well-known scholar of corporate and organizational deviance. His coedited text on corporate deviance is widely regarded as a classic in the field. Ermann, M. David, & Richard J. Lundman (1996), *Corporate and governmental deviance: Problems of organizational behavior in contemporary society*, 5th ed., New York: Oxford University Press. The experimental study was published: Hans, Valerie P., & M. David Ermann (1989), Responses to corporate versus individual responsibility, *Law and Human Behavior, 13,* 151–166.

30. On the first day of the study, ten groups of subjects (sixty people in all) received a "high-liability" version of the Wilson scenario, in which Mr. Wilson or the employee admitted that the rip had been known about for some time and that others had tripped over it. This proved to be such clear evidence for negligence that there was little variation in subjects' responses either between or within experimental conditions. Furthermore, the videotaped deliberations centered almost exclusively on the award rather than on issues of negligence. Because we were interested in encouraging discussion of negligence, we decided to consider these groups a "pilot study." We modified the scenario to a "moderate-liability" version, in which the defendant claimed to have no prior knowledge of the carpet rip. The data presented in Figures 4-3 and 4-4 and discussed in the text pertain to the mock juries who decided the moderate-liability version.

31. The difference in individuals' negligence judgments was statistically significant: $F = 13.83$, $p < .03$.

32. The difference in awards was statistically significant at both the individual level ($F = 21.91$) and the group levels ($F = 5.49$) (both p's $< .03$).

33. For a discussion of the use of a series of questions to structure jury decision making, particularly in complex cases, see Cecil, Joe S., Valerie P. Hans, & Elizabeth C. Wiggins (1991), Citizen comprehension of difficult issues: Lessons from civil jury trials, *American University Law Review, 40,* 727–774.

34. See the discussion of licensees and invitees on pp. 412–432 in Keeton, W. Page, Dan B. Dobbs, Robert E. Keeton, & David G. Owen (1994), *Prosser and Keeton on the law of torts*, 5th ed., St. Paul, Minn.: West.

35. The experiment also varied the financial wealth of the parties. Those findings are presented in Chapter 7.

36. The overall defendant identity effect is statistically significant. To examine the hypothesis that the group versus individual nature of the defendant influenced judgments of negligence and recklessness, the individual condition responses were tested against the combined responses in the other two conditions in a planned contrast. The contrast was statistically significant, indicating that the group identity of the defendant resulted in higher judgments of negligence and recklessness. In addition, a second contrast comparing the responses of the business defendant with the nonbusiness group and individual conditions revealed that the business defendant is treated differently from the nonbusiness entities.

37. The interaction between defendant identity and the type of case was statistically significant.

38. Of the six cases MacCoun used, four of them varied defendant identity along the lines of the

example in the text. In a fifth case, an auto accident case, the individuals were not involved in a business at the time of the accident, but the corporate defendant was. In the sixth and final case, also an auto accident, the rich individual was operating the car outside a business context, but the accidents involving the poor individual and the corporate defendant were both described as occurring right after a business activity. MacCoun, Robert J. (1996), Differential treatment of corporate defendants by juries: An examination of the "deep-pockets" hypothesis, *Law & Society Review, 30*, 121–161.

39. Sanders, J., V. Lee Hamilton, & Toshiyuki Yuassa (1994), Corporate actor responsibility in three societies, Paper presented at the annual meeting of the Law & Society Association, Phoenix. For a fuller description of the study methodology, see Hamilton, V. Lee, & Joseph Sanders (1996), Corporate crime through citizens' eyes: Stratification and responsibility in the United States, Russia, and Japan, *Law & Society Review, 30*, 513–547.

CHAPTER 5 A Different Standard for Corporations

1. Coleman, James S. (1982), *The asymmetric society: Organizational actors, corporate power, and the irrelevance of persons,* Syracuse, N.Y.: Syracuse University Press.
2. Black, Donald (1987), Compensation and the social structure of misfortune, *Law & Society Review, 21,* 563–584.
3. There is a vast literature on the subject. Citations include: Braithwaite, John (1984), *Corporate crime in the pharmaceutical industry,* London: Routledge and Kegan Paul; Brickey, K. (1984), *Corporate criminal liability,* Wilmette, Ill.: Callaghan; Cullen, Francis T., W. J. Maakestad, & G. Cavender (1987), *Corporate crime under attack: The Ford Pinto case and beyond,* Cincinnati: Anderson; Ermann, M. David, & Richard J. Lundman (1996), *Corporate and governmental deviance: Problems of organization behavior in contemporary society,* 5th ed., New York: Oxford University Press; Levi, Michael (1987), *Regulating fraud: White-collar crime and the criminal process,* London: Tavistock Publications; Paternoster, Raymond, & Sally Simpson (1996), Sanction threats and appeals to morality: Testing a rational choice model of corporate crime, *Law & Society Review, 30,* 549–583; and Sutherland, Edwin H. (1983), *White collar crime: The uncut version,* New Haven: Yale University Press.
4. In keeping with the request of the judges in the jurisdiction to mask the cases and jurors as much as possible, I am not identifying the parties in this case. That includes the car manufacturer.
5. Another juror, however, did sympathize with the plaintiff because of a similar experience: "My heart went out to him. . . . I had a car one time and within twenty months, because it was a lemon, I got rid of it and, you know, lost a great deal of money. Now this was before lemon laws and things like that. So we put these laws in place to protect the consumer and then you have a fancy dealership say we'll fight you, and there are lemons out there" (C25-J3).
6. Hart, H. L. A. (1968), *Punishment and responsibility,* New York: Oxford University Press.
7. Hamilton, V. Lee, & Joseph Sanders (1992), *Everyday justice: Responsibility and the individual in Japan and the United States,* New Haven: Yale University Press; Kelman, H. C., & V. Lee Hamilton (1989), *Crimes of obedience: Toward a social psychology of authority and responsibility,* New Haven: Yale University Press.
8. Kelman & Hamilton, *supra* note 7.
9. Coleman, *supra* note 1.

10. These percentages correspond to the number of jurors who were asked this question, with the exception of jurors in medical malpractice cases. Because so many jurors in medical malpractice cases were unaware that a corporation was a party to the case, we experimented with the corporate standard question, sometimes asking whether the juror thought that doctors should be held to a higher standard than other individuals, or whether the medical context required a higher degree of care.

11. Hamilton, V. Lee, & J. Sanders (1996), Corporate crime through citizens' eyes: Stratification and responsibility in the United States, Russia, and Japan, *Law & Society Review, 30,* 513–547.

12. Shaver, Kelly (1985), *The attribution of blame: Causality, responsibility, and blameworthiness,* New York: Springer-Verlag.

13. Ermann & Lundman, *supra* note 3. See also Diane Vaughan's (1995) account of the Challenger disaster: *The Challenger launch decision: Risky technology, culture, and deviance at NASA,* Chicago: University of Chicago Press.

14. Although there were no significant differences in the judgments of liability, in the judgments of recommended awards MacCoun found a complex interaction between whether the defendant was described as an individual or a corporation and the purpose of the activity. When the activity that generated an injury was for personal use, the wealthy individual was expected to pay lower damages than the wealthy person who was engaged in a commercial activity and lower damages than the corporation in both the personal-use and the commercial-use situations. MacCoun concluded that commercial activity affected awards against wealthy individuals but was not the prime reason that corporations are treated differently from individuals. The MacCoun study could understate the effect of commercial activity, though. The personal use that was attributed to the corporation was the development of a summer cottage for corporate executives to use during retreats and vacations. Because the corporation's business might be (at least for the retreats) conducted at the summer cottage, it could have been construed as at least partly commercial in nature. MacCoun, Robert J. (1996), Differential treatment of corporate defendants by juries: An examination of the "deep-pockets" hypothesis, *Law & Society Review, 30,* 121–161.

15. McClellan, Frank M. (1993), *Medical malpractice: Law, tactics and evidence,* Philadelphia: Temple University Press. See also the discussion in Vidmar, Neil (1995), *Medical malpractice and the American jury: Confronting the myths about jury incompetence, deep pockets, and outrageous damage awards,* Ann Arbor: University of Michigan Press, pp. 123–126.

16. Vidmar, Neil (1993), Empirical evidence on the deep pockets hypothesis: Jury awards for pain and suffering in medical malpractice cases, *Duke Law Journal, 43,* 217–266. See also Keeton, W. Page, Dan B. Dobbs, Robert E. Keeton, & David G. Owen (1984), *Prosser and Keeton on the law of torts,* 5th ed., St. Paul, Minn.: West. The section on pp. 185–193 takes up the issue of professional malpractice, concluding that the law demands that professionals must use the knowledge and care that would be employed by members of good standing in their professions.

17. Vidmar, *supra* note 16, at 252.

18. Vidmar, *supra* note 15, at 37–45, where Vidmar presents plaintiff success rates in medical malpractice cases in a variety of studies (p. 39) and compares them to the rates in other types of cases (pp. 43–44). In several of the larger studies presented by Vidmar, malpractice success rates are around 30%, while other torts produce 50% or higher success rates on average.

Vidmar reminds us that success rates are not highly informative in that they do not reflect the effects of case selection and settlement practices, which may differ dramatically across types of cases. Vidmar, Neil (1994), Making inferences about jury behavior from jury verdict statistics: Cautions about the Lorelei's lied, *Law and Human Behavior, 18,* 599–617.

19. The original study is Walster, E. (1966), Assignment of responsibility for an accident, *Journal of Personality and Social Psychology, 3,* 73–79. Several good reviews analyze the research on this issue. In one meta-analysis, Burger found that six out of twenty-one studies of the link between severity and responsibility produced significant differences. Burger, J. M. (1981), Motivational biases in the attribution of responsibility for an accident: A meta-analysis of the defensive attribution hypothesis, *Psychological Bulletin, 90,* 496–512. Other discussions of the empirical literature include: Fincham, F. D., & J. M. Jaspers (1980), Attribution of responsibility: From man the scientist to man as lawyer, in L. Berkowitz (Ed.), *Advances in Experimental Social Psychology* (vol. 13, pp. 81–138), New York: Academic Press; and Karlovac, M., & John M. Darley (1988), Attribution of responsibility for accidents: A negligence law analogy, *Social Cognition, 6,* 287–318. Hamilton and Sanders, *supra* note 7, found in their multinational scenario study that varying the consequences of an action affected both judgments of responsibility (p. 111) and recommended punishment (p. 168). See also Hans, Valerie P., Joanne Nigg, & Melvin D'Souza (1994, March 11), Contextual effects on responsibility judgments, Paper presented in the symposium "Whose responsibility, for what, when? Responsibility judgments for disaster consequences," at the annual meeting of the American Association for the Advancement of Science, San Francisco.

20. The analysis was conducted in the following manner. Jurors from cases other than medical malpractice suits who had been asked at least one of the questions about the impact of the corporation in their cases were included in the analysis. If the juror responded positively to either of the two questions about the impact of the corporation in his or her own case, we identified that juror as a "yes." Otherwise, if the juror responded with a "no" to one or both of the questions, we identified that juror as a "no." We then correlated these responses to the jurors' responses to the corporate standards question, using just the jurors who answered definitively yes or no. Because of missing data and ambiguous answers, the subset of jurors who could be included in this analysis was smaller than the overall sample (140 of the 194 jurors in the cases that did not involve medical malpractice). However, for those jurors whom we were able to categorize as giving yes or no responses, the relationship between the two variables was powerful (Chi square [1 d.f.] = 10.48, p = .001).

21. We examined only respondents from the moderate-liability mock juries, which provided a more sensitive measure of the potential impact of attitudes. In that group, the correlation between response to the item about corporate standards and the person's initial individual judgment of liability was .30, $p < .05$.

22. The correlation was .21, $p < .05$, based on the 150 individuals in the business corporation conditions.

23. Hamilton and Sanders found this effect only in the U.S. sample. In Japan, there was no relationship between attitudes that corporations should be treated differently and judgments of responsibility for corporate actors. In Russia, views of corporate accountability were unrelated to judgments of responsibility in three of the four stimulus cases, and in the fourth case (one involving factory pollution), those who saw the corporation as special were actually less likely to find the corporate actor responsible. There is a technical difference between the

judgments studied by Hamilton and Sanders and my project: Hamilton and Sanders studied
judgments of responsibility to an individual within the corporation, whereas I analyzed judgments of negligence to the corporate entity itself. This is not necessarily a crucial difference,
because there is typically a relationship between the liability of corporate actors and the corporation as a whole. Judgments that a corporate actor is responsible for an injury are often
associated with judgments that the corporation as a whole should be liable. Hamilton and
Sanders, *supra* note 11.

24. Hamilton & Sanders, *supra* note 11, at 536.

25. t (174) = 2.302, p = .02. The average age differed by five years (forty-seven years for those
who claimed that the corporate party had no effect, compared to forty-two years for those who
said that the corporate identity had an impact).

26. Of the managers and professionals, 17% acknowledged a difference due to corporate identity,
compared to 39% of jurors in other job classifications; Chi square (1 *d.f.*) = 7.363, p = .007.

27. Just 12% of union members said the corporate identity had made a difference, compared to
36% of other jurors; Chi square (1 d.f.) = 5.539, p = .019. Political conservatism was higher
for jurors who said that the corporation had an impact on their thinking; t (172) = −2.638,
p = .009.

28. As before, these analyses were conducted with the 194 jurors in cases other than medical
malpractice. For Political Efficacy, t (140) = 2.195, p = .03. The other results were not statistically significant.

29. The statistical relationships between endorsement of a higher standard for corporations and
the other variables were as follows: education r = −.163, p = .001; income r = −.193, p <
.001; and union membership t (252.848) = 2.203, p =.028.

30. The correlation between endorsement of a higher standard for corporations and income was
negative and significant: r = −.151, p = .029.

31. The correlation was r = −.113, p = .096.

32. The relationship between Political Efficacy and endorsement of a higher standard was negative and significant: r = −.142, p = .038.

33. The mean rating for minorities was 3.81, compared to 3.29 for whites, t (35.600) = 2.573, p =
.014; the mean civil jurors' rating was 3.79, compared to 3.29 for those who had not served,
t (41.788) = 2.694, p = .01.

34. For mock jurors, there were significant correlations between endorsement of a higher standard and the Business Attitudes scale (r = −.279, p < .0001) as well as an item tapping concern about business power (r = −.183, p = .007). In the public opinion poll, the Business
Attitudes scale (r = −.236, p < .0001) and confidence in big business (r = −.097, p = .043)
were significantly and negatively related to endorsement of a higher standard.

35. Keeton et al., *supra* note 16, at 185 (footnotes omitted).

36. Whether the reasonable person standard should be particularized to take into account the
specific characteristics of the parties is a matter of some debate. Although Prosser and
Keeton's classic text (Keeton et al., *supra* note 16) argues that such characteristics as blind-
ness, infirmity, and age need to be considered in the reasonable person standard, the development of the reasonable woman test in sexual harassment cases in some jurisdictions
(e.g., Ellison v. Brady, 924 F.2d 872 [9th Cir. 1991]) has been heavily criticized. For example, it is charged with being too broad, failing to recognize the many differences between
women, and offering an overly generalized view of the reasonable woman, relying on mislead-

ing stereotypes of women's behavior. See Gutek, B. A., & M. O'Connor (1995), The empirical basis for the reasonable woman standard, *Journal of Social Issues, 51,* 151–166; Blumenthal, Jeremy (1998), The reasonable woman standard: A meta-analytic review of gender differences in perceptions of sexual harassment, *Law and Human Behavior, 22,* 33–57.

CHAPTER 6 Are Jurors Anti-Business?

1. Earlier versions of some of the arguments presented in this chapter may be found in Hans, Valerie P. (1998), The illusions and realities of jurors' treatment of corporate defendants, *DePaul Law Review, 48,* 327–353.
2. McGunnigle, George F., Jr. (1992), Representing the corporate defendant in the courtroom: Reflections of a veteran advocate, in *Views from the courtroom* (Brookings Institution/American Bar Association Section of Litigation).
3. *Id.* at 3.
4. Lande, John (1995), *The diffusion of a process pluralist ideology of disputing: Factors affecting opinions of business lawyers and executives,* Ph.D. dissertation, University of Wisconsin, Madison (hereinafter *The diffusion of a process pluralist ideology*). See especially pp. 104–116. Lande conducted telephone interviews with fifty senior executives, fifty-eight inside corporate counsel, and seventy outside counsel, and some face-to-face interviews with members of each group. A summary of his findings is published in Lande, John (1998), Failing faith in litigation? A survey of business lawyers' and executives' opinions, *Harvard Negotiation Law Review, 3,* 1–70.
5. Participant E-3: 47, from Lande, *The diffusion of a process pluralist ideology, supra* note 4, at 112–113.
6. Participant I-2: 47, from *id.* at 112.
7. Participant O-4: 52, from *id.* at 113.
8. The judge, however, is not immune from public opinion. The outcomes of judicial elections are shaped by public opinion, and even in states without direct election of judges, selection and retention can still be affected by public opinion. See Dubois, Philip L. (1980), *From ballot to bench: Judicial elections and the quest for accountability,* Austin: University of Texas Press; McFadden, Patrick M. (1990), *Electing justice: The law and ethics of judicial campaigns,* Chicago: American Judicature Society.
9. See, for example, the important role reserved for preexisting opinions and world knowledge in the "story model" of juror decision making. Pennington, Nancy, & Reid Hastie (1986), Evidence evaluation in complex decision making, *Journal of Personality and Social Psychology, 51,* 242–258; Pennington, Nancy, & Reid Hastie (1992), Explaining the evidence: Tests of the story model for juror decision making, *Journal of Personality and Social Psychology, 62,* 189–206.
10. See the discussion of this controversy in Cutler, Brian L. (1990), Introduction: The status of scientific jury selection in psychology and law, *Forensic Reports, 3,* 227–232.
11. See Diamond, Shari S. (1990), Scientific jury selection: What social scientists know and don't know, *Judicature, 73,* 178–183; MacCoun, Robert (1993), Inside the black box: What empirical research tells us about decisionmaking by civil juries, in Robert E. Litan (Ed.), *Verdict: Assessing the civil jury system* (pp. 137–180), Washington, D.C.: Brookings Institution. See especially p. 151 and accompanying footnotes. See also Wrightsman, Lawrence L.,

& Saul M. Kassin (1985), *The importance of evidence and trial procedure,* Beverly Hills, Calif.: Sage.

12. Ellsworth, Phoebe C. (1993), Some steps between attitudes and verdicts, in Reid Hastie (Ed.), *Inside the juror* (pp. 42–64), Cambridge: Cambridge University Press.

13. Field, H. S., & L. B. Bienen (1980), *Jurors and rape,* Lexington, Mass.: Lexington Books.

14. Ellsworth, *supra* note 12.

15. Another example is Hamilton, V. Lee, & Joseph Sanders (1996), Corporate crime through citizens' eyes: Stratification and responsibility in the United States, Russia, and Japan, *Law & Society Review, 30,* 513–547.

16. Although the lemon law case discussed in Chapter 5 also included punitive damages, I do not include it here, in order to avoid repetition.

17. By the end of the case, she seemed to have changed her opinion about the legitimacy of lawsuits against doctors:

Interviewer:	Do you still think that it's true that there are too many lawsuits against doctors?
Juror:	No. I think that doctors need to be more careful.
Interviewer:	So maybe this case changed the way you thought about that issue?
Juror:	Oh yes. It changed my opinion of what I think of doctors, how I seek advice and how I trust them. I don't look at them as God anymore, not that I always did. (C12-J1)

18. Cases 4 and 26, with nine and twelve plaintiffs, respectively, resulted in relatively low awards. The average award was less than $100,000 per case and less than $10,000 per plaintiff. The third asbestos trial in the sample, Case 22, included six plaintiffs and resulted in an award around $950,000, nearly ten times the awards in the other two cases. By way of comparison, a national study of state-court jury awards in toxic substance cases (predominantly asbestos trials) found that the median award in such cases was $101,000 and that the mean award was $530,000. See Ostrom, Brian J., David B. Rottman, & John A. Goerdt (1996), A step above anecdote: A profile of the civil jury in the 1990s, *Judicature, 79,* 233–241. See p. 238, figure 8, for data on toxic substance trials.

19. Laufer, William S. (1995), A study of small business compliance practices, In the Proceedings of the Second Symposium on Crime and Punishment in the United States, *Corporate crime in America: Strengthening the "good citizen" corporation* (pp. 135–137), Washington, D.C.: United States Sentencing Commission.

20. Davis, James Allan, & Tom W. Smith (1991), *General social surveys, 1972–1991: Cumulative codebook,* Principal investigator James A. Davis, Director and Co-Principal Investigator Tom W. Smith, Chicago: National Opinion Research Center.

21. I chose to use the 1990 General Social Survey poll results, because that was the year in which the bulk of the juror interviews were conducted.

22. Lipset, Seymour Martin, & William Schneider (1987), *The confidence gap: Business, labor, and government in the public mind,* rev. ed., Baltimore: Johns Hopkins University Press; McClosky, Herbert, & John Zaller (1984), *The American ethos: Public attitudes toward capitalism and democracy,* Cambridge: Harvard University Press; Page, Benjamin, & David Shapiro (1992), *The rational public: Fifty years of trends in Americans' policy preferences,* Chicago: University of Chicago Press.

23. McClosky & Zaller, *supra* note 22, chapter 4.

24. Roper, Burns W., & Thomas A. W. Miller (1985), Americans take stock of business, *Public Opinion, 8,* 12–15; see also The public is willing to take business on (1989, May 29), *Business Week,* p. 29.

25. America, land of the shaken *(Business Week/*Harris poll) (1996, March 11), *Business Week,* pp. 64–65.

26. Niemi, Richard, John Mueller, & Tom W. Smith (1989), *Trends in public opinion: A compendium of survey data,* New York: Greenwood Press.

27. Davis, James Allan, & Tom W. Smith (1993), *General social surveys, 1972–1993: Cumulative codebook,* Principal investigator James A. Davis, Director and Co-Principal Investigator Tom W. Smith, Chicago: National Opinion Research Center. Over the time span of 1972–1993, 51% of national poll respondents expressed "a great deal" of confidence in medicine, 43% expressed "only some" confidence, and 7% expressed "hardly any" confidence. The percentage expressing a great deal of confidence in medicine was higher than for any other social institution. See pp. 205–208.

28. Niemi et al., *supra* note 26.

29. McClosky & Zaller, *supra* note 22.

30. The 1990 GSS data are comparable to the average responses by GSS respondents in the 1972–1991 survey years. The 1991 GSS data were more polarized than the other years; more people expressed both "a great deal" (38%) and "hardly any" (18%) confidence in big business in 1991 than in prior years.

31. For a qualitative assessment of the civil jurors' views of lawyers, see Hans, Valerie P., & Krista Sweigart (1993), Jurors' views of civil lawyers: Implications for courtroom communication, *Indiana Law Journal, 68,* 1297–1332.

32. Munsterman, Janice, G. Thomas Munsterman, Brian Lynch, & Steven D. Penrod (1991), *The relationship of juror fees and terms of service to jury system performance,* Arlington, Va.: National Center for State Courts; Diamond, Shari S. (1993), What jurors think: Expectations and reactions of citizens who serve as jurors, in R. E. Litan (Ed.), *Verdict: Assessing the civil jury system* (pp. 282–305), Washington, D.C.: Brookings Institution.

33. Hans, Valerie P., & Jonathan D. Casper (1997), Trial by jury, the legitimacy of the courts, and crime control, in Lawrence M. Friedman & George Fisher (Eds.), *The crime conundrum: Essays on criminal justice* (pp. 93–106), Boulder, Colo.: Westview Press.

34. Lipset & Schneider, *supra* note 22.

35. Van Voris, Bob (1998, November 2), Civil cases: Jurors do not trust civil litigants. Period, *National Law Journal,* p. A24.

36. *Id.*

37. Results of the study samples and the national poll overlapped, with 50%, 50%, 48%, and 48% of the four studies' participants saying that labor had too much power. However, labor had a minority core of strong support in the state poll, with 28% of the state poll respondents expressing the view that labor had too little power in society today, compared to 19% of jurors, 4% of mock jurors, and 13% of the national poll respondents.

38. Cullen, Francis T., William J. Maakestad, & Gray Cavender (1987), *Corporate crime under attack: The Ford Pinto case and beyond,* Cincinnati: Anderson; Levi, Michael (1987), *Regulating fraud: White-collar crime and the criminal process,* London: Tavistock Publications.

39. The public is willing to take business on, *supra* note 24.

40. Page & Shapiro, *supra* note 22, at 159.

41. Jurors made some comments on safety issues. In the conveyor-belt case, the facts of the case led one of the jurors to question the safety standards the company used: "I know some people who work at this plant, and I just know, from and after talking about the case afterwards, I realize that [the defendant company] was very lax in their safety regulations. They did not file a safety report when this happened, which I thought was strange. And that was brought up several times. They didn't really have anybody there that night from [the defendant company] representing them from the safety department, in case something did happen. I thought that was a little strange. So I really felt that their safety procedures were very lax" (C14-J6).

42. See Hans, Valerie P., & William S. Lofquist (1992), Jurors' judgments of business liability in tort cases: Implications for the litigation explosion debate, *Law & Society Review, 26,* 85–115. See particularly pp. 98–99 n. 7.

43. Louis Harris and Associates (1987), *Public attitudes toward the civil justice system and tort law reform* (survey conducted for Aetna Life and Casualty). The "don't know" responses for the Aetna poll included both "not sure" responses and refusals to answer the question.

44. The nine specific items were the following: (1) How much confidence do you have in the people running major companies? (2) Do you think that business and industry in this country has too much power or too little power? (3) As they grow bigger, companies usually get cold and impersonal in their relations with people. (4) Big business in this country is adequately concerned with the safety of its workers. (5) Competition in the marketplace keeps costs down for everyone. (6) Ensuring the safety of products sold to the public is so important that regulations and standards cannot be too high. (7) A company should be required to tell the public about any possibility, however small, that its products might be unsafe. (8) Companies should not be responsible for defects in their products if they used the best scientific and safety information available at the time. (9) Requiring that products be 100% safe is just too expensive. All responses were coded or recoded so that high numbers indicated more positive views of business. The alpha for the scale was acceptable across all three studies: .64 for the jurors; .67 for mock jurors; and .55 for the state poll.

45. Although the exact values of each of the items in the rotated factor matrices differed somewhat across the three studies, the factor structure was remarkably similar. Confidence in big business, concern about business power, the impersonality of large companies, and business concern for worker safety all clustered together in the Business Support factor. Two items on product safety consistently loaded on the Business Safety factor, while the competition item and the liability item clustered together on Business Regulation across the three studies. A few additional items had high loadings in one study or another but were not consistent correlates of the factors across the studies.

46. In an earlier analysis using a different set of items to measure attitudes toward business among tort jurors, we found a similar trend toward lower awards among juries whose members held more pro-business attitudes. See Hans & Lofquist, *supra* note 42, at 99–100. The specific items in the Business Attitudes scale were chosen to maximize the reliability of the scale across all three studies. During scale development, several different collections of items were employed, and although the Business Attitudes scale used here appeared to be the best choice in terms of scale reliability, there were no huge changes in the relationships of business attitudes and case judgments across the scales. They all produced similar results:

small to modest correlations in a similar direction, with more pro-business attitudes associated with more pro-business defendant decisions.

47. For ease of interpretation, all items were recoded as necessary so that higher numbers on each of the items or scales reflected higher values for the factor or more positive views of business.

48. The correlation between business attitudes and negligence judgments was $-.27, p = .001$, for the worker injury, but for the slip-and-fall case it was just $-.07, ns$.

49. For the worker injury condition, the correlation for the individual defendant was $-.39, p = .001$; for the nonprofit, it was $-.41, p < .001$; and for the business, it was $.02, ns$.

50. The mock jury sample included ten groups that decided a high-liability version of the scenarios and twenty-four that decided a moderate-liability version. I report data testing the impact of attitudes and defendant identity for the twenty-four groups only, because these groups provide a more sensitive test of attitudes and case factors. I tested this assumption by comparing correlations of attitudes and case judgments for all mock jurors and for the moderate-liability mock jurors. As predicted, when all mock jurors were used, the correlations between attitudes and judgments were smaller. Looking at the high-liability cases only, there was no statistically significant relationship between business attitudes and judgments (r's were $-.06$ and $.09$ [both ns] for negligence and award judgments, respectively). Thus, it appears to be primarily in trials with ambiguous evidence that jurors' business attitudes make a difference, consistent with general research on the role of attitudes in jury decision making, which shows that jurors' attitudes and values have more impact when the facts of the case are ambiguous. See Kalven, Harry, & Hans Zeisel (1966), *The American jury,* Boston: Little, Brown; Hans, Valerie P., & N. Vidmar (1986), *Judging the jury,* New York: Plenum.

51. For predicting jury awards, using a zero award value for defense verdicts, the linear regression beta weight for the jurors' mean Litigation Crisis score was $-.46$ ($p = .005$), whereas the beta weight for the jurors' mean Business Attitudes score was $-.15$ ($p = .34, ns$).

52. The finding reported in the text is based on mock juries who heard the moderate-liability scenario. For the moderate-liability scenario the linear regression beta weights were similar for the two variables ($-.28$ for Litigation Crisis and $-.26$ for Business Attitudes, both p's = .001). When all mock juries are used in the analysis, Litigation Crisis attitudes remain significant (beta = $-.27, p = .001$), but Business Attitudes are no longer a significant predictor (beta = $-.11, p = .12, ns$).

53. The linear regression beta weights were $-.18$ ($p = .0001$) for Litigation Crisis scores and $-.16$ ($p = .001$) for Business Attitudes scores.

54. $F (2, 21) < 1, ns$.

55. $F (2, 24) = 3.39, p = .05$.

56. Regression analyses included a range of demographic and attitudinal variables. All mock jurors (including the high-liability jurors) were employed for the regression analysis. The multiple r for the regression analyses in the three study samples, with beta weights for education, politics, and gender, were as follows. For jurors, the multiple r was .44; beta weights were .17, .19, and $-.14$ for education, politics, and gender, respectively. For mock jurors (using the full sample), the multiple r was .47, and the beta weights were .27, .25, and $-.17$ for education, politics, and gender, respectively. For the state poll, the multiple r was .35, and the beta weights were .19, .13, and $-.13$ for education, politics, and gender, respectively.

57. Among jurors, age (beta = .21) and a sense of political efficacy (beta = .16) were also related to business attitudes; older jurors and those who had a sense of political efficacy were more positive about business. Among the full complement of mock jurors, mock jurors who had never sued anyone showed greater support for business (beta = .18). Finally, in the state poll, belief in a just world was associated with more support for business (beta = .18).

58. Lipset & Schneider, *supra* note 22. See especially chapter 10, The social and political bases of attitudes toward business, labor, and government. The chapter focuses on education, occupation, and class and does not include a discussion of gender and its possible role in business attitudes.

59. Diamond, Shari S., Michael J. Saks, & Stephan Landsman (1998), Juror judgments about liability and damages: Sources of variability and ways to increase consistency, *DePaul Law Review, 48*, 301–325. See p. 308, table 2.

60. *Id.* at 309.

CHAPTER 7 The Robin Hood Jury

1. Huber, Peter (1988), *Liability: The legal revolution and its consequences*, New York: Basic Books. The quotation is from p. 11.

2. Broder, John M. (1997, September 10), Stares of lawyerly disbelief at a huge civil award, *New York Times*, pp. D1, D2. The quotation is from p. D2.

3. Sensible solutions #3—Civil justice: Balance the scales, Material presented on the Web by the Mobil Corporation at http://www.mobil.com/this/news/opeds/sensible/ss3.html (downloaded June 17, 1997). It originally appeared in the *New York Times*, February 16, 1995, at A15.

4. Chin, Audrey, & Mark A. Peterson (1985), *Deep pockets, empty pockets: Who wins in Cook County jury trials*, Santa Monica, Calif.: Rand Corporation.

5. *Id.* at 28, table 3.7.

6. *Id.* at 41–44; see particularly p. 43, table 4.5.

7. Ostrom, Brian J., David B. Rottman, & John A. Goerdt (1996), A step above anecdote: A profile of the civil jury in the 1990s, *Judicature, 79*, 233–241. See figure 6, p. 237. For the same kind of pattern, see Ostrom, Brian J., David Rottman, & Roger Hanson (1992), What are tort awards really like? The untold story from the state courts, *Law & Policy, 14*, 77–106.

8. Vidmar, Neil (1994), Making inferences about jury behavior from jury verdict statistics: Cautions about the Lorelei's lied, *Law and Human Behavior, 18*, 599–617; Saks, Michael (1992), Do we really know anything about the behavior of the tort litigation system—and why not? *University of Pennsylvania Law Review, 140*, 1147–1292.

9. Chin & Peterson, *supra* note 4; Hans, Valerie P., & Neil Vidmar (1986), *Judging the jury*, New York: Plenum (see discussion on pp. 161–163); Clermont, Kevin, & Theodore Eisenberg (1992), Trial by jury or judge: Transcending empiricism, *Cornell Law Review, 77*, 1124–1177.

10. See Vidmar, *supra* note 8, for fuller discussion of the ways settlement practices and other differences between cases could produce divergent awards.

11. Priest, George (1991), The modern expansion of tort liability: Its sources, its effects, and its reform, *Journal of Economic Perspectives, 5*, 31–50.

12. Escola v. Coca Cola Bottling Co., 24 Cal. 2d 453, 462 (1944). See also the discussion in

chapter 14 (pp. 584–615) in Keeton, W. Page, Dan B. Dobbs, Robert E. Keeton, & David G. Owen (1984), *Prosser and Keeton on the law of torts*, 5th ed., St. Paul, Minn.: West.

13. Huber, *supra* note 1, at 75.

14. Ellis, Dorsey (1982), Fairness and efficiency in the law of punitive damages, *Southern California Law Review, 56*, 1–78.

15. See, for example, the discussion in Daniels, Stephen, & Joanne Martin (1995), *Civil juries and the politics of reform*, Evanston, Ill.: Northwestern University Press, at 200–205. For the argument that punitive damages do not effectively deter, see Peters, Susan M. (1982), Punitive damages in Oregon, *Willamette Law Review, 18*, 369–432. For a defense of punitive damages on deterrence and other grounds, see Galanter, Marc, & David Luban (1993), Poetic justice: Punitive damages and legal pluralism, *American University Law Review, 42*, 1393–1463. A special 1998 issue of the Wisconsin Law Review, "The future of punitive damages," provides a number of superb analyses of the political and empirical issues surrounding punitive damages (*Wisconsin Law Review, 1998*, no. 1).

16. See the discussion on equity research on pp. 67–70 in Wrightsman, Lawrence S., Michael T. Nietzel, & William H. Fortune (1998), *Psychology and the legal system*, 4th ed., Pacific Grove, Calif.: Brooks/Cole.

17. Chin & Peterson, *supra* note 4, at ix.

18. Much has been written on the components of damage awards, and my brief presentation only scratches the surface. The reader is referred to Daniels & Martin, *supra* note 15, and Saks, *supra* note 8, for more extended discussions; see also Vidmar, Neil, Felicia Gross, & Mary Rose (1998), Jury awards for medical malpractice and post-verdict adjustments of those awards, *DePaul Law Review, 48*, 265–299.

19. Greene, Edith (1989), On juries and damage awards: The process of decisionmaking, *Law and Contemporary Problems, 52*, 225–246.

20. Kalven, Harry, Jr., & Hans Zeisel (1966), *The American jury*, Boston: Little, Brown (see pp. 63–65); Kalven, Harry, Jr. (1964), The dignity of the civil jury, *Virginia Law Review, 50*, 1055–1075.

21. Hans, Valerie P., & Neil Vidmar (1991), *The American Jury* at twenty-five years, *Law and Social Inquiry, 16*, 323–351.

22. See Saks, Michael J., Lisa A. Hollinger, Roselle L. Wissler, David Lee Evans, & Allen J. Hart (1997), Reducing variability in civil jury awards, *Law and Human Behavior, 21*, 243–256; Peterson, Mark A. (1984), *Compensation for injuries: Civil jury verdicts in Cook County*, Santa Monica, Calif.: Rand Corporation; Wissler, Roselle L., David L. Evans, Allen J. Hart, Marian M. Morry, & Michael J. Saks (1997), Explaining "pain and suffering" awards: The role of injury characteristics and fault attributions, *Law and Human Behavior, 21*, 181–207. Wissler et al. find, using experiments, that the nature and severity of the injury influence the amounts of awards in the expected manner, with more severe injuries receiving greater damage awards for pain and suffering.

23. See summary of the research on pp. 1218–1223 in Saks, *supra* note 8: "This pattern of overcompensation at the lower end of the range and undercompensation at the higher end is so well replicated that it qualified as one of the major empirical phenomena of tort litigation ready for theoretical attention" (p. 1218).

24. See pp. 63–66 in Bell, Peter A., & Jeffrey O'Connell (1997), *Accidental justice: The dilemmas of tort law*, New Haven: Yale University Press.

25. The means were 3.55, 3.34, and 3.28 for no information, low assets, and high assets, respectively (F [2, 402] = 1.06, ns).

26. The means were 3.82, 3.80, and 3.79 for no information, low assets, and high assets, respectively (F [2, 432]= .025, ns).

27. F (2, 435) = 28.91, $p < .001$.

28. The no-information and low-assets conditions are indistinguishable ($M = 2.83$ for no information and $M = 2.52$ for low assets). Both differ from the high-assets condition ($M = 3.50$).

29. For a discussion about the problems of making scientific inferences from results of "no difference" in the context of breast implant litigation, see pp. 90–110 in Angell, Marcia (1996), *Science on trial: The clash of medical evidence and the law in the breast implant case*, New York: Norton.

30. MacCoun, Robert J. (1996), Differential treatment of corporate defendants by juries: An examination of the "deep-pockets" hypothesis, *Law & Society Review, 30*, 121–161.

31. Vidmar, Neil (1995), *Medical malpractice and the American jury: Confronting the myths about jury incompetence, deep pockets, and outrageous damage awards*, Ann Arbor: University of Michigan Press. The deep-pockets studies are described in chapter 18, pp. 203–220.

32. *Id.* at 217.

33. Landsman, Stephan, Shari Diamond, Linda Dimitropoulos, & Michael J. Saks (1998), Be careful what you wish for: The paradoxical effects of bifurcating claims for punitive damages, *Wisconsin Law Review, 1998*, 297–342.

34. *Id.* at 319–320, table 4.

35. Greene, Edith, Jane Goodman, & Elizabeth F. Loftus (1991), Jurors' attitudes about civil litigation and the size of damage awards, *American University Law Review, 40*, 805–820. See particularly pp. 811–813 for presentation of the correlation between million-dollar-award estimates and mock juror damage awards.

36. Syverud, Kent D. (1994), On the demand for liability insurance, *Texas Law Review, 72*, 1629–1654.

37. Saltzburg, Stephen A., Daniel J. Capra, & Michael M. Martin (1999), Commentary on United States Code Service, Federal Rules of Evidence, Rule 411, downloaded from LEXIS-NEXIS.

38. Broeder, D. W. (1958), The University of Chicago Jury Project, *Nebraska Law Review, 38*, 744–761. See also discussion in Hans, Valerie P., & Neil Vidmar (1986), *Judging the jury*, New York: Plenum, at 124–125.

39. Chin & Peterson, *supra* note 4.

40. The mention of insurance might be undercounted in the corporate defendant condition, because the research assistants summarized the discussions.

41. Mott, Nicole L., Valerie P. Hans, & Lindsay Simpson (2000), What's half a lung worth? Civil jurors' accounts of their award decision making, *Law and Human Behavior, 24* (forthcoming).

42. For further discussion of the undercompensation effect, see Saks, *supra* note 8, at 1216–1223; Bell & O'Connell, *supra* note 24.

CHAPTER 8 Myths and Realities of the Civil Jury in Business Cases

1. Huber, Peter (1988), *Liability: The legal revolution and its consequences*, New York: Basic Books. The quotation is from p. 185.

2. Angell, Marcia (1996), *Science on trial: The clash of medical evidence and the law in the breast implant case*, New York: Norton. The quotation is from p. 74.

3. Sensible solutions #3—Civil justice: Balance the scales, Material presented on the Web by the Mobil Corporation at http://www.mobil.com/this/news/opeds/sensible/ss3.html (downloaded June 17, 1997). It originally appeared in the *New York Times*, February 16, 1995, at A15.

4. Participant E-3: 47, pp. 112–113, in Lande, John (1995), *The diffusion of a process pluralist ideology of disputing: Factors affecting opinions of business lawyers and executives*, Ph.D. dissertation, University of Wisconsin, Madison. A summary of his findings is published in Lande, John (1998), Failing faith in litigation? A survey of business lawyers' and executives' opinions, *Harvard Negotiation Law Review, 3*, 1–70.

5. Other highly likely causes of the variability are differences in state law and different settlement strategies across jurisdictions, which would create distinctive case mixes. For a discussion, see Daniels, Steven, & Joanne Martin (1995), *Civil juries and the politics of reform*, Evanston: Northwestern University Press, at 72.

6. Engel, David (1984), The oven bird's song: Insiders, outsiders, and personal injuries in an American community, *Law & Society Review, 18*, 551–581.

7. The studies, all discussed in Chapter 7, include: the Los Angeles project, MacCoun, Robert J. (1996), Differential treatment of corporate defendants by juries: An examination of the "deep-pockets" hypothesis, *Law & Society Review, 30*, 121–161; the North Carolina project, Vidmar, Neil (1995), *Medical malpractice and the American jury: Confronting the myths about jury incompetence, deep pockets, and outrageous damage awards*, Ann Arbor: University of Michigan Press (the deep-pockets studies are described in chapter 18, pp. 203–220); and finally, the Illinois project, Diamond, Shari S., Michael J. Saks, & Stephan Landsman (1998), Juror judgments about liability and damages: Sources of variability and ways to increase consistency, *DePaul Law Review, 48*, 301–325.

8. For a survey of the judicial surveys, see pp. 261–265 in Hans, Valerie P. (1993), Attitudes toward the civil jury: A crisis of confidence? in R. E. Litan (Ed.), *Verdict: Assessing the civil jury system* (pp. 248–281), Washington, D.C.: Brookings Institution. As described in Chapter 7, the judge-jury agreement rate in civil trials in the Kalven and Zeisel project was approximately 78%. Kalven, Harry, Jr., & Hans Zeisel, *The American jury*, Boston: Little, Brown. A more recent study of Arizona civil trials found a similar rate of judicial agreement with jury verdicts. See Hans, Valerie P. (1998), The illusions and realities of jurors' treatment of corporate defendants, *DePaul Law Review, 48*, 327–353.

9. Vidmar, *supra* note 7. Vidmar's survey of research comparing negligence judgments of jurors and experts may be found on pp. 161–173.

10. Lempert, Richard (1993), Civil juries and complex cases: Taking stock after twelve years, in Litan, *supra* note 8. The quotation is from p. 234.

11. For reviews, see Cecil, Joe S., Valerie P. Hans, & Elizabeth C. Wiggins (1991), Citizen comprehension of difficult issues: Lessons from civil jury trials, *American University Law Review, 40*, 727–774; Hans, Valerie P., & Andrea J. Appel (1999), The jury on trial, in Walter F. Abbott & John Batt (Eds.), *Handbook of jury research*, Philadelphia: American Law Institute; Vidmar, Neil (1998), The performance of the American civil jury: an empirical perspective, *Arizona Law Review, 40*, 849–899.

12. Thompson, William C. (1989), Are juries competent to evaluate statistical evidence? *Law*

and Contemporary Problems, 52, 9–41; Smith, Brian C., Steven D. Penrod, Amy L. Otto, & Roger C. Park (1996), Jurors' use of probabilistic evidence, *Law and Human Behavior, 20,* 49–82.

13. Brief amici curiae of Neil Vidmar et al., Kumho Tire Company v. Carmichael, 1997 U.S. Briefs 1709 (1998). I was one of the amici who wrote this brief.

14. Saltzburg, Stephen A. (1993), Improving the quality of jury decisionmaking, in Litan, *supra* note 8. The quotation is from p. 365.

15. The range of jury trial innovations is presented in Munsterman, G. Thomas, Paula L. Hanna-ford, & G. Marc Whitehead (Eds.), *Jury trial innovations,* Willamsburg, Va.: National Center for State Courts. For background on the Arizona jury reforms, see The Arizona Supreme Court Committee on More Effective Use of Juries (1994), *Jurors: The power of twelve.*

16. Hans, Valerie P., Paula L. Hannaford, & G. Thomas Munsterman (1999), The Arizona jury reform permitting civil jury trial discussions: The views of trial participants, judges, and jurors, *University of Michigan Journal of Legal Reform, 32,* 349–377; Hannaford, Paula L., Valerie P. Hans, & G. Thomas Munsterman (2000), Permitting jury discussions during trial: Impact of the Arizona reform, *Law and Human Behavior, 24* (forthcoming).

17. Shanley, Michael G., & Mark A. Peterson (1987), *Posttrial adjustments to jury awards,* Santa Monica, Calif.: Rand Corporation; Vidmar, Neil, Felicia Gross, & Mary Rose (1998), Jury awards for medical malpractice and post-verdict adjustments of those awards, *DePaul Law Review, 48,* 265–299.

18. Galanter observes that establishing the going rate can often be a challenge. Galanter, Marc (1993), The regulatory function of the civil jury, in Litan, *supra* note 8.

19. For examples of several methods for guiding awards, see: Baldus, D., J. C. MacQueen, & G. Woodworth (1995), Improving judicial oversight of jury damage assessments: A proposal for the comparative additur/remittitur review of awards for non-pecuniary harms and punitive damages, *Iowa Law Review, 80,* 1109–1267; Saks, M. J., L. A. Hollinger, R. L. Wissler, D. L. Evans, & A. J. Hart (1997), Reducing variability in civil jury awards, *Law and Human Behavior, 21,* 243–256.

20. Schuck, Peter H. (Ed.), *Tort law and the public interest: Competition, innovation, and consumer welfare,* New York: Norton. The quotation is from Schuck, Peter H., Introduction: The context of the controversy, at 18.

21. Galanter, *supra* note 18.

22. De Tocqueville, Alexis (1835/1969), *Democracy in America* (Edited by J. P. Mayer; Translated by George Lawrence), Garden City, N.Y.: Doubleday. The quotation is from pp. 274–275.

23. The mean rating was 7.37, and the mode was 8. Just 3.8% of the jurors rated their experience below the midpoint of 5.

24. The literature is vast. Several excellent treatments of these important questions about the civil justice system may be found in Bell, Peter A., & Jeffrey O'Connell (1997), *Accidental justice: The dilemmas of tort law,* New Haven: Yale University Press; Schuck, *supra* note 20; Huber, Peter W., & Robert E. Litan (1991), *The liability maze: The impact of liability law on safety and innovation,* Washington, D.C.: Brookings Institution. Steven Garber's economic analysis of the product liability system nicely conveys the complexities (and perhaps the impossibility) of evaluating the multiple effects of the system. Garber, Steven (1998), Product liability, punitive damages, business decisions and economic outcomes, *Wisconsin Law Review, 1998,* 237–295. Issues relating to the jury's role within the civil justice system are also

discussed in a special issue of the *University of Chicago Legal Forum* (1990): The role of the jury in civil dispute resolution, vol. 1990 (entire issue). For the perspective that the civil jury's role should be reconsidered, see Priest, George (1993), Justifying the civil jury, in Litan, *supra* note 8.

25. Vidmar, *supra* note 7.

26. Galanter, Marc (1974), Why the "haves" come out ahead: Speculations on the limits of legal change, *Law & Society Review, 9,* 95–160.

27. Kafoury, Gregory (1998), Raiding the initiative: Corporations vs. citizens, *Willamette Law Review, 34,* 729–732. The quotation is from p. 730.

28. See Hastie, Reid, & W. Kip Viscusi (1998), What juries can't do well: The jury's performance as a risk manager, *Arizona Law Review, 40,* 901–921; Adversarial Forum, *Law and Human Behavior, 23,* 703–730.

29. Lempert, Richard (1999), Juries, hindsight and punitive damage awards: Failures of a social science case for change, *DePaul Law Review, 48,* 867–894. Shuman and Champagne list other disadvantages of removing cases from juries in Shuman, Daniel W., & Anthony Champagne (1997), Removing the people from the legal process: The rhetoric and research on judicial selection and juries, *Psychology, Public Policy, and Law, 3,* 242–258.

INDEX

Adler, Stephen, 11–12, 13
advertising campaigns, for tort reform, 15, 73–74, 76–77
Aetna Life and Casualty, 58, 60, 170
Alschuler, Albert, 74–75, 242n64
ambulance chasers, image of lawyers as, 65
American Bar Foundation, 19
American Consulting Engineers Council, 52
American Tort Reform Association (ATRA), 51–52, 74
Angell, Marcia, 13
anti-business jury, as myth, 217–219
anti-business prejudice, 138–177 *passim*
anti-plaintiff bias, 39; mentioned, 22–49 *passim*
Arizona, jury reform in, 39, 223
asbestos cases, 29, 31, 57; and company awareness of hazards, 167, 169–170; corporate visibility in, 86; filing statistics for, 57; financial resources considered in, 195–196; juror influence in, 88; negative jury views in, 149–153; standard of responsibility in, 119, 120, 123, 132
assumption of risk, 38, 47
Asymmetric Society, The (Coleman), 112
ATRA. *See* American Tort Reform Association
attitudes: toward business, 138–177 *passim;* toward death penalty, 140
attorneys. *See* lawyers
auto accident cases: corporate "ghosts" in, 85; juror influence in, 88; standard of responsibility in, 119
availability heuristic, 74

Bailis, Daniel, 73
Baptists, on ethics of litigation, 70

Barculo, Judge, 22
Bell, Peter, 183–184
Bellah, Robert, *Habits of the Heart,* 41
Bendectin: and birth defects, 14, 23; and expert witness testimony, 16
Benlate cases, 1–4, 9, 10–14, 222
Benlate DF. *See* Benlate cases
bias, anti-plaintiff, 39
big business, public confidence in, 158–160
birth defects: Bendectin and, 14, 23; Benlate and, 4, 12–13
black lung cases, filing statistics for, 57
blaming of victim, 22–49 *passim*
Blue Cross and Blue Shield, 201
breast implant cases: Dow Chemical and, 74; in federal courts, 57
Breyer, Justice Stephen, 16
Business Attitudes scale, 170–177, 254n46; and juror sample, 171; and mock jury experiment, 173–175; significant predictors in, 175; and state poll participants, 171–173
Business Jury Project, 17–21

CALA. *See* Citizens Against Lawsuit Abuse
California: study of potential lawsuits in, 55; survey on frivolous lawsuits in, 58
California Supreme Court, and *Summers v. Tice,* 92
capitalism, public confidence in, 157–158
career, as juror influence, 134–135
Chicago Jury Project, 183; insurance study, 213–214
Chin, Audrey, 182
Citizens Against Lawsuit Abuse (CALA), 52; survey on frivolous lawsuits, 58

win rate, 19, 73; vs. awards, 179

witnesses: badgering, 35; credibility of, 140; expert (*see* expert witnesses)

worker injury cases: juror influence in, 88–89; standard of responsibility in, 119

worker safety, opinions about, 165–166

workers' compensation: origins of, 8; rules, 94

Yale University, 39

Zeisel, Hans, 39, 183